Donald R. Bardill, PhD

The Relational Syste[m]
for Family Ther[apy]
Living in the Four Realities

*Pre-publication
REVIEWS,
COMMENTARIES,
EVALUATIONS . . .*

"**T**his book springs from the depths of a very effective, experienced therapist and educator, and incorporates a lifetime of practice and theoretical wisdom. The concepts have been tested with students and families repeatedly, and are honed and fine-tuned for maximum therapeutic effectiveness.

Bardill's clarification of very complex concepts, such as differentiation of self, are most gratifying and elucidating as he shows how the concepts are used in therapeutic situations. His discussions of the triune brain and the reticular activating systems are novel in traditional family therapy literature. Bardill demonstrates the courage to deal forthrightly with spirituality issues that must be faced when working with families–something most authors fail to do.

Some of the most valuable and informative aspects of the book are the exercises incorporated within the text that assist the reader in integrating the material. Bardill brackets and highlights the central issues presented in each chapter, which also provides a good, quick review. Finally, his 'Helping Principles' draw together the threads running throughout the book into specific, organized, handy treatment implications for all therapists who are working with families."

Allie C. Kilpatrick, PhD
Professor, School of Social Work,
University of Georgia

"**I**n his new book, *The Relational Systems Model for Family Therapy,* Dr. Bardill combines the best of Aristotle and Tom Bodet. By pulling together his and others' perceptions of interpersonal family 'realities,' he has managed to present some extremely complex concepts in a very readable and understandable way.

His 'Relational Systems' model provides a particular paradigm for the conduct of family therapy that makes sense (even to a jaded practitioner with over 40 years of practice). By including in his model a conceptualization of the so-called 'four realities of life,' he provides a view of the human 'elephant' that encompasses more than just the 'trunk' or 'hind quarters.' Dr. Bardill's premise is that patients and therapists have a better chance of achieving congruity in interpersonal system(s) if they are playing with a 'full deck'–if they are aware of and deal with all the essential elements.

Of particular interest is Bardill's inclusion of the spiritual (as opposed to religious) component, along with a discussion of the other essential components of 'self, other, and context.' The inclusion of the spiritual is unique and definitely provides an essential but often ignored element.

In a somewhat less conceptual mode, the reader will find useful the assessment and intervention profiles/models in chapters on 'Life Stances' and the 'Family Grid.'

I once had a philosophy professor who maintained that in everyone's life there is one book that can replace all the others–this may be the one in family therapy."

Jerry L. McKain, PhD, DSW
Tir Na Nog Family Therapy Institute
Steilacoom, WA

"**D**onald R. Bardill is one of the few people in the field who have continued to remain very relevant in his training in family therapy. For more than two decades, he has challenged those of us in the field to integrate our personal value systems as family therapists with the models we use in therapy. This book provides relevant new information, is very usable, and courageously deals with the spiritual aspects of family therapy as an important dimension. I believe this book will be very helpful for therapists, as well as patients/clients. It is a pleasure to recommend this book."

Ralph H. Earle, PhD, ABPP
President, Psychological Counseling
Services, Ltd., Scottsdale, AZ

The Haworth Press, Inc.

The Relational Systems Model for Family Therapy
Living in the Four Realities

HAWORTH Social Work Practice
Carlton E. Munson, DSW, Senior Editor

New, Recent, and Forthcoming Titles:

The Relational Systems Model
for Family Therapy
Living in the Four Realities

Donald R. Bardill, PhD

The Haworth Press
New York • London

The Haworth Press, Inc., 10 Alice Street, Binghamton, NY 13904-1580

Cover designed by Donna M. Brooks.

Library of Congress Cataloging-in-Publication Data

Bardill, Donald R.
    The relational systems model for family therapy : living in the four realities / Donald R. Bardill.
       p.   cm.
    Includes bibliographical references and index.
    ISBN 0-7890-0183-7
    1. Contextual therapy. I. Title.
RC488.55.B37 1996
616.89'156–dc20
                                       96-4072
                                         CIP

CONTENTS

ABOUT THE AUTHOR

Donald R. Bardill, PhD, MSW, is Professor in the School of Social Work at Florida State University in Tallahassee, where he was Dean for fifteen years. The former President of the American Association of Marriage & Family Therapy, Dr. Bardill is the co-author of the books *Family Group Casework* and *Thank God I'm a Teenager.* The author of more than thirty articles appearing in journals such as *Social Work, Social Casework,* and *Social Thought,* he is currently the Editor of the *Journal of Family Social Work* and serves on the Editorial Board of *Social Work & Christianity.* During his distinguished career, Dr. Bardill has conducted over 120 family therapy workshops in both the United States and Europe. He holds memberships in the National Association of Social Workers, the American Family Therapy Association, and the American Association of Marriage & Family Therapy.

Acknowledgments

I wish to express my appreciation to all who have contributed to the content of this volume. After over forty years of work with families–teaching family therapy to graduate students and fellow professionals, engaging in dialogue with graduate students, conducting workshops, attending workshops, and reading journals and books–it is impossible to give proper credit to everyone who contributed to the thinking in this book. Over the years, I have used the ideas of many people in an effort to develop an effective treatment model.

I am aware that in the early 1960s, William Vogel, PhD, a psychologist at The Walter Reed General Hospital in Washington, DC, introduced me to a systemic approach to family problems. The early contributions of John E. Bell, Virginia Satir, and Murray Bowen provided the necessary theoretical basis for sorting out some of the vital dynamics in family systems. Later, Frank Pittman and Gus Napier served as mentors from a far distance. Videotapes by such key family therapists as Harry Aponte, Virginia Satir, and Salvador Minuchin continue to provide direction to theoretical and practice considerations.

I am always aware that in the final analysis, it is the clients who have provided the depth of insight needed to understand family dynamics. I so vividly remember the client at Walter Reed who, when asked what his feelings were about certain information that came out in the interview, looked me squarely in the eye and said, "Feelings? What do you mean feelings?" It was at that moment years ago when I realized that the therapist's engagement in the self-differentiation process was vital to an effective treatment process. I continue to learn from my clients.

The ideas of Ed Friedman and, most recently, the directions provided by David Schnarch have been valuable to me.

My own family has always been an inspiration to me. My wife Joyce, and my daughters, Amanda and Amy, support and confront me in ways that have added to my range of knowledge about family dynamics. My daughter Amy provided very valuable insights into some of the early manuscript material.

While I am aware that it is not politically correct to talk about one's spiritual side in this day and age, I would not model the integrity I value so much if I did not mention the enormous strength I get from my connection to God through my faith relationship to Jesus Christ. In the true spirit of the Relational Systems Model presented in this volume, I neither impose my spiritual beliefs on others nor do I deny their power in my life.

Finally, I wish to thank Carlton Munson of The Haworth Press for his encouragement and support. A special debt of gratitude goes to Margaret (Maggi) A. Vanos-Wilson, who had the task of deciphering my notes and endless revisions.

CHAPTER 1

THE RELATIONAL SYSTEMS MODEL

A Concept of Human Relationships
    Locations, Labels, and Human Relationships
    Relational Truth
    Past and Present Choices
    Relational Choice
    Separateness, Connectedness, and Differentiation

A Concept of Human Systems
    Vertical and Horizontal Systems
    Emotional Systems
    Linear and Circular Dynamics
    Multisystems

A Concept of Models
    Relational View
    To Emulate
    Universal and Specific in Nature
    Differentiation

Summary

As we penetrate into matter, nature does not allow us to isolate building blocks, but rather appears as a complicated web of relations between the various parts of a unified whole.

H.P. Stapp[1]

A CONCEPT OF HUMAN RELATIONSHIPS

Out of changes in the basic theories in modem physics and biology have come new ways of examining human relationships. We now know reality has a basic relationship dimension as well as a basic matter dimension. Human beings in every known culture exhibit a need to relate to other human beings. Human relationships may be thought of as that without which you cannot experience your existence. As humans, we live in a complex web of relationships with ourself, others, our natural and social context, and the spiritual dimension of life.

Locations, Labels, and Human Relationships

Take a moment to imagine a little girl holding a large, beautiful, smooth rubber ball with an X on it. Now, imagine that the little girl starts to toss the ball into the air, catches it, and tosses it back into the air repeatedly. As you observe, in your imagination, the little girl tossing the ball you are asked, Where is the X on the rubber ball?

If you are like most people, you will have difficulty coming up with the words to pinpoint the location of the X on the ever-turning, moving rubber ball.

Now, imagine that I take the ball and put an O opposite the X and give it back to the little girl who once more starts rapidly tossing the ball into the air. If I ask you, where is the X on the ball, what would you say? My experience has been that almost everyone will say that the X is opposite the O.

One characteristic of human beings is that we locate things in relation to other things. We locate ourselves in relation to other people, other systems, other ideas, other places, etc. The locations we use include such notions as labels, categories, roles, and time and distances. Locations give us a frame of reference for making connections to people, events, and places.

Roles, times, and labels provide a position from which to relate within a complex world. Locations are vital to the process of human relationships. Relationships are complicated, and we need a perspective from which to approach them.

There are down-sides to the need to relate from distinguishable locations. For instance, in the use of roles there is a tendency to not see the *person* who is in a particular role. Often we just do not see the human being who occupies a role or position. We relate more to the role than to the person in the role. All of us are much more than the roles we occupy. For instance, a person may change over time while occupying the same role. I am not the same person in my father role today that I was twenty years ago. On the other hand, roles also change for the same people within families. The child becomes an adult; parents who took care of us when we were children grow old and need to be cared for by their "children." The care receiver becomes the caregiver.

Locations give each of us a unique view of the world. In our relational existence, each one of us occupies a unique position, complete with our own views about the human condition. We come to our own perspective from our individual capacities, personal experiences, and our unique interpretations of human events. By implication, we are who and what we are in relation to other people.

Relational Truth

Often, I begin a workshop or graduate course in family work with the following announcement, "Let me share something very important about this course. When I talk about family activities and family therapy, I do not tell *the* truth." After a short pause, I repeat the statement in a very forceful manner. After another pause I ask, "Why is that so?" Most of the time no one says anything for a minute or so. At some point, someone will venture a comment about words reflecting a particular point of view. The discussion that follows ordinarily is lively and informative for everyone. We learn that we are limited in the view we have by the perspective from which we operate.

When we use words to describe concepts, social events, or human relationships, we reflect a particular perspective. Words limit how and what we say. When we put something into language it is not *the* truth. Human language is not designed to tell *the* truth. I inform the students that in human affairs *they* do not tell *the* truth either.

It is essential for the students to examine the idea of relational truth. A perspective carries with it a preoccupation with certain activities and selective inattention toward other activities. In our limited human perspectives, we know reality or truth only in part. When we are children, we relate as children; when we are adults, we relate as adults. In our professional roles we interact as professionals. There is a bigger picture than the one we see from our limited perspectives. We only see parts of the *truth.* The height of illusion is to take part of the truth and make it *the* whole truth.

Relationship truth in the human reality does not exist. When we put language to an activity, it is only a point of view.

I tell the students that if I do not tell *the* truth, then it follows that I do not *know* anything either. Intellectually, we can deal with the notion that we do not *know* anything. Intellectually, we sense that our words represent our estimate of reality. Emotionally, it is difficult not to know. For survival purposes we need to know. When it comes to human relationships, we don't know. I don't know exactly how close or distant to be with my wife or children at certain times. How close or distant should one be to one's teenage child, or adult child? Not knowing is emotionally troublesome to us, but as finite humans, we only have our perspectives as a basis for truth in the arena of human relationships.

Most people understand that in matters of human activities, we do not have the final answer or *the* truth. For some, it is intellectually comforting to know that when we deal in human affairs, there is no *one* truth we should seek to uncover.

As relational therapists, we deal in theory and practice application on a probability basis. Research and practice wisdom guide us, but they are based on probabilities and perspectives, not *the* truth. Therapy, like all of life, is a problem-solving process wrapped in probabilities. In human relationships we often know what is likely to happen, but we don't know for certain.

It is essential to make the distinction between spiritually based moral absolutes and the dynamics of relational truth. In relational truth we are dealing with the inherent limits on the human capacity to deal with reality. From our human position in life, we see what we see and know what we know, but we see through the glass of life darkly and partially.

Therapy, like all of life, is a problem-solving process wrapped in probabilities.

Imagine driving through a large city in our country. Why do we choose to obey the speed limits and traffic signals? We know that if we generally obey the traffic rules, it is likely that we will safely make it from one place to another. Now, imagine driving through the same large town going 100 miles per hour and disobeying all the traffic signals. It is quite likely that either you will have an accident or that you will be stopped by the police. Your probabilities for making it from one place to another are quite low. If we walk along the side of a tall building with one foot over the edge of the building, the probabilities of falling are higher than if we stay several feet from the edge. Sometimes, we enjoy walking close to the edge, the thrill of danger is a pleasure to us. Some of us are very conservative when we play the probabilities of life; we never walk close to the edge if we can avoid it.

It is clear to many people that, given the nature of human beings, we cannot always accurately predict the behavior of either ourselves or other people. We can, and we do, use probability thinking as we engage the human problem-solving process. This means that in matters of human activities, we use probability dynamics rather than deterministic outcomes.

Past and Present Choices

In family matters, we know that the past influences the present and the present influences the future. Because of continuity through time, we can make fairly accurate assessments about the future. What I am doing at this moment is a selection of activity out of the many possibilities that were available to me at a point in the past. This process is called dynamic causation by Capek.[2] In dynamic causation, life is a continuous present act of selection from among possibilities that have been provided from the past. If we know the pattern of choices made in the past, our ability to predict accurately for the future is high. Past behavior is a good predictor of future behavior. Choice then becomes a crucial dynamic in the ongoing flow of life. Self-awareness includes awareness of our choices and our pattern of choices. So, put another way, choices made in the past influence the choice possibilities for the present that, in turn, influence the choice possibilities for the future.

Relational Choice

Humans exert will and volition in matters of human relationships. We are not automatons; the extent of our will and volition is limited by our human nature. We do what humans do. We are designed to do that which serves our survival, safety, and growth, both physically and psychologically. We seek pleasure and anything we associate with pleasure; we avoid pain and anything we associate with pain. A major governing mechanism underlying the processes of all relationships is our natural avoidance of pain and affinity for pleasure.

We are not bound by narrow instinctual restrictions, nor are we wholly conditioned by social forces. We are capable of degrees of subjection to and freedom from raw instinctual control, social and emotional conditioning, traumatic events, powerful external forces, and internalized past experiences. We have in us a powerful push to grow to our full physical, mental, and emotional capacities. The push to maturity is part of our human heredity.

Separateness, Connectedness, and Differentiation

In the world of human beings, we see much of life in terms of relationship distances. How often do we say, "I feel close to her" or "I feel distance from him"? The forces of togetherness and the forces of separateness are powerful and unrelenting. We want to be individuals, and we want to be close to others. Murray Bowen made the processes of separateness and togetherness the cornerstones of his conceptualization of the emotional, relational world of humans.[3]

There is separateness and connectedness in the functioning of the physical world as there is in the emotional, relational world.

P. L. Steinke[4]

In Bowen's scheme of things, all of us struggle with the basic life processes of maintaining a strong sense of exactly who we are individually and staying in close touch with others. Bowen calls the separation/togetherness struggle part of "the differentiation process." In his writings, he pointed out that differentiation is part of nature itself. Differentiation is a fundamental life force in which something struggles to be itself. Both molecular biology and quantum physics have discovered the importance of boundary concerns in the life process.

Human relationships are inherently anxious. There is a part of each of us whose purpose is survival. Survival concerns are not easily put to rest. It is in our relationships to others that we demonstrate the emotional survival processes of our very being. We are never at ease for very long in our relationships with others. The intense need for separateness and togetherness in human relationships inevitably draws us into boundary issues. Where do I begin and where do I end in my relationships with others and the world around me? How close and how distant should I be to my wife?

To understand family functioning is to understand how each individual family member, as well as the larger family unit itself, deals with human boundary dynamics. Issues of personal space, intimacy, and emotional distancing and responsibility form the essence of relational systems considerations. Working at life's boundary points in human relationships takes us into the enormous complexities of the emotional relational world of human existence.

The crucial test of emotional maturity is tied to our struggle to be separate from and close to other people. A major factor in marriage is each person's ability to be an independent self while developing a close intimate relationship to one's spouse. Clearly, the dynamic forces toward both separateness and togetherness create a vital relationship tension in the activities of families. Ideally, there is a balancing force that promotes emotional survival, safety, and growth for everyone involved. Separation is not isolation. We need to be distinct from others, not distant from them.[5]

The complex world of human relationships is not easy to understand. The history of humankind attests to each human's struggle to be distinct from others, and to be close to others. In our relationships with others, we are capable of the most brutal and the most loving actions imaginable. The purpose of the Relational Systems Model (RSM) is to identify and energize the life processes that enable each individual human being and aggregates of human beings to realize the full potential that life has to offer.

A CONCEPT OF HUMAN SYSTEMS

Humans form various aggregates of people who are in interaction and interdependent; in such groups, what affects one member of the set effects other members. In other words, humans exist in social and emotional systems. Minuchin points out that the theory of family therapy is predicated on the fact we are not individual isolates. We are acting and reacting members of social groups–to say that people are influenced by their social contexts, which they also influence, may seem obvious.[6] Families demonstrate social systems characteristics. They are organized, have boundaries, and have identifiable communications networks.

Humans are, and exist in, social and emotional systems.

Vertical and Horizontal Systems

Systems may be viewed vertically. Viewed vertically, each system is a subsystem of larger systems. Life is made up of systems with subsystems and suprasystems. Individual family members may be thought of as subsystems within the family system (see Figure 1.1).

On the other hand, the family is a subsystem of the larger surrounding culture. For instance, larger society sets the broad outlines of family structure and functioning. Yet, each individual family develops its own unique family form and style.

Systems may also be viewed horizontally. There are systems at the same conceptual level, such as families interacting with other families (see Figure 1.2). Within the family subsystem network, brothers and sisters interact with each other.

In our relational perspective we are interested in the points of intersection between and among larger and smaller systems as well as the interaction between systems at the same conceptual level. The relational system model concerns itself with a multisystem perspective.

Emotional Systems

Bowen-thinking, as reflected by Ed Friedman, proposes the idea of the family as an emotional system.[7] An emotional system refers to any aggregate of people that has developed an emotional inter-

FIGURE 1.1

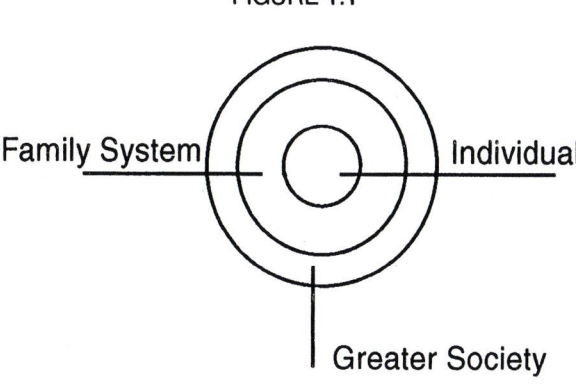

FIGURE 1.2

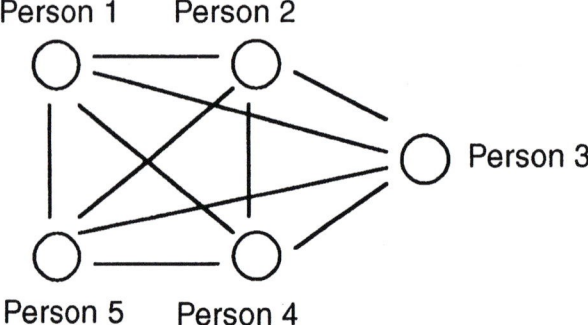

dependence to the point that the resulting system has evolved its own principles and energies of organization. Out of the emotional system comes an influence on the functioning of its members that is stronger than any of the components of the system. A family emotional system includes the members' thoughts, feelings, emotions, fantasies, and their past connections, individually and together. Friedman's discussions of Bowen theory posit that an emotional system is not to be equated with a relationship system or a communications system although it includes them. In the Bowen/Friedman scheme, the vital dynamics of the emotional system are the focus of the treatment process. The Bowen point in this regard is well taken. The focus of treatment at the systematic level must be on the driving dynamics of the system. For Bowen, differentiation, interlocking triangles, and anxiety constitute the vital energies of the family system.

Linear and Circular Dynamics

Systemic considerations allow us to escape linear type thinking. Systemic thinking moves us to consider more than straight line cause-and-effect logic. Linear logic assumes that we can objectively identify discrete events with set beginnings and endings ($A \rightarrow B$). In other words, A causes B. Systemic thinking recognizes that we are a part of events rather than just the cause or effect ($A \leftrightarrow B$). We influence the drift of events as we are influenced by other events.

Systemic thinking allows us to help families see that while we are affecting the family we are being affected by the family.

In systemic thinking, the flow of the therapy process is the result of ongoing feedback interchanges between the family and the therapist. The notion of reciprocal feedback has universal application. For instance, the process of teaching a class is greatly influenced by the teacher, the class response, the teacher's response to the class response, the class's response to the teacher's response to the class response, and on and on and on.

Another way to describe systemic thinking is that it steers away from event-driven thinking only. Systemically, we realize that the connection between events and outcome may not be immediate. It enables us to see beyond events and develop a more expansive view. The cumulative effect of events may take years to show. The effect of smoking tobacco may take years before it becomes painfully apparent. In systemic thinking, we see the larger picture. Highly skilled automobile drivers always drive with the entire road in view, not just with a view of the car immediately in front of them.

Human observation shows that we experience linearly and explain holistically. We respond to experiences immediately. When asked a question in class, a student will respond to the professor very quickly. When we are asked to explain the cause of a particular behavior, a much more expansive and comprehensive answer is usually forthcoming. If you are asked why are you reading this material, you may give an immediate one-variable answer, but upon reflection, you probably will decide the answer requires considerable explanation. Thus, systemically, we do not use the single variable approach to understand human functioning. We know that there are multiple reciprocal influences to behavior. We think ecologically, configuratively, and holistically. Knowing the complexity of human behavior, systemic thinkers are as likely to ask *how* something happened as *why* something happened.

Humans experience events linearly and explain them holistically.

Systemic thinking, with its holistic view, also allows us to get beyond emotional right/wrong thinking in human relationships. Linear thinking is steeped in emotionalized right/wrong, black/white, cause/effect absolute logic. Systemic thinking helps us see the breadth of an event or situation. While systemic considerations are vital to understanding human functioning, it is important to remember that linear logic, individual dynamics, and single variable thinking are part of the total configuration of human events. Systemic thinking includes linear thinking as part of the whole.

Environments–contexts–are often set up to influence people toward certain actions. Soft music, wine, and special food are thought to be an appropriate context for romance. Yet, we must always honor individual choice. We may have a gun put to our head and be told to push the button that will destroy the world. Such a choice might be very different from everyday choices, but the choice to push the button is ours. We may be under intense influence to conform to specific group actions, yet each person exerts individual choice. Individual choice is crucial to the differentiation process. The relational systems perspective simultaneously looks at various systems levels; human nature is whole, and within the whole are separate parts.

Multisystems

As human beings we live in relation to numerous social arrangements. We are part of many social systems such as family, work, community, and society. We are affecting and being affected by the various social contexts of which we are a part.

Sometimes, the different social systems make contradictory demands on us. Meeting the material expectations of our economically intense society may require long work hours away from home. Hours away from home may put stress on the individual need to be home with one's family. Organizations and philosophies that push for individual freedom may conflict with one's desire to have close relationships within one's marriage and family. It is at the interface-boundary of our different life systems that human problems and opportunities arise. The natural differentiation process is founded in remaining a distinct entity while connected to all vital supra- and sub-systems. Complex systems generate complex problems, and complex problems demand complex solutions. Systems thinking moves us forward into the complexities of life.

A CONCEPT OF MODELS

A model provides a perspective from which it is possible to view human events. It is a starting place or an overall framework on which to stand. A model may be both universal and specific in its focus of attention. A model can also serve as something to follow or emulate.

Relational View

The Relational Systems Model (RSM) provides one way to consider family functioning. It provides a frame from which to organize our attention and from which to make meaning as we consider the complexity of family dynamics. It has been said that when you have a workable frame for viewing family dynamics, you have a workable way to examine a family and to conduct the family therapy process.

A major goal for the therapy process is to get family dynamics into a form you can use. The questions therapists ask serve (1) to reinforce the particular frame of reference they are using, and (2) to create a particular perspective within which the family can begin the work of therapy.

When you have a workable frame for viewing family dynamics, you have a workable way to examine a family and to conduct the family therapy process.

The treatment model used to work with families is critical to the process of therapy. The model organizes information in a specific way. It satisfies the therapist's need to make sense of events. Ideally, it moves the family toward new and additional views of the events taking place in the family. All humans have a need to make meaning out of everything; the search for meaning is a powerful inherent force in our life. The therapist's point of view underlying conducting the helping process is one of the most powerful forces in the therapy process.

The RSM provides possibilities from which to view family functioning. The RSM is just a view. It is not *the* view, it is *a* view of important family dynamics. When I talk about *a* view and not *the* view, recognition is being given to the limitations inherent in language and in human perspectives. The relational systems model recognizes that each client enters the treatment process with a personal worldview, or model, which directs his or her life. A first task of the therapist is to understand the client's worldview. In the process of understanding the client's personal worldview, the client is helped to bring into clear awareness the fundamental nature of the worldview that directs his or her life.

Some humans attempt to find *the* right world-view or *the* truth about human affairs in this world. Yet, in our humanness we have such limited perspectives. I am certain that absolute truth exists, but not in the realm of humanness. It certainly does not exist in the domain of family therapy. The RSM is designed to allow you to see some new things in families and to do some new things in your work with families.

To Emulate

Another view of a model is that it is something to emulate. An ongoing goal of RSM is to identify both family and treatment dynamics that offer the best hope for creating highly effective therapeutic understanding and technologies. Success leaves clues. What are the clues about successful family work that are, and have been, provided to us by the masters in family therapy, our patients, our students, and our own individual creativity?

Universal and Specific in Nature

The dynamics that form the basis for understanding the Relational Systems Model are relevant to understanding *all human relationships*. In that sense, the RSM is a universal human relationship model. The presentation of the content within the emotional/social context called the family may be thought of as simply an entry point along the road to understanding complex human relationships in general. The RSM is about human life, rather than just the family unit. What we observe in all human relationships, including those in the family, is the intense drive toward survival, safety, and the realization of our inherent potentials. In the process of pushing toward survival and a full life, we seek to avoid pain and to enhance pleasure. Moment by moment, we deal with the opposing and complementary forces inherent in the human condition–the yearning to be a part of and to be separate, to be loving and to be loved, and to be valuable and to give value.

One universal dynamic is that human interactions within a social system are subject to the unique considerations of that specific context. For instance, each family unit demonstrates the unique characteristics of a specific family, in a specific community, in a specific society, and at a specific time in history. Even so, human nature is human nature, and human needs are human needs. In other words, human nature abides. The emotional issues of love, worth, and identity abide in all human contexts. So, we are faced with the importance of systemic distinctiveness and the vital universal human dynamics at different levels of abstraction. The RSM moves to identify the vital dynamics that include all variations in human aggregates, i.e., race, gender, culture, religion, environment, etc., while giving the systemic variations the unique attention they demand. The question is, What are the *variables that are essential?* Which variables are helpful and which ones are distractions in the therapeutic process?

Differentiation

From the RSM perspective, the essential dynamics are to be found in the way human systems meet basic human emotional needs in the relational dynamics of the realities of self systems, dyadic and triadic systems, and larger social systems or contexts, as well as the spiritual realm of existence. Thus, we are concerned about human relationships within, between, and among various social systems as they are influenced by the different perspectives that flow out of complex human interactions. The very nature of the Relational Systems Model discussion highlights our unique human struggle *to be a part of and separate from the many reality systems* in which we exist. Bowen's attention to the process of differentiation provides a valuable entre' point for examining the many systems of which humans are a part. The concept of self-differentiation turns out to be a fundamental human dynamic, and as such, it is a core therapeutic consideration in the affairs of all human beings, especially the affairs of family living.

On a broader systems level, differentiation is the systemic integrity necessary for any human system to survive–be it family, marriage, community, or country. The capacity to be a solid self with systemic *integrity* and *internal direction,* while being open to new ideas and new relationships on a measured basis, is an attribute necessary for systemic survival and growth. All systems are either limited or enhanced by the degree to which the differentiation process is part of the foundation of the system. It occurs to me that only differentiated systems, individuals, couples, families, societies, etc. will be able to survive the challenges in today's increasingly complex world.

SUMMARY

The Relational Systems Model posits that human beings live in complex sets of relationships with the realities of ourself, others, social contexts, and the spiritual realm. We are unique individuals, members of various aggregates of people, and we are subject to powerful social contexts and spiritual considerations that impinge on our life.

In the journey of life, we take positions and locations in our many relationships. Positions and locations provide us with points from which we may view events. From our point of view and social contexts, or systems, we give meaning to life's events. Remember, humans *are* meaning-making creatures.

The journey of life also includes the never-ending process differentiating our self from, *and* remaining connected to, all that exists, including our impulses, our emotions, our thinking, our social and emotional conditioning, other people, social contexts, and the spiritual realm. In other words, there are relational realities to which all humans must connect in some way. The following section discusses the relational realities with which we must connect and from which we must remain differentiated.

NOTES

1. Stapp, H.P. (1971). S-Matrix Interpretation of Quantum Theory, *Physical Review*, pp. 347-366.

2. Capek, M. (1961). *In Philosophical Impact of Contemporary Physics*. Princeton, NJ: D. Van Nostrand, p. 340.

3. Bowen, M. (1978). *Family Therapy in Clinical Practice*. New York: Jason Aronson.

4. Steinke, P.L. (1994). *New Creation*. Austin, Texas, Vol. 1, No. 1.

5. Steinke, P.L. (1993). *How Your Church Works*. Washington, DC: The Allan Institute, p. 28.

6. Minuchin, S. (1979). *Families and Family Therapy*. Cambridge, MA: Harvard University Press, p. 2.

7. Friedman, E. (1990). "Bowen Theory and Therapy," in A. Gurman and D. Kniskern (Eds.). *Handbook of Family Therapy*, Vol. II, New York: Brunner/Mazel, pp. 134-170.

CHAPTER 2

THE REALITIES: SELF, OTHER, CONTEXT, AND SPIRITUAL

The SOCSp Triangle
   Self
   Other
   Context
   Spiritual

The Human Being
   Human Uniqueness
   Worldview
   The Triune Brain
   Mind-Set
   Life Filter
   Reticular Activating System
   Emotional Rightness

A working premise of the relational systems model is that reality is. Reality is defined as what is. As humans, we constantly distinguish those parts of reality that serve our survival, safety, and growth needs. The relational systems model posits that in this world, there are three human realities and a spiritual reality that account for all that exists. All events, then, reflect the relational realities in some way.

As an approach to assessing family relationships, Virginia Satir (Satir, Stachowiak, and Jaschman, 1980) developed a family therapy model designed to identify common communications patterns among family members.[1] In Satir's model, a person's mode of communication is based on the degree to which self, other people, and context are taken into account in the communications process. For example, a person who *diminishes* the self reality will communicate differently than someone who *highlights* the self reality. A person who organizes his or her life around the context reality will differ from someone who seldom accounts for the context reality in his or her human transactions.

When Satir's original work with self, other, and context is combined with some of the ideas implied in the pioneering work of Sir John Eccles, the basis for a new paradigm for examining family function emerges (Eccles, 1973).[2] Eccles proposed that in this existence there are three worlds that are easily defined. The three worlds take care of everything that is in existence and in our human experience. World 1 consists of physical objects and states. Included in this world is everything organic and inorganic. World 2 is human states of consciousness as subjective knowledge and experiences. This world includes the self, the basis of our unity as an experiencing being throughout our lifetime. World 3 is a knowledge in the objective sense, including records of intellectual efforts and theoretical systems. Included in this world is the whole of civilization and culture. It is a world unknown to other earthly creatures other than humans. Finally, Eccles speaks of the mystery of the uniqueness of each self: that which goes beyond a mindless universe. Out of the ideas of Satir and Eccles then comes the notion of life realities. The fundamental premise of the relational systems model rests on the notion that the self (world 2), other (world 1), context (world 3), and spiritual (the mystery) dimensions of human experience encompass all that is in the human realm of existence. Thought of as life realities, self, other, context, and spiritual considerations (SOCSp) form the basis for a working paradigm for the RSM. The many ways life realities are identified and used in the therapy process are fundamental to the Relational Systems Model.

THE SOCSp TRIANGLE

The SOCSp triangle provides a way to visualize, understand, and internalize family activities. The three human realities—self, other, and context—and the spiritual reality are depicted in the SOCSp Triangle in Figure 2.1. In the SOCSp Triangle, the realities of self, other, and context form the inner triangle and the spiritual reality surrounds the three human realities. While the SOCSp triangle sim-

FIGURE 2.1. The SOCSp Triangle

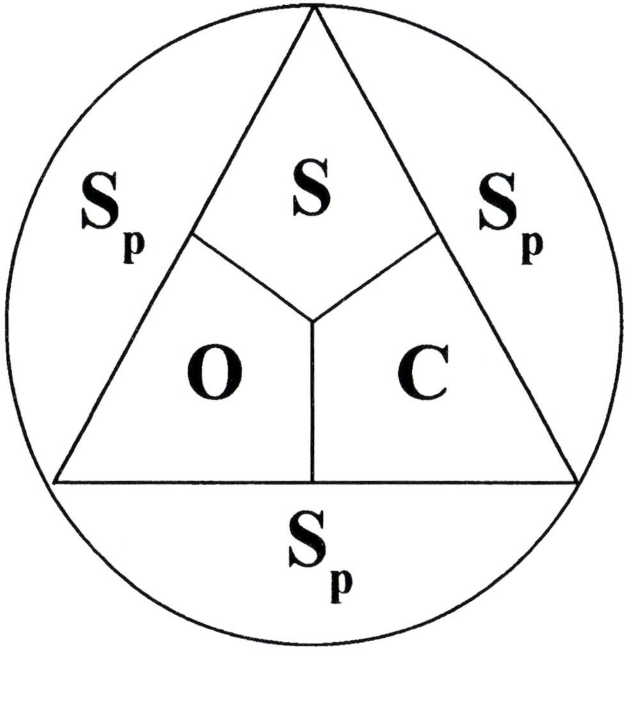

plifies a complex set of human dynamics, it provides a way to account for some fundamental family issues.

Self

The reality of self is not easy to explain. Yet human beings know they exist as a self. Do you know that you exist? Do you experience that you are real? Self-consciousness, or consciousness of the self, has been described as a unique attribute of human beings. It is how you know that you are alive. I, as a self, relate to the world of experiences that I encounter. I do things; I think; I feel; I reflect. I have a self image, and I make choices. Self may be thought of as subjective reality. I have subjective knowledge about the world. Self is the place where the process of life and the content of life come together.

Self may be regarded as the personal context, or the position, from which one's life is viewed. It is the personal context that organizes one's experiences of life; it is the basis of our unity as human beings. It is the self that is required to answer the question What is the purpose of life and how will I respond in view of that purpose?

Self is the source of all my identities and it is none of them.

Our awareness of our self means that we are conscious beings who know that the self is the position from which we view life. My conscious self not only knows, but it knows that I know. There are many ways to put words to the notion of the self. It can be called the process of our unity since all humans have selves. It is the uniqueness that is me in my lifetime.

Self may be thought of as the context for all my identities. It is the space for all my identities, my labels, my views, my images, my definitions, etc. Self is the source of all my identities, yet *it is none of them.*

Let's try something that may help us grasp the essence of self. Take a moment to imagine a giant clear plastic balloon with a large hole at the top. Think of identities, labels, or "I ams" that you held as part of your existence. For instance, I am a teacher, I am an American, I am a father, I am a mother, I am a brother, I am a sister, I am a psychologist, etc. Put all the I ams into the balloon: name, race, religion, degrees, beliefs, etc. Imagine that you toss each one of the I ams you hold into the balloon. Take the time to throw all of the I ams into the balloon.

Have you thrown all the I ams into the balloon? Throw those last few I ams into the balloon. Now, observe the balloon once more. I have a question for you. Who is observing the balloon?

The nameless, timeless, placeless observer is the true you. You are the context of your life, the place from who all your positions and views emanate. You are the context of your life, the matrix for self. Self contains the screen of life but never appears on it.[3]

In the RSM, it is important to understand that the self is not a belief, it is not a value or ideology that you hold, though they are *part* of a larger view toward life that you hold. Humans get attached and committed to certain values, beliefs, ideologies, and traditions. We begin to think that we *are* our views and rigidly defend them. The point is not to lack views. The point is not to get rigidly stuck in specific narrow human perspectives. To be stuck in such a position is to lose creativity, to be unable to assume other viewpoints, or to be locked in narrow thinking. Again, and very importantly, self is more than any value, belief, ideology, tradition, role, etc. The well-differentiated self has the function of not getting locked into one of the above in such a way as to regard anyone of them as *the* self. If a value, belief role, etc. is regarded as *the* self, we defend it on a survival basis. It is the self that has the task of not allowing the mind to be *taken over* by emotions, feelings, or thinking *and* at the same time allowing for the expression of emotions, feelings, and thinking. Self is the personal context for all that I am.

The self is dependent upon the functioning of the brain, yet it clearly is more than the genetic instructions that run the brain. I am more than my genetic coding, my experiences, and my education.

We are self-differentiated beings to the extent that: (1) we can know our positions, viewpoints, contexts, and internal demands, *and* we transcend them; (2) we can assume various view points, be creative, open to other viewpoints, *and* not be stuck or frozen in a position; *AND*–a very big *AND*, (3) we know who and what we are from considerations of love, caring, and integrity. The self is the major player in my life. I am real! I am a reality!

Other

The second reality is everything organic and inorganic in the world. Included in the reality of other are all living creatures (Eccles, 1973).[4] Of special concern to family relationships is the reality of other human beings–the reciprocal of self. Other human beings exist in the world of human relationships and experiences. All humans have the same basic thoughts, needs, fears, hopes, yearnings, and desires. These common human features may manifest themselves differently from person to person.

The challenge of emotional maturity is to experience close, caring, and loving relationships with others and maintain a clear, solid sense of self.

I am an other for you and you are an other for me. Other people live together in this world of amazingly complex transactions and relationships. *Other* people are a source of both pain and pleasure for each other. We influence others and others influence us. We need other people, and we often fiercely compete with other people. Other people meet some of our survival needs, and they may be a threat to our survival needs. Some of the most loving acts and some of the most savage acts in the world characterize human relationships.

The requirement of life is that we relate to other human beings. The challenge of emotional maturity is to experience close caring and loving relationships with others *and* maintain a clear, solid sense of self. Humankind is connected to each other in a complex web of relationships that cannot be avoided. Even the hermit chooses an isolated way of existence in relation to other human beings–to get away from other people.

Do you believe that other people exist? Do you know that they are real? Throughout your entire life, you will deal with the reality of other people and your relationship to other people. Embedded in the realities of self and other is the question How do you deal with the need to be separate from, and connected to, other human beings?

Context

The third human reality is everything that exists in the objective sense (Eccles, 1973). It is the manufactured part of existence that comes from the dynamics created by the patterns, structures, and transactions of human beings; it is the organized part of social existence.

One of the unique and powerful dynamics of the context reality is that it serves as a frame of reference for making meaning of events.

We come into the world with a predetermined set of social contexts. Our context is laid upon us in such entities as government, bureaucracy, culture, religion, communities, families, and other institutions created by people. These people-created contexts have been handed down from generation to generation. The content of the context reality is a learned reality. Humankind learns about values, expectations, beliefs, and morals through the socialization process. All societies have contextual factors that serve to regulate and define behavior.

The context reality is an agreement reality. We can't see a context, yet it exists. Contexts, or social systems, have a force of their own that transcends their constituent parts. We are controlled by the context reality to the extent that there is agreement or disagreement with its traditions, values, and beliefs. It is an agreement reality.

One of the unique and powerful dynamics of this reality is that context serves as a frame of reference for making meaning of events. The social context gives meaning to words. The word "dummy" has a different meaning depending upon the context. In one context, the word "dummy" refers to one's intellectual capacities in a negative sense. In another context, being a dummy means that you and your bridge partner have won the bid and may be the winners of a particular game.

The social context of concern in this book is the family system. A family system generates a power of its own that exerts influence on its members, now and in future generations. The dynamics of the family life cycle demonstrate the effect of structural and role changes over time. Family members function not only according to their individual patterns, but also in relation to their position and expectations within the family context.

At another level we are influenced by the position of the family in the wider social context. Within limits, a change in the structure of a specific social context will encourage different interactions for family members. Context serves as an extremely *powerful* reality for human relationships. It is a powerful *meaning maker* for all that is!

Spiritual

The fourth reality refers to the existence of a creator, or ruler, of the universe. Here we are talking about a reality that presupposes the existence of a sentience (a state of awareness) beyond the human senses, a reality capable of acting outside of the observed principles and limitations of the natural sciences *and* a force that makes demands upon its adherents. This human sense of a transcendent authority, an ultimate context, has been found in all known human cultures. Surveys in our country have consistently found that over 90 percent of the people in the United States believe in God.

People connect to the spiritual reality in a variety of ways. Satir often referred to the spiritual as a life force. In referring to The Life Force, she said, "When we forget our spiritual dimension there is a feeling of loss because we then have no connection with the life force or the universal mind" (Satir, Stachowiak, and Jaschman, 1980). The spiritual reality is like electricity, always there, often not seen, but ready to be used for beneficial purposes. For some people, the spiritual is a profound mystery (Eccles, 1973).[5] Some people reject the spiritual as a fabrication of the mind. Viktor Frankl spoke of the spiritual in its provision of ultimate meaning to life for the individual (Frankl, 1975)[6] The spiritual reality is the connecting link to the supernatural creator of all that is. For the Christian, the spiritual reality is found in a faith relationship to Jesus Christ. While the spiritual reality exists, the content of its reality for humans varies in many ways.

The spiritual reality is *subject to great misunderstanding,* especially when identified as religion. Spiritual reality shows up in the *context* of religion—when a group of humans apprehend themselves to stand in relation to whatever they consider divine and share beliefs and practices relative to sacred things that unite them into a single moral community (Carter, 1993).[7]

The spiritual reality, when subject to the forms of institutional religion, is a part of the reality of context. Religion is based on the human context. The spiritual reality and religion are not the same. Religion serves as a humanmade overlay, or screen, in relationship to the spiritual reality.

The range of ways people connect to the spiritual realm varies. For many people, the spiritual is an organizing frame for all that they think, feel, see, and do. For these people, spiritual connection provides a morally correct approach to existence—a powerful reality indeed!

A failure to account for the spiritual reality in therapy means that a powerful reality of life has been ignored.

The spiritual domain is a *very personal reality* for each person. For many, spirituality is part of their very essence and, as such, is often a highly emotionally charged area. For anyone who has worked in the death and dying area, the power of the spiritual is obvious. The human connection to the spiritual reality often is exhibited powerfully as life on this earth draws to an end.

A failure to account for the spiritual reality in the therapy process means that *a powerful reality* of life has been ignored. Consistent experience in dealing with the spiritual reality has demonstrated that it is easy to misinterpret comments about the spiritual part of life. Some mental health professionals fail to relate to the spiritual part of family work because they have strong negative feelings about religion. Professional self-awareness about one's emotional maturity in all areas of life includes knowing who and what you are in the domain of the spiritual. Ethical professional behavior by mental health professionals requires that the uniqueness of clients be respected.

It is important to realize that in our current society, expressing one's spiritual beliefs may be regarded as "politically incorrect" in many contexts. In understanding family activities, the pressure from society pushes the religiously faithful to act as if their spiritual side does not matter. When a therapy process does not account for a reality, the understanding of family functioning will have little depth. The therapy process must allow the spiritual reality to emerge in its own form and content.

The *reality is that the spiritual matters to people*; it is real and influences our very being. For some people, the spiritual reality is the ultimate context; God is active in their lives.

Appropriate behavior is based on complete consideration of the relationships between and among self, other, context, and the spiritual.

How do you relate to the spiritual part of life? Self awareness demands that we work in full recognition of our specific connection, or lack of connection, to all of the realities—including the spiritual reality. Our awareness or lack of awareness about the spiritual does not alter the existence of the spiritual reality. Sir John Eccles, winner of the Nobel Prize for Medicine in 1963 is reported to have said, "I believe that there is a fundamental mystery in my existence, transcending any biological account of my body with its genetic inheritance and its evolutionary origin" (Eccles, 1973).

The life realities provide a basic paradigm for examining human relationships at the personal, interpersonal, contextual, and spiritual level. Effective human functioning requires that all realities be taken into account. The RSM posits that *appropriate behavior* is based on a complete consideration of the relationships between and among self, other, context, and the spiritual. A failure to account for any one, or combination, of the realities results in activities out of congruence with what is reality.

The self, other, context, and spiritual (SOCSp) paradigm places the examination of family activities squarely in the human relationship domain. We are rooted in our biology, guided by our connections to the world around us, refined by our evolving self, and made whole by our connection to the spiritual. How we manage those complex realities guides us in our journey through life.

THE HUMAN BEING

The reality of the human being as part of all life in this world is fundamental to the SOCSp model. Humans are real! We live in relationship to each other, to the world around us, and to our human and spiritual natures.

As part of the biological domain, we are similar to other life forms. Bowen's theory conceptualized the family as a naturally occurring system that exhibits patterns of emotional functioning just as those of subhuman species (Kerr and Bowen, 1988).[8] In the realm of survival, we show the emotional characteristics of all life. Within that conceptualization, the family unit is thought of as an emotional system.

Human Uniqueness

While the human being shares many fundamental characteristics with all life forms, it is generally accepted that the human is unique among the animal species. First, we are not as rigidly bound by our instinctual drives as other animals. Our nature provides us with the capacity for a wide range of *choices* in our interactions with the environment. Second, the human brain enables us to be self-aware. We have the ability to *observe* ourself in our interactions with our environment. We are self-conscious human beings. Third, like all living systems, we live in a state of constant interchange of energy and information with our environment. But for humans, the specific impact, or *meaning*, of particular events is often not self-evident. It is left up to us to find the meaning. Indeed, it is in the nature of humans to make meaning out of every information interchange. Satir often referred to humans as meaning-making machines. We rely on our memory system for much of that meaning.

We not only seek out specific events, we learn about the events. We give them meaning.

Fourth, from the sum total of meanings we make of our life experiences, we evolve a unified view of our world. This *worldview* provides the context from which to make meaningful premises about our existence. The personal and unique nature of our relationships to self, other, and our environment will be determined by these premises (Watzlawick, Beaven, and Jackson, 1967).[9] John Eccles has observed that central to our experienced existence is our personal uniqueness (Eccles, 1973).[10]

Worldview

So, based on life experiences, evolving values, beliefs, and assumptions; and our unique physical predisposition, each of us formulates a unique worldview. It is a philosophy of life designed to enable us to meet our physical and psychological survival and growth needs. Out of the context of our worldview, we *actively* seek that part of life we regard as necessary to survive and to enhance our innate potential. We formulate our own roadmap by which to traverse the road of life.

We not only seek out specific events, we learn about the events; we give them meaning. We learn what to look for, *how* to look for it, and what meaning to give events. In the process of taking a family therapy class, we not only learn the content, we learn *how* to learn the content. We never cease to seek knowledge about experiences, to understand its meaning for our existence, and at the same time, interpret all that we experience according to our worldview. The physical basis of much of our uniqueness is found in the nature of our brain.

The Triune Brain

Recent findings concerning how the brain works indicate that the brain is made up of many modules, each having its own unique functions. Like a computer, the brain is busy doing many things at once, and the output presents a unified pattern of how the brain works.

American neuroscientist Paul MacLean discusses the "triune brain" (MacLean, 1985).[11] In his scheme, the whole brain is divided into three structures; each structure has its own unique function although the three function as a unit. At the base of the brain is the reptilian complex, which connects with survival processes. Just above it is the mammalian brain, or limbic septum, which connects with the emotional processes. The top and largest area is the neocortex, or the cerebral hemispheres, which connect with our thinking processes (see Figure 2.2).

Reptilian Brain—At the base of the brain are two nodes, or stems, referred to as the reptilian brain. These two nodes are like the brain of reptiles. The reptilian brain regulates autonomic processes. Instinctual reactions, reflexes, and habits, are located here; it is the place of automatic survival processes. In the reptilian brain no thought processes are involved, nor are there any language capabilities.

The seat for loving, caring, and nurturing in humans and other mammals comes from the cortex, a part of the brain not present in reptiles. Thus, reptiles do not care for their young; they step on them, they ignore them, they eat them, or they leave them. Reptiles

FIGURE 2.2

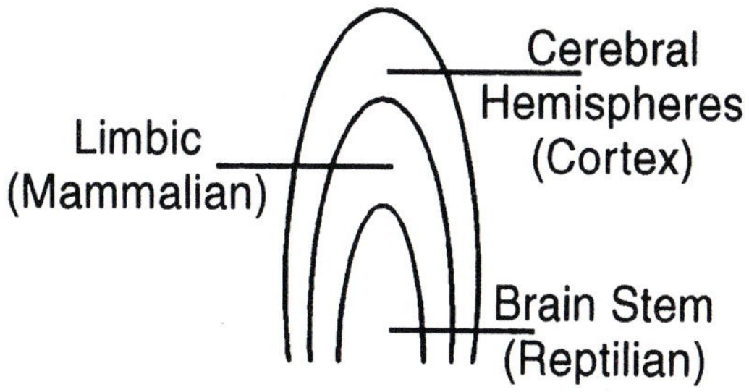

are incapable of playful behavior and do not make cuddly pets. They are *serious* in their behavior. The reptilian brain is a primitive brain. It is the repository for programmed action behavior. It operates in an automatic, instinctual manner that provides for routine and ritual.

Limbic Brain–As the seat of powerful emotion, sexual instincts, and the sense of smell, the limbic brain functions as the site of affective behavior and ensures that emotional responses will be influenced by relationships. Research indicates that this part of the brain plays a mediating role between pain-pleasure, tension-relaxation, and flight-fight (Steinke, 1993).[12]

The processes for loving, caring, and nurturing in humans and other animals come from the cortex, a part of the brain not present in reptiles.

Reactions out of the limbic brain are based on emotional impulses that are not informed by external realities. The motto for the limbic brain might be, "Don't confuse me with facts, they interfere with my emotions!" Steinke says about the reptilian and mammalian brains:

> They are well connected by neurons. Involved with involuntary reactions they operate like "clockwork." But being automatic, they cannot be inventive; being reactive, they cannot be creative. They are slaves to precedent and strangers to novelty. (Steinke, 1993)

Cerebral Cortex–The cerebral cortex, or higher brain, is designed for thoughtfulness, planning, reflection, playfulness, insights, and creativity. It is capable of new learning. It is the site concerned about the survival and maximum potentiation of the human being. Leadership complete with a vision and the capacity to share that vision come out of the cortex.

As the executing part, ordinarily, the cortex is in charge of the human brain and nervous system. However, when the human is threatened and anxious, it is possible for the limbic system to take over. The problem gets worse when the cortex thinks it is still in charge when it is not. We cannot assume people are not anxious because they appear to be thinking in a reasonable manner. Friedman points out that a person may have mental activity, but it may not be rational thought (Friedman, 1991).[13] It is mental activity in reaction to real or imagined threat.

Under intense threat, a regression to the reptilian brain may occur. Operating primarily out of the instinctually driven functions of the reptilian brain, behavior may be characterized by an intolerance for difference, dichotomous rigidity, extreme seriousness or bland affect, and an inability to receive new learning (Steinke, 1993).[14]

It is out of the functions of the neocortex that we are distinctly human beings. The neocortex enables us to live in self-awareness, to reflect on events, and to create for the future. We are more than reactive toward life. We are more than lower animals who live in a survival mode. We can respond through our thinking processes. We evolve a process that uses our whole brain.

Mind-Set

Every living system functions within the parameters of its particular survival instincts, but for humans, survival is more than a physical concern. We have both physical and psychological needs and capabilities that require fulfillment. Our particular world-view provides the general frames of reference from which to seek out specific situations. This generalized state of readiness to respond selectively to life events may be called a mind-set. Thus, our mind-set is a predisposition to perceive, distort, and/or keep out of awareness certain parts of life events for the purposes of survival, safety, and growth. Our mind-set, and its concomitant filtering process, is designed to operate in the service of our worldview.

It is out of the functions of the neocortex that we are distinctly human beings.

In a reciprocal feedback operation, our worldview, which shapes the mind-set, is shaped by the filtering process of our mind-set. Like a quantity of liquid that has changing shapes, our worldview, which programs our mind-set, is in turn shaped by the mind-set through which experiences are poured. What and how we abstract out of life events, how we react to events, and thus, what we consequently learn about living is governed by the interactive feedback process between our worldview and our mind-set. The practical result is that we actively pick and choose what we think, feel, and do and what we think, feel, and do in turn influences what we pick and choose to think, feel, and do.

Life Filter

The life filter is a conceptualization of the complex process whereby, in our own unique way, we experience the world in which we live and exist. The life filter may be thought of as an inborn psychological process that distinguishes certain events for survival purposes. It is an unconscious screening process whereby parts of events are experienced, and other parts are not consciously experienced. Each of us encounters enormous amounts of information every second. At best, we can process only a few items at one time. So, we experience only information seen as essential to our survival, well-being, and growth. In a real way, our life filter determines what our experiences of the world will be and, in turn, what choices we make available to ourselves.

The life filter is the psychological equivalent of the way the body responds to a disruption in its physical state of equilibrium. Any change in the steady state of our body generates an organic response of some kind. Certain stimuli in the surrounding environment activate human sensory receptors such as the eyes, ears, nose, etc. In the interest of survival, the stimuli are picked up by the appropriate sense receptor. For instance, the human will respond to intensely bright light by narrowing the pupil of the eye, and/or closing the eyelid, and/or turning the head away from the light. It is important to note that the adjustment of the pupil of the eye takes place instantaneously so that the eye does not consciously experience a harmful amount of light. It is as if there is a set prescreening point operating to protect the eye from physically harmful amounts of light. The set prescreening point operates according to the dictates of the self with its philosophy of life (worldview) and its mind-set.

The life filter operates similarly when dealing with psychological survival information. Sensory input that would overwhelm psychological survival requirements is screened and either recorded out of conscious awareness or altered into a more psychologically acceptable form. This process of change in the nature of information available to us is essentially what takes place when we use defense mechanisms such as repression, denial, projection, etc.

Reticular Activating System

The reticular activating system located in the central core of the brain stem is a small bundle of cells about the size of one-fourth of an apple. This network of cells, which serves as a sensory filter for the brain, is called the reticular activating system. It is the physical source for the functions of the conceptualization of the life filter. It is an electric powerhouse, a spark of the mind, and a protector of our psychological survival. In its role as our protector, it sifts, filters, and sends forward information necessary for our survival. The brain is assaulted with millions of impulses every second. Only a small number are allowed to influence the brain; only a small number are needed for survival. If a fire alarm sounds, the reticular activating system functions to bring that information to our attention. The reticular activating system lets us know what we need for survival. The reticular core runs our behavior patterns and monitors all the nerves connecting the brain with the rest of the body. It filters incoming stimuli and decides from millisecond to millisecond what information is going to become part of a person's experience of the world. Its function is to filter incoming information according to the dictates of our mind-set and to operate like a homing device to seek that which conforms to our survival and growth needs.

Basically, we strive to see that part of events that is congruent with our mind-set.

This means that once you have adopted certain values, beliefs, and assumptions, your reticular activation system acts accordingly.

Thus, over time, as we operate from a particular mind-set, complete with belief structures that organize our "reality," we evolve specific patterned stances from which we view the world.

This predisposition to view the world in a particular way is an active seeking-out process. We seek to distinguish certain aspects of events. Basically, we strive to see that part of events that are congruent with our mind-set. And, our mind-set is congruent with our worldview.

Information, or feedback, is the energizer of the living human system. We constantly seek information about how we are doing in our efforts to survive, find safety, and grow. Through the feedback process, humans work to control what they see and what they do not see. The goal is to see that which, at a minimum, does not threaten survival. Also, we *do* what is consistent with our perception of what is congruent with our mind-set, worldview, and life filter processes. We are exactly who and what we are. Our way of seeing the world and our actions reflect us as we are.

As humans, we make meaning out of events. For instance, an event takes place such as lightning in the sky. The event has no inherent meaning; we make the meaning out of the event. For some, lightning in the sky is frightening and something to fear. For other people, lightning is beautiful and thought of as the fireworks of God. How an event is perceived is a manifestation of the operations of our mind-set, worldview, and life filter processes (i.e., *who we are*).

Psychological and emotional needs are enormously complex. The pressures of survival, safety, and growth move us to deal with conflicts concerning pain and pleasure, desires for loving and being loved, being a part of and being separate, and being valuable and finding value in others. We are, by nature, socially competitive creatures; conflict is built into our being (Glasser, 1981). The complex mind-set activities of the reticular activating system are designed to enable us to survive and prosper in an unpredictable world according to our worldviews. As Scott Peck has said, "Life is difficult."[15] We constantly seek the answers to the questions, What is life all about and What must I be to take it in this worldly existence? And we live out the answer in our lives.

Emotional Rightness

Human beings are designed for survival, safety, and growth, both physically and psychologically. The genetically based characteristic that has provided the essential spark of life throughout the history of humankind, *the survival instinct,* also contains the ingredients for *the most destructive part of human existence.* Embedded in the survival instinct is the human mind's drivenness to establish the correct physical and psychological conditions for survival. Only people with the instinct to do what is physically correct have survived.

In the *physical domain,* the built-in autonomic body functions and the mind-set work together to discover *the correct* actions needed for survival. Natural laws in the physical domain are consistent and predictable enough that it is relatively easy to establish the right survival patterns or actions. Water is always water, gravity always works the same way, and the body's response to certain temperatures is quite predictable.

In the *psychological domain,* survival matters are not so predictable. For instance, the correct patterns for meeting love, worth, and identity needs are not so easily identified. Humans exhibit an enormous range of behavior patterns in the course of human experience. Some of the behavioral patterns seem to work for some people but not for other people. Some patterns seem to work on a short-term basis and not on a long-term basis. Knowing what is correct and, if known, the willingness to do what is correct in the psychological domain are complicated matters for human beings.

We have choices within the broad constraints of human behavior. Freedom of choice is the source of our uniqueness. It is also the human capacity for freedom of choice that makes life unpredictable and threatening.

The genetically based characteristic that has provided the essential spark of life throughout the centuries, the survival instinct, also contains the ingredients for the most destructive part of human existence.

We seek the freedom to do as we wish and the predictability of knowing what is right in human affairs. Genetically, we are driven to sense that we are correct in our survival actions. Instinctively, we require the "correct" mind-set from which to deal with all that goes on around us. Unfortunately, human history demonstrates that when past and present life experiences have been and/or are painful and life threatening, the demand to be correct in matters of survival sometimes becomes forced and emotionalized. When threatened, the human fight or flight response demands to know what to do to survive. Under conditions of acute or chronic pain, threat, and vulnerability, the psychological need to find the correct survival conditions becomes an *emotionalized* demand to be right. The emotionalized demand to be right assumes a primary survival position. Physical and psychological survival needs become fused. The limbic brain, which houses our feelings and emotions, spills over into the executive functions of the higher brain, the cortex. The emotion of fear has the capacity to overwhelm the thinking function of the brain. The biologically driven mind-set locks in on specific thinking patterns as the "right" survival actions (Glasser, 1981).[16] It is at those very times when flexibility of thinking and actions are needed that the emotionalized demand to be right moves us to react with rigid automatic processes.

At such times we may think we are in control, yet an emotionalized demand to be right has moved to the forefront of our behavioral considerations. Emotionalized rightness makes reflective behavior and creativity impossible because the mind is set to defend, *on a survival basis*, anything the mind-set regards as right. The worldview, primarily based in the cerebral cortex, comes under the domination of reactions located in the limbic and/or reptilian brain. Being psychologically right assumes a survival demand. Under the domination of the subcortex, then, we lose our uniqueness as human beings. Anxiety rules! We revert to automatic survival reactions, and our capacity to be fully human is greatly diminished.

NOTES

1. Satir, V., Stachowiak, J., and Jaschman, H. (1980). *Helping Families to Change*. New York: Jason Aronson, pp. 41-42.

2. Eccles, J. (1973). *The Understanding of the Brain*. New York: McGraw-Hill, pp. 188-194.

3. See Smotherman, R. (1980). *Winning Through Enlightenment*. San Francisco, CA: Context Publications, p. 57.

4. Eccles, p. 190.

5. Eccles, p. 219.

6. Frankl, V.E. (1975). *The Unconscious God*. New York: Simon and Schuster, p. 13.

7. Carter, S.L. (1993). *The Culture of Disbelief*. New York: Basic Books.

8. Kerr, M. and Bowen, M. (1988). *Family Evaluation*. New York: Norton.

9. Watzlawick, P., Beavin, J.H., and Jackson, D. (1967). *Pragmatics of Human Communication: A Study of Interactions Patterns, Pathologies and Paradoxes*. New York: Norton, p. 260.

10. Eccles, p. 223.

11. MacLean, P. (1985). Brain Evolution Related to Family, Play and the Isolation Call, *Archives of General Psychology, 42*, 405-417.

12. Steinke, P.L. (1993). *How Your Church Works*. Washington, DC: The Allan Institute, p. 16.

13. Friedman, E.N. (1991). "Bowen Theory and Therapy," in A. Gurman and D. Kniskern (Eds.). *Handbook of Family Therapy*, Vol. II, New York: Brunner/Mazel, p. 140.

14. Steinke, p. 73.

15. See Peck, S. (1978). *The Road Less Traveled*. New York: Simon and Schuster.

16. Glasser, W. (1981). *Stations of the Mind*. New York: Harper and Row.

CHAPTER 3

NECESSARY BUT NOT SUFFICIENT CONSIDERATIONS: PART ONE

Managing the complex web of relational realities is not easy for the human being. Life demands that we establish a distinct self that: (1) is separate from, *and* in relationship to, other people; (2) is connected to, and not controlled by, the many social contexts in which humans live; and (3) finds its relationship to the spiritual realm.

We are like all life, and we are unique in our capacities for survival and full potential. We are uniquely equipped to manage the complex web of relational realities. At the same time, the very capacities that serve our survival needs turn against us when they do not work together with our total being.

You can be as reactive with your thinking brain as you can with your feeling brain.

Our primitive survival instincts, which enable us to react to immediate life threatening events, also may be counterproductive in the ongoing processes of living and moving toward full potential. The basic survival instincts of the lower brain are appropriate as immediate reactions to real or imagined threat. But, reactions out of the lower brain are automatic and are not mediated by the cortex. For the full potential of cortical activities to be realized, instinctual activity must give way to the thinking, creative processes of our higher brain.

On the other hand, when anxiety is intense, the activities of our higher brain can be captured by survival functions. The thinking processes are used in the service of survival activities. When anxiety is high, what we think may be merely mental activity, rather than cognitive processes. You can be as reactive with your thinking brain as you can with your feeling brain.

The process in which people flourish best is one that maximizes each individual's ability to keep the thinking and emotional systems in an appropriate balance. The core manifestation of such appropriate balance is the extension of choice and considered responses in the process of life. Clearheaded choices based on thinking and feelings are the basis for productive life decisions—decisions that have a high probability of working well for all the realities.

Given the nature of the relational systems model for examining family activities, some necessary but not sufficient considerations are proposed as a way to create a treatment atmosphere in which there is a high probability for therapeutic success.

In the RSM, "necessary but not sufficient" means that to have a high probability for treatment success there are key considerations that require therapist attention during the treatment process. If these considerations are not given adequate attention, an effective treatment process is not likely. To the extent the considerations are accounted for, an effective treatment process is likely. Taken as a whole, the necessary but not sufficient considerations provide a therapeutic stance for the therapist.

The necessary but not sufficient considerations take into account two powerful forces in the therapeutic atmosphere. Each force is important as a separate entity and at the same time both are intertwined with each other. Taken together, both forces exert enormous control over the atmosphere in which the treatment will take place.

The *first* therapeutic force to be considered is the person-of-the-therapist. The therapist is the basic change agent for the family system. The introduction of the therapist into the ongoing family process lets the possibilities for change to take place. The therapist's use-of-self becomes paramount in the whole process (Satir et al., 1991).[1] Bowen systems thinking also provides us with a powerful model for looking at the self-of-the-therapist. For Bowen, the concept of self-differentiation is not only basic to the treatment process, it is a treatment technique in and of itself (Friedman, 1991).[2] Given the importance of the self-of-the-therapist, the maturity level of the therapist is a vital factor in the treatment process. The work of the therapist will be limited to the extent that the therapist is stuck at a particular level in the self-differentiation process.

The *second* powerful force in the treatment atmosphere is a set of interrelated relational dynamics that form *core considerations for all human relationships*. In the therapeutic context, the power of the core considerations is magnified. The nature of the therapy event heightens anxiety for every participant. Survival reactions are set to be brought into play if viewed as necessary by the client. Therapy looks at client behavior. The threat of being wrong or "at fault" for problems in a family is fearful to all human beings. The core considerations are the processes of right/wrong, worthiness, responsibility, purpose, worldview, and communications. To the extent that the core considerations are given full attention in the treatment process, the likelihood of an effective treatment process is enhanced.

SELF-DIFFERENTIATION

The concept of differentiation in family systems thinking was first introduced by Murray Bowen. It has been expanded upon by family therapists who have followed the Bowen Systems Model. It is a term borrowed from biology. It looks at the interrelatedness of parts. For instance, it deals with how parts of our own body perform separate but related functions to make up a whole person. In family systems thinking, self-differentiation is about the integrity and self-regulation of an individual as he or she relates to the complex set of realities that are part of human life. In that sense, differentiation is a universal life process.

The process of differentiation is a universal life process.

Self-differentiation is concerned about one's uniqueness or self-definition in the face of pressure toward groupness. It is the capacity to be a solid self throughout various human encounters and social situations.

Friedman talks about differentiation as "the capacity to become oneself out of one's self with a minimum reactivity to the positions or reactivity of others. It is charting one's own way by means of one's own internal guidance system rather than perpetually eyeing the 'scope' to see where others are located" (Friedman, 1991).[3]

Self-differentiation also involves self-regulation. It is the capacity to manage reactivity when survival anxiety arouses the autonomic responses of the lower brain. The basic level of differentiation of self is manifest in the degree to which an individual manages to keep thinking and emotional processes separate, or differentiated. It is the capacity to retain *choice* between behavior governed by thinking and behavior controlled by emotional reactivity, and to set a life course based on carefully thought out principles and goals (Papero, 1990).

To be self-regulated means to maintain a life long process of standing on your own two feet in human relationships. It is the capacity to articulate a self, to know where you end and the other begins, and not to be reactive to pathology.

In summary, self-differentiation is the process of responding to life events in a distinct clear-headed manner. Responding in a clear-headed manner means that the emotional and thinking parts of functioning have to be accounted for under the direction of our higher brain. It is an antidote to chronic and acute anxiety.

Self-Differentiation Scale

It is possible to consider the self-differentiation process through the use of a self-differentiation scale ranging from zero to one hundred. The self-differentiation scale in Figure 3.1 provides a bipolar continuum with differentiated at the high end of the scale and undifferentiated at the low end of the scale. The scale shows that depending on the extent to which one has the capacity for

FIGURE 3.1. Self-Differentiation Scale

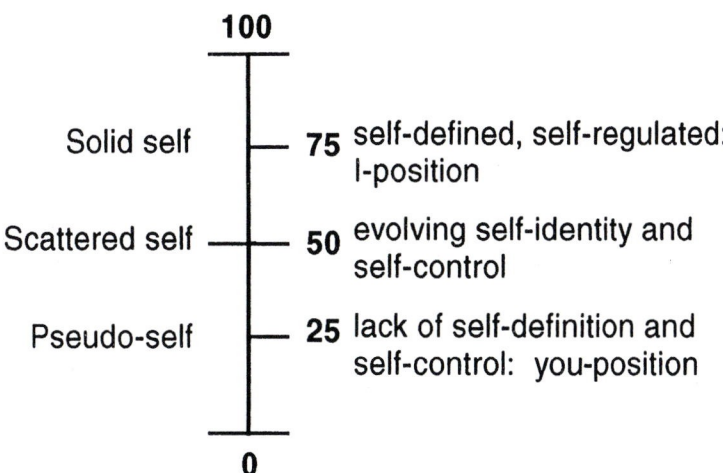

differentiating, his or her life is influenced either by higher brain activities or by the survival-driven dictates of the limbic and reptilian parts of the brain.

Those of us with strong differentiating capacities are located at the higher end of the scale. We are likely to make decisions in a thoughtful, clearheaded way that fully accounts for our feelings and emotions. We are likely to operate from an I-position that is based on our life principles and goals. At the higher levels on the scale, we know who and what we are and act accordingly. We tend toward a solid self.

Those of us located at the lower end of the self-differentiation scale are driven by automatic survival reactions. The lack of self-definition and self-regulation exposes us to the anxieties of the world around us. The lower we are on the scale, the more likely we are to operate out of a stuck you-position in which we blame others and the environment for our problems. Not knowing who and what we are, we are prone to adopt the latest trend or fad of the day. We need to be politically and socially correct. We have a pseudo-self.

Most of us are located somewhere in the mid-range on the self-differentiation scale. We have some sense of who and what we are, but we are open to the pressures of our surrounding culture. At times, we succumb to such enticements as power, money, position, and social acceptability as proofs of worth. We have a scattered self. We evolve certain values and beliefs, and emotionally defend them when they are questioned. At a higher level of the mid-range of differentiation, we know our operating values and beliefs, and as needed, we transcend them.

At our best, we operate out of an I-position, and at our worst, we react to stress and anxiety by taking a you-position. We are not likely to be stuck in any position; we have a scattered self. Most of us locate somewhere on the mid-range of the self-differentiation scale.

Self-Regulation, Self-Definition, and Self-Differentiation

The forces of self-regulation and self-definition symbolize the whole differentiation process. Each is unique and each requires the other in the process of self-differentiation. The entire process flows out of (1) the life forces that push for separateness and togetherness and (2) the survival, safety, and growth needs that control the activities of our brain. At its best, the differentiation process brings human emotional and thinking processes together under the overall direction of the neocortex. To the extent that the differentiation process is engaged by the therapist, there will be a tendency toward the following related responses by the therapist:

A. *There will be a capacity to take a stand in an intense emotional situation.* In one sense, emotions are catching. It is difficult for an individual not to get caught up in the emotions of a situation especially when the emotion is triggered by a perceived threat to the self; the therapist remains clearheaded and yet connected to the emotional activity;

B. *Closely related to the first activity is the capacity to maintain a nonanxious presence in the face of anxious others.* There is a balancing dynamic that takes place as the therapist becomes a kind of transformer for the flow of anxiety. If emotions need to be calmed *or* energized, the therapist can help by his or her nonanxious presence;

It is difficult for an individual not to get caught up in the emotions of a situation, especially when the emotion is triggered by a perceived threat to the self.

C. *The capacity to be an "I" when others and the context are demanding a "we."* Operating primarily out of one's own internal guidance system, the I-position reflects what fits for the particular person. The I-position is a caring, nonblaming, nondemanding clear statement about where "I" stand at a particular time. The I-position is predicated on a nonjudgmental relationship with clients. Taking an I-position is basic to the self-differentiation process. It means being congruent at all levels–verbal and nonverbal. Virginia Satir was a master of the I-position;

D. *There will be clarity about where one begins and ends.* The personal boundary issue in the therapy process includes the therapist-client boundary. Boundary dynamics often show up in a therapist's responsibility concerns. It is easy to become so concerned about the outcome of a counseling situation that I, as therapist, start to intrude in matters that belong to the decision domain of clients. Choice remains with the client;

E. *There will be a conscious effort to maintain a distinction between thinking and emotions.* Emotions arise in the process of treating clients. Emotions are appropriate in the context of counseling. The goal is to manage our automatic responses so that they are helpful when needed, but not beyond the point of need. The process of self-regulation rests on clarity between emotional and thinking processes;

F. *There will be clarity about one's values and beliefs.* A self that is solid and well-grounded is aware of the worldview that organizes her or his activities. If I do not know what my values and beliefs are, I am vulnerable to control by those who are fully aware of their organizing worldview. Self-definition requires self-awareness about my organizing values and beliefs. Knowing *where* I stand in life gives me a place *to* stand in life;

G. *The capacity to think systemically and to avoid polarizations.* The relational dynamics of the world are both broad and deep as well as complex. The mind-set that includes lineal and circular thinking will have a flexibility that serves survival, safety, and growth needs;

H. ***And,*** *being fully connected to others and the surrounding contexts.* The *and* here is vital to the differentiation process. Self-regulation and self-definition are vehicles for fully relating to others and the surrounding contexts.

From the relational systems perspective, a differentiating therapist is essential to the creation of a therapeutic atmosphere.

While we have been discussing self-differentiation for the worker/therapist, identifying the process of differentiation in a troubled family is critical to the therapy process. Most Bowen family systems therapists actively seek out and work with the family member who is functioning at the highest level of self-differentiation in the family unit. Much of the initial work is with the most differentiating family member. Starting with the strength in the family is congruent with an emphasis on the processes of health rather than pathology.

Relational Systems and Differentiating

From the relational systems perspective, a differentiating therapist is essential to the creation of a therapeutic atmosphere. So, to the extent that I am a differentiating therapist, I am engaged in a present process of knowing who and what I am from a context of love, caring, and integrity. Let us examine each part of the process.

Present Process–This means that in the here and now I have a direction in life that is evolving rather than stuck in a fixed state.

Of Knowing–This means that I am self-aware about my values, priorities, and beliefs. This is not a momentary self-awareness; it is a process that gives substance to my connection to myself. I am acquainted with me.

Who and What I Am–This means that my values, priorities, and beliefs form a conscious worldview for me. It means that I have a personal context from which I view the world, and I am acquainted with it. I have a self-definition that guides me in my self-regulation process and vice-versa.

Context–There is a context, an organizing frame of reference in my worldview or life paradigm to which I am connected and from which I get my meaning. It serves as the background for all that I do. The meaning of my personal life context evolves from the answer to the question, What is the purpose of what and who I create myself to be? The forces of love, caring, and integrity engage the vital processes of growth and full potential.

Loving, Caring, and Integrity–The essential forces of my context are:

a. *Love.* This means to actively build up others and the world around. It means to focus unconditionally on strengths and build up the positive creative parts of self, others, and context. It is an active, doing direction. Love recognizes that the forces for health, strength, and growth–life itself–are inside each of us.

b. *Caring.* Caring means the process of being concerned about another through the expressions of empathy, honesty, and connectedness. The caring forces push connectedness when the activities of the lower brain push for separation and disconnectedness. Caring draws people together.

c. *Integrity.* This means to be honest and congruent in everything.

It means to show who and what I am, and to be who and what I am and who I say I am. The forces of integrity let me be me.

In the relational systems model, differentiating is a conscious activity used by the worker/therapist to enhance the effectiveness of the therapeutic process. Differentiating involves self-awareness and goes beyond the awareness of self. It is a *direction* in life that manifests who and what the therapist is as a person. One is never differentiated; we are always in the process of differentiating.

The process of differentiating is difficult. Differentiating involves growth, and growth is not easy. Navigating the developmental stages of life for individual, family, and wider social systems means change amidst sameness. The task of attention to self without creating overdetermined self-centeredness and self-concern is the essential process of differentiating. In the growth process, attention to self is for the purposes of integrity, not for narcissistic enhancements.

Self-Differentiation Exercise

As an exercise, estimate where you might be located on the self-differentiation scale. Take a few moments to recall some recent situations that were highly stressful. How did you handle the stress? What was the basis for the way you handled the situation? Be honest! ("I needed to do it this way." "It was the right thing to do for my reputation!") Think carefully about how you handled the situation, what you did, and how you explained to yourself the basis for your decisions. (See Figure 3.2.)

FIGURE 3.2

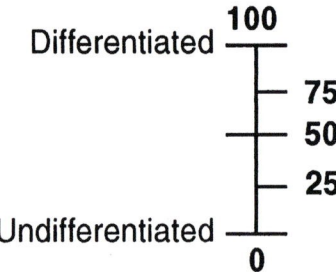

Reflect on your decisions. How do the decisions *tell* you exactly who and what you are? Everything you do, feel, and think is you! ("I thought about the situation." "I felt my anxiety." "I will make this particular decision because it reflects clearly who and what I am." "Where do I locate myself?")

Think about people who are important to you in your life. Who is the most differentiating person you know? Who is the most undifferentiating? (See Figure 3.3.) Give specific reasons for your evaluation of each person.

Knowing who and what you are in the present context of love, caring, and integrity is a powerful force in the creation of an effective therapeutic atmosphere.

Differentiation and Health

Friedman's ideas about differentiation focus on health. The characteristic that all pathogens have in common is the absence of a factor that regulates their own growth and behavior (Friedman, 1991).[4] The characteristic of all troubled activities is an inability to say no when it is required. For instance, all of us have pathogens in our body. It is not the presence of pathogens that causes disease in the body; it is a lack of health. Likewise, it is not the presence of troubling activities that results in dysfunctional behavior; it is the lack of coping capacities to deal with the problems. Continuing the medical metaphor, the goal is to strengthen the immunological possibilities. Enhancing the differentiating capacities of family members serves to optimize the conditions necessary to energize the

FIGURE 3.3

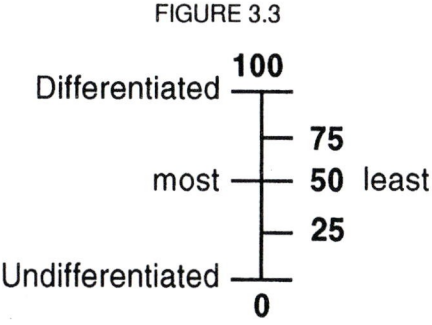

coping processes. The Bowen systems perspective rests on the idea that to the extent the differentiating is not active in the treatment process, all tactics and techniques of therapy are limited.

Identifying the forces of health becomes a major goal of the treatment process.

The health of the client is in the client system. Identifying and energizing the forces of health become major goals of the treatment process. It means creating a therapeutic atmosphere where the client system can locate its own strengths and solutions. The emphasis on strength means that the differentiating therapist values and gives attention to the differentiation process both for himself or herself and for the family system.

NOTES

1. Satir, V., Banman, J., Gerber, J., and Gomori, M. (1991). *The Satir Model.* Palo Alto, CA: Science and Behavior Books, Inc., p. 26.

2. Friedman, E.N. (1991). "Bowen Theory and Therapy," in A. Gurman and D. Kniskern (Eds.). *Handbook of Family Therapy*, Vol. II, New York: Brunner/ Mazel, p. 138.

3. Friedman, p. 141.

4. Friedman, see entire article.

CHAPTER 4

NECESSARY BUT NOT SUFFICIENT CONSIDERATIONS: PART TWO

CORE CONSIDERATIONS FOR CREATING
AN EFFECTIVE THERAPEUTIC ATMOSPHERE

To the extent that there are individual, couple, and family-unit problems in the differentiation process, dysfunction will show up in the core considerations necessary for creating an effective therapeutic atmosphere. The differentiating therapist will actively address the core-considerations. He or she will not get entangled in the dysfunctional manifestations of these powerful core dynamics.

Relational Right/Wrong

When I talk about right/wrong in the therapeutic context, I am not talking about a moral sense or a standard for the good of society. I am not talking about rules or the lack of rules. I am not talking about making correct or incorrect decisions as part of problem solving. I *am* talking about a position, a view, or frame of reference toward the right/wrong dynamic that exists in all human relationships.

The frame for our consideration of the right/wrong dynamics is the helping process that takes place in a therapeutic context. I am addressing the right/wrong dynamic in the sense of the psychological survival issues in a relationship process in which there is an "I win, you lose" outcome. It is a win/lose transaction in which to win is to be right and to lose is to be wrong, and to lose threatens one's psychological survival. Under threat, lower brain activities take over and anxiety becomes a powerful motivating force. The right/wrong dynamic becomes emotionally charged. It becomes emotionalized right/wrong.

I have observed that all human beings have a dreaded fear of being wrong, of not being right. From the earliest age there is absolute attention on the need to be right, all of the time. For instance, the educational process awards being right. Papers are to be written right; the answers to quiz questions are to be right.

Encouragement and approval, which are emotionally necessary for young children to grow, are used as rewards for being right. ("You did that right; you are such a good girl.") Being wrong means being rejected by parents, teachers, and peers. Being right quickly gets tied into self-esteem. Being wrong is a matter of shame. Being wrong quickly becomes a threat to our well being. We cannot accept that we are wrong; it's a matter of psychological survival. As a survival issue, the right/wrong dynamic has become emotionalized.

All humans have a dreaded fear of being wrong, of not being right.

Some years ago, a particular high school experienced an excessively high drop-out rate, falling grades, and high absenteeism. In response to these concerns, a strict dress code was adopted. The dress code was approved by the parents and the school officials. Each student was restricted to $150.00 per year for clothing costs. That meant that there were no designer jeans, shirts, etc. It was difficult to be unacceptable or wrong because of the clothes one wore. Student grades went up, the drop out rate was lowered, and absenteeism virtually disappeared. While being wrong is threatening to all of us, it is especially threatening to teenagers.

There is a group of people who establish their rightness by being wrong all of the time. These people are sometimes referred to as the "poor me" people. "I'm right. I told you I could not do it. I am right again." "I am always wrong, and I knew I would be wrong again."

There is the story of the rat-in-the-maze looking for cheese. You place a rat in a maze with ten tubes. The cheese in at the end of tube ten. The rat will quickly explore all the tubes until the cheese is found down tube ten. Later, if you put the rat in the maze again, the rat will explore the tubes very briefly until the cheese is again found down tube ten. After about the third experience in the maze, the rat will quickly go down tube ten to find the cheese. Now, if the cheese is moved to tube five, the rat will first go down tube ten, come out, scratch its nose, go down tube ten again. After about two or three trips down tube ten, the rat will start to explore the other tubes in search of the cheese. When confronted with the same situation, the human being will continue to go down tube ten muttering something to the effect that "I know it's down tube ten. It's always been down tube ten. I know I am right; the cheese is down tube ten." Humans all too often continue to go down tube ten hoping to be proven *right*. We get to be right, but we don't get the cheese. Emotionalized right/wrong is a survival issue.

There is one demand in life that ranks higher than physical survival–the psychological demand to be right.

Humans have a dreaded fear of being wrong! All of us seek to survive, physically and psychologically. Our bodies are designed to make use of food, water, air, love, etc. All living systems seek to survive. Only those systems with the survival instinct have survived over the centuries. It may be observed that one demand in life often ranks higher than physical survival–the psychological demand to be right. Some people have died in order to be right. Duels, wars, and gang battles are examples of the power of the emotionalized demand to be right. Rightness is given incredible survival value.

Some years ago I saw a client whose whole life was organized around the demand to be right. He was professionally educated and had an IQ of around 160. With an IQ that high, he often proved himself to be right in arguments with other people. He came in for one session expressing frustration about his relationship with his girlfriend. He related story after story where he had argued with his girlfriend, proven her wrong, and ended up in even more troublesome disagreements with her. Toward the end of the session, he concluded with a statement to the effect that he did not know how to make things more positive with his girlfriend because he had "time after time showed her how she was wrong." When I pointed out to him that it seemed that the only thing he was getting out of the relationship was that he was right, he was ready to begin examining his drivenness to be right. The question in many relationships may come down to a choice: Do you want a positive relationship or do you want to be right all the time? We cannot have it both ways.

A relationship pattern in which one person is right and the other is wrong all of the time has a low probability of providing satisfaction and growth to either person.

A relationship pattern in which one person is right and the other is wrong all of the time has a low probability of providing satisfaction and growth to either person. The party who is "proven" wrong must find some way to deal with the survival threat that accompanies being emotionally wrong. The probability of either social, emotional, or physical dysfunction in the relationship is very high.

In the emotionalized right/wrong dynamic we are not talking about rules in life. Clearly, certain actions are unacceptable. There are actions that break the law. In my view, any activity that is destructive to self, others, or the environment is wrong. It is unacceptable because of the destructive consequences. People are hurt and our world is damaged. On a moral basis, certain activities are wrong. Life is full of choices. We are required to make decisions, some of which work out well and some do not. That is a reality of life!

Some years ago I treated a couple for rather severe marital problems. The husband worked in the state legislature, and the wife was a legal secretary. The wife's threat to divorce the husband motivated both of them to seek marital therapy. From the very beginning of the treatment process, emotionalized right/wrong was a powerful dynamic in the problems between the couple. During therapy, their relationship improved slowly but consistently as they both worked to put their emotionalized right/wrong concerns aside in order to get to the resolution of other problems.

Eight weeks into the treatment, the husband came to a scheduled session alone. With an extremely angry voice and an equally angry look on his face, he announced that he was filing for divorce. He had gone through a terrible experience with his wife. She was wrong in how she treated him, and she was unaware of how awful she had treated him. ("Doc, I don't care what you say, she was wrong!") After a short period of time, I asked him to tell me what had happened to make him so angry. He told me that several days ago he came home excited and announced to his wife that he was on the verge of legislative success concerning a bill coming up for a vote the next day. His wife's rather bland response to his excitement made him angry. ("She was wrong in her response to me.") The next morning as he was getting ready to go to the legislature, his wife said she was not feeling well and asked him to drop their daughter off at the nursery school. ("Can you believe it? I am going in for one of my most successful days, and she blandly asks me to take our daughter to the nursery school.")

The legislation he was involved in passed that morning. He called his wife to invite her to a celebration luncheon. She told him that she had already made other plans that she could not break. ("She is so insensitive to me and what I want.") Later that day a second bill that he had written passed. Beyond himself in excitement, he again called his wife to tell her that a big party was being planned for the evening and he wanted her to go with him. ("She really wasn't excited about it but she agreed to go.") That evening when they attempted to drop their daughter off at the home of the babysitter, the babysitter was sick and could not care for their daughter. When his wife wanted to go back home with their daughter, he told her she and the daughter were going to the party. He took both of them to the celebration, but he was angry that his wife stayed out of most of the celebrating to care for their daughter. ("Can you believe it? She stayed in the corner with our daughter. She showed no excitement about what we had accomplished that day. She is insensitive. She treats me wrong, and she won't admit it!")

When my client had finished, I asked him to try something. I asked him to tell me the story of yesterday's events again. I further asked him to tell the story without making his wife wrong. With an angry response he said, "I got up, went to work, and came home." I told him I had a bit more in mind than what he had just told me. We worked on other versions of the story until he was able, on his own, to tell about the events of the previous day without making his wife wrong.

When he finally told me what had happened and did not make his wife wrong in telling the story, he paused, looked into the distance, and with tears in his eyes said, "You know, when I came here this morning, I was determined to divorce my wife. Right now, I can't wait to get home and hug her." It was one of those rare times when as a therapist you feel goose pimples on your body. It was a time of an emotional breakthrough for the client.

***

Tell me the story of yesterday's events without making your wife wrong.

When emotionalized right/wrong overrides all other consider-ations, it is very difficult to bring the thinking functions into the relationship process. If, as the therapist, you have refused to get caught in the emotionalized right/wrong dynamic, your very non-anxious presence is therapeutic in itself.

In over a third of a century as a therapist/change agent, I have never seen a troubled client where the emotionalized right/wrong dynamic was absent. In the therapeutic situation, the vital elements of emotionalized right/wrong show up almost immediately. The therapeutic process is fearful to most clients. Basic to the healing process is your intention as a therapist to deal with the right/wrong dynamic in a way that does not energize emotionalized right/wrong. Rules or behavior that do not work need to be faced by the client. Problems must be confronted. Destructive behavior requires identi-fication, but not as part of an emotionalized process. The therapist works against emotionalizing any part of the relationship processes that take place in the treatment atmosphere. By not being a part of the emotionalized right/wrong process, the therapist is better able to be a non-anxious presence.

The therapeutic stance deals with the right/wrong dynamic in a way that does not energize emotionalized right/wrong.

The therapeutic atmosphere is a climate that offers a place to deal with the tough questions that face a family. The process of facing relationship issues in a straightforward nonblaming way is part of the power of the therapeutic process. Therapy *is* the place to con-sider alternative ways to relate and problem solve. The goal is to move out of the emotionalize right/wrong framework for relation ships. The therapist is most powerful when he or she is a nonanxi-ous presence that does not locate in the emotionalized right/wrong dynamic.

When working in the therapeutic domain, you are not primarily concerned with such issues as right or wrong, guilt or innocence, hero or heroine, etc. The purpose is to promote activities that will enable the client to consider new and different activities. From this perspective, the language of right/wrong, victim or victimizer is not likely to be helpful.

For instance, in a child abuse situation, will establishing the wrongness or guilt of an abusing parent be therapeutically helpful? Remember we are speaking about the therapeutic context. Will making the abuser "bad" likely reduce the chances of abuse happening again? It is a fine line between establishing in detail what happened without exacting the pound of "you are bad to the core" flesh. Yet, the behavior must be confronted as part of owning what is one's to own.

If you are working in a context that is not therapeutic in purpose, the view of right/wrong may be different. For instance, if the decision to be made is primarily administrative or legal, your purpose may be to clearly identify the behavior and to determine the legal or administrative ramifications of the abusive behavior. Even in those situations, therapeutic help is most likely to come from an atmosphere that does not energize the psychological survival forces that fuel emotional right/wrong. Establishing exactly what happened *by whom* in detail confronts the issue.

In the therapeutic context, will establishing the wrongness or guilt of an abusing parent be therapeutically helpful?

The context for communication is important. Right/wrong language often has to do with morality and, as such, is moral language. For instance, it is morally wrong to abuse another, no matter what the provocation might be. There are rights and wrongs in the domain of morality. There are moral absolutes that guide the activities of many people.

In the legal domain there is the language of right and wrong, crime, guilt, innocent, perpetrator, and victim. In the legal domain there are the guilty and there are the innocent. The guilty must pay for their crimes.

In the problem-solving domain of life we make many decisions; some of them work out well and some of them do not. We learn from consequences what works and what does not work. In the domain of decision making, we see more clearly if we do not make incorrect decisions a measure of our worth. In such a nonjudgmental approach, we operate in the realm of the present in which we examine *what* happened and only *what* happened. There are no personal judgments that raise the question, Am *I* wrong as a person because of the outcome? The process remains in the realm of deciding, decision making, outcomes, and consequences. When we add the personalized judgmental filter to life's constant flow of decision making, we increase the probability of emotionalizing decisions into the right/wrong domain. The built-in reaction in emotionalized right/wrong is to determine what is *wrong* with me, you, or the context. The mind will not let *me* be wrong because emotionalized right/wrong operates at the level of survival; the pain of being wrong is too much for me to handle.

In the therapeutic domain, there are the dynamics of complex human relationships. The purpose of the therapeutic domain is to provide a place where humans can sort out the nature of their relationships in ways that offer hope for alternative ways of being with themselves and others. The goal is to promote change, to empower clients, and to assist them in identifying alternative behaviors. It has been said that the height of dysfunction is to continue doing the same thing over and over, again and again, and expect different results. We engage the client in an examination of his or her life. We include in that examination a clear look at the client's personal worldview and what exactly he or she does to live out the personal worldview. We also look at the outcomes for particular activities. The ultimate purpose of therapy is to get everyone on their own two feet. Therapy inherently is a push toward self-differentiation. The goal of therapy is to get change going for the client. Bringing the right/wrong dynamics under control is necessary to the change process and to the creation of an effective therapeutic atmosphere.

My part as the therapist, in dealing with the right/wrong dynamics, is to remain committed to who and what I am within the context of love, caring, and integrity. I actively work on my own differentiating process. My actions as a therapist are correlated to who and what I am, rather than to the anxious processes before me. I am committed to the growth process within the client. I am totally connected to the client, but I will not be part of the anxious processes brought to the therapy context. It is not easy to be a nonanxious presence in the face of enormous anxiety that has a powerful past history and present momentum.

The ultimate in dysfunction is to do the same thing over and over, again and again, and expect different results.

Responsibility Consideration

The overwhelming fear of being wrong shows up in our lifelong struggle with personal responsibility. Personal responsibility has to do with the volitional part of our existence. It is our willingness to claim our autonomy. It is a recognition of the choices available to us as human beings. The story of Adam and Eve found in the book of Genesis in the Holy Bible identifies the fundamental place the responsibility dynamic holds in human relationships.

Relational responsibility means the willingness to own one's part in our activities with other people, nothing more and nothing less.

As the story goes, Adam and Eve lived in the Garden of Eden. Their living conditions were perfect. Excellent climate. Plenty of food and water. They had a personal relationship with God. They walked and talked with God. They could do just about anything they wanted to do except that they were not to eat the fruit of two particular trees in the center of the Garden.

One day Eve was out for a morning stroll when she found herself talking to a serpent. After some initial pleasantries, the serpent asked Eve why God had told her not to eat of the fruit of the particular trees in the center of the Garden. When Eve told the serpent what God had said, the serpent told Eve that God was lying. The serpent said that the only reason God did not want Adam and Eve to eat fruit from the tree was that the fruit would make Adam and Eve "be like Gods, knowing good and evil." In other words,

God was doing a con job on Adam and Eve for the purpose of keeping them lower than God.

Later, when Eve looked at one of the trees, the fruit looked good and she wanted the "wisdom" the serpent told her would be hers if she ate the fruit. She ate the fruit from the tree. She gave Adam some of the fruit and he ate it. The result was immediate! When God called for them, they were fearful and hid from God. When God questioned Adam about what he had done, Adam said, "The woman whom thou gavest to be with me, she gave me of the fruit of the tree and I did eat." Adam denied responsibility for his actions. He first blamed God, "that *you* gave me" and then he blamed Eve. ("She gave me of the bit of the tree and I did eat.") When God turned to the woman she said, "the serpent beguiled me and I did eat." Eve also denied any responsibility for her actions.

The story of Adam and Eve is the story of who we are as human beings. We are fearful of being wrong; we try to hide much of what we do, and we tend to deny responsibility for the choices we make. The story of Adam and Eve and their reaction to God when He questioned them about eating the fruit has been played out over and over, again and again, throughout the centuries. "It is not my fault." "I did not do it." "It was someone or something else that did it to me." It is also our story as we meet the anxieties of living. We hid from all four life realities: our self, others, the context, and God.

When we talk about our escape from freedom, we are talking about denying the choices available to us.

Relational responsibility means the willingness to own one's part in our activities with other people. It is a recognition of the implicit and explicit agreements we make with other human beings. It is the willingness to own one's part in the family unit. There is a recognition of the self within the family and our connectedness to the family. Relational responsibility is the willingness to own our own experiences, even those we do not like. It puts us at choice. When we accept personal choice in our experiences, it means noticing what we are doing about our circumstances.

Troubled people do not claim their autonomy. When we talk about our escape from freedom we are talking about denying the choices that are available to us. Scott Peck says in *The Road Less Traveled*[1] that the psychopath takes no responsibility for anything. The neurotic takes responsibility for everything and, in essence, takes responsibility for nothing. Both extremes are ways of avoiding responsibility.

Systemic thinking notes that we are both the cause and effect for actions. I am influenced by others and my environment while I am influencing others and my environment. We are co-creators of our actions and circumstances.

The reality is that chance is a player in all of the games of life. In a card game, chance determines the hand we get dealt. How we play our particular hand is our personal responsibility.

For most people, taking a responsible position is both stressful and extremely satisfying.

In relational responsibility we are not talking about fault, blame, or praise. There are no judgments or evaluations along the lines of good/bad or right/wrong. There are no heroes or heroic victims. Relational responsibility means owning what is mine to own, nothing more and nothing less. It means that I own what I do, think, feel, see, and hear. Blame is not part of relational responsibility.

Relational responsibility may be thought of as perspective that seeks to be clear about my part in any activity. It is empowering in that it is a self-directed, self-examining process that comes out of knowing who and what I am. For most people, taking a responsible position is both stressful and extremely satisfying. I fear that I might be wrong. I find it joyful to more fully see what I do and feel.

The therapeutic context is inherently an anxious situation. The fear of being found to be the cause of family difficulties is deep. Fear arouses survival reactions and an emotionalized responsibility dynamic is energized. Therapist sensitivity to emotionalized responsibility is an essential part of the creation of an effective treatment atmosphere. Being nonjudgmental and recognizing that whatever the situation, the client has done the best he or she can do is fundamental to dealing effectively with the emotionalized responsibility dynamic.

The power of emotionalized responsibility is pervasive. It does not show up only in the client. The responsibility issue may show up in the therapist as well. There are two places therapists have trouble with the responsibility dynamic: (1) putting one family member at fault for family difficulties, and (2) directing the decision-making processes of a client. Taking responsibility for client functioning takes away basic client responsibility.

How many times in case conferences or supervisory sessions have we heard a therapist talk about the ways one particular family member is "at fault" for the family difficulties? In such situations, the therapist has become a part of the emotionalized process of attaching blame to family interactions. Blame is a direct indication of an emotionalized responsibility reaction. Adam blamed Eve and Eve blamed the serpent for the purpose of denying responsibility for their actions. Little children, when found out for some mishap in interactions with other children, usually blame someone or something for "causing it." Blame is a survival reaction. Examining what happened or is happening in descriptive nonblaming language is an appropriate response to concern about any activity within a family. The therapist owns the responsibility for setting up an effective treatment atmosphere, not for finding fault.

Therapist anxiety about a client's failure to make progress tends to set in motion emotionalized reactions to the client. When the client's failure to progress in treatment is taken as a threat to the therapist's sense of competence or value, the therapist's ability to maintain a nonanxious presence is diminished greatly. The moment the therapist owns the client's responsibility for treatment progress, the client becomes disempowered and dependent on the therapist. In reality, the mechanisms for growth and maturity reside in the client. The therapist owns the responsibility for setting up an effective treatment atmosphere, not taking over for the client. I am not responsible for the client. As a therapist I am responsible for my conduct in the treatment context.

A mind-set driven by a belief that other people or circumstances are doing it to me lives in a world of effect. "I am effect, not cause."

Therapeutic progress is not likely to take place as long as the therapist does not deal with the responsibility dynamic. The world is made up of people doing things, of actions, reactions, and responses. Troubled people have well-defended stories that show how other people or circumstances are doing it to them. My wife is doing it to me. My children are doing it to me. My boss is doing it to me. I am doing it to me. Someone or something is at fault. It is not my responsibility! A mind-set driven by a belief that "people are doing it to me" lives in a world of effect. "I am effect, not cause." It is a world oriented to demonstrating how "they" are doing it to me. In such a mind-set, we live in a world of deception.

Owning what is mine to own, nothing more and nothing less, means that what others are doing is real. *And*, I am positioned to examine closely what I am experiencing and how I am reacting to and responding to the activities around me. I remain in a differentiating mode as I sort out all that is taking place with *me*.

It is not easy to take a responsible position. Avoiding responsibility and blaming has become culturally acceptable in our modern world. The distinction between facing what is in a nonjudgmental atmosphere and avoiding what is in a judgmental atmosphere goes to the crux of the helping process. The facing "what is" drives us to deal in illusion and self-defeating behaviors. The therapy atmosphere is one where it is safe enough to risk owing "what is" one's to be owned, nothing more, nothing less.

My failure in the realm of responsibility keeps me from seeing what I need to do in order to take growth-enhancing actions.

Recall the Adam and Eve story. The most self-destructive part of the story is not that Adam and Eve ate of the forbidden fruit, but that they tried to hide what they had done by blaming someone else. Eating of the forbidden fruit did not make Adam and Eve gods. They were deceived by the serpent. Apparently, eating the forbidden fruit brought them the fear of being wrong. They felt threatened. In the automatic survival process of fight or flight that followed, they hid themselves from God.

The refusal to own what is mine to own is a failure to face exactly what I do. My failure in the realm of responsibility sets me on a path of denial and illusion and fosters an inability to see what I need to do to take corrective action. The creation of the therapeutic atmosphere seeks to overcome the fear of facing ourself with a nonjudgmental, caring, and confronting context.

Identifying new and creative parts of reality is difficult in anxious situations. The survival-based drive to be right tends to distort reality. The underlying purpose of all actions is mobilized in the service of being right. Certain parts of reality are not seen and other parts of reality are highlighted in order to not be wrong. The survival-based mechanisms attempt to see only that which are needed to avoid being wrong. Survival reactions result in blame, rationalizations, denial, etc. in order to be right.

Judgmentalness tells more about the person judging someone that it does about the person being judged.

There is no need to "attack" what the survival mechanisms serve up for reality. There is a need to examine *exactly* what is being said and what is being done in specific situations. Anxious people do not see the inherent contradictions and self-destructiveness in their actions. Anxious people need to be helped to surface other possible ways to examine the issues at hand. The goal is to energize new possibilities for growth.

Part of the genius of Virginia Satir was her ability to convey her nonjudgmental, caring approach to clients. Being nonjudgmental is a process that is (1) nonevaluative in the matters of the value or worth of the person, and (2) nonevaluative in the examination of behavior of family members. Judgmentalness is an evaluative process whereby someone is relationally right or wrong, better or worse so that a person or persons can be considered good or bad in their very essence. They are less or more valuable as human beings. If they are wrong they are not OK in their core of existence. Judgmentalness is directed to our value as a being rather than to an examination of our activities. Judgmentalness directed to our essence as a human being panics our brain's survival mechanisms. Negative judgments are psychologically threatening and arouse anxiety. Our right to exist as valued beings is at risk; thus, defensive psychological mechanisms are put into place.

Positive judgmentalness that is global in nature puts the brain's survival mechanisms on alert. Global judgmentalness that is positive tells the brain that judgments about one's value or worth are in play. The next evaluation may be negative. Remember, judgmentalness tells much more about the person judging someone than it does about the person being judged. A judgment is merely an evaluative process; it is not the truth. Judgmentalness as a relational mode is a two-edged sword. Functional families tend to speak in terms of positive or negative behaviors, not positive or negative global evaluations. It is the difference between a global "you are a good kid" and "I saw you help your friend with his homework."

In the process of helping clients feel comfortable enough to take responsibility for their experiences, the focus is on specific activities and the apparent outcomes associated with those activities.

In all activities there is a condition called consequences, the result of what we do. The nonjudgmental position is a therapeutic stance that says "I see what happened. What do you want to do *now*?" The focus is on what happened in clear descriptive language and what do you plan to choose as your next action? The purpose of the nonjudgmental position is to allow the client to move beyond where he or she is now. It is a move toward grasping something more specific than highlighting a sense of wrongness or failure on the part of the client. There is a meta-message that says: You have been doing your best; you are doing what you have learned to do; there are understandable reasons for what took place; there are some things you haven't noticed; now what do you want to change?

Within the nonjudgmental approach helping becomes a process of adding, rather than getting rid of, possibilities for action. The therapy process takes on a breadth as well as a depth. New roads, new considerations, and new perspectives become possible. As mentioned, Virginia Satir enabled people to more easily own their activities when she identified positive intentions behind outwardly-appearing negative behaviors. Satir's work conveyed her belief that ordinary people do not intentionally seek to harm others. The job of the therapist often is to make manifest the caring part of seemingly negative actions. Indeed, the secret of all therapy may be the process of making manifest what is missing in the interactions between and among people.

Owning what is mine to own, nothing more and nothing less, is the dynamic of personal responsibility. There will always be consequences or outcomes attached to human activities, enabling clients to look clearly at the flow of transactions between and among people, without baggage, if an emotionalized responsibility dynamic is basic to creating an effective therapeutic atmosphere.

Worth Consideration

The survival anxieties that flow out of the fear of being wrong and being found out, or being responsible, show up in the dynamic of worth. Our sense of worth is a driving force with which all of us deal throughout our life. Our concern about our value or worth is always present. We yearn to experience high value and worth. There are few, if any, times in our life when we are not processing what a bit of information means to our sense of value or worth. We are always dealing with worth consideration! Low worth is experienced as exceedingly painful; high worth is experienced as pleasure. We seek pleasure and we avoid pain.

Our concern about worth is part of our survival function. As such, worth is closely tied to our emotional reactions. A threat to our worth quickly triggers defensive reactions. At times a threat to our sense of worth may be registered by our brain quite out of our awareness. The mind registers it, the body reacts, and our anxiety builds. We are in a defensive state and it is out of our awareness. We are anxious and we are not sure why. In an instant, we are set to react to the pain of a loss of a sense of worth.

There are few, if any, times in our life when we are not processing what a bit of information means to our sense of value or worth.

How does our sense of worth get to be so important to our psychological survival? From our earliest times in life, we observe that to be of great value is to be loved, protected, and cared for by others. Items, including people, that have high value have a positive place in the scheme of life. We quickly realize that to survive and to have psychological security in life we must be able to sense that we are valued. To not be of value is to risk not being loved, not being protected, not being wanted, and being discarded. Our worth gets tied to our very survival fears. Thus, humans possess a deep lifelong yearning to sense value, to feel good about one's self and the surrounding world. Worth is an active dynamic in family life.

In the best of situations, a solid sense of high worth is internally based. We possess a strong sense of self-validation. That is, we have an internal appreciation of who and what we are as a particular human being. Our sense of our worth flows from inner pictures of ourself as valuable. We have a sense that the world is a better place because of our existence. This sense of value extends to pictures of others as valuable. We not only self-validate, we validate others and the world around us. A solid sense of worth includes my sense of my value, your value, and the value of the many people with whom we associate.

Much of what goes into our sense of worth has been learned. I have a reservoir of memories that feed into my worth considerations. The problem with the worth issue is that it is a lifelong process. We never settle, once and for all, the issue of our worth. Internally, I may feel good about myself, others, and the world around me, but the events of life may shatter that sense of value. Loss of various kinds, such as health, family, job, or social position may unsettle our internal sense of value. In such situations, our ability to self-validate is crucial to our sense of value.

Our overall sense of well-being ranges from being energetic to feeling down and discouraged. The difference between the variations in our sense of well-being and our basic sense of worth is that it is natural for our sense of well-being to shift and change. The down feelings and the up feelings are OK and subject to change. When we have a solid sense of worth, we acknowledge the down feelings as temporary and move forward in life. Feeling down is OK! Our overall solid sense of value enables us to soothe ourselves as needed.

For most people, the need to seek therapy for themselves or their family is a threat to their sense of worth. Their deepest fears of failure threaten to break through into our awareness. The survival defenses are poised for reaction, if needed.

In the relational systems model, the focus of therapeutic attention is on the promotion of an overall sense of respect, value, and worth. The attention to worth is not just a thinking or doing process on the part of the therapist. It is based on the establishment of a particular therapist stance toward the client. It is a stance or position that actively searches out the value and worth part of the client in life transactions. The worth position involves energizing a context of *worthness.*

---

*The culture of narcissism says that it is necessary to have a positive sense of self-worth **before** it is possible to sense others as valuable. It is a linear approach to the issue of value.*

Worthness is a process in life that simultaneously seeks to find the value in self, other, and context. It's a caring and building up of self, others, and the surrounding world. It's a systemic view that has wide-angle lenses that are used to get the whole picture of the value and worth for everyone in the family. It seeks the *value* in all human transactions.

Worthness has more breadth and depth than self-worth. The culture of narcissism says that self-love is an indispensable prerequisite to a happy life. It is necessary to have a positive self-image or sense of self-worth *before* it is possible to sense others as valuable. It is a linear kind of thinking that says first, give attention to the self and then, when I feel good enough about myself, I can reach out to others in love and caring. The linear approach to self-worth is a self-centered process that turns in on itself if taken to its logical conclusion. Thus, we hear stories that, in essence, say, "I can't reach out to her or him because I don't feel good enough about myself." In such a perspective each of us becomes self-concerned entities working on our own self-worth. The linear view also includes an other-validated approach to worth. Thus, we feel valuable *after* someone or something praises us or meets a need we have. Other-validated worth is appropriate when we are very young. As we mature, we are better able to self-validate our worth.

Worthness says that it is my active intention to seek the value in myself, others, and my world. And, I intend to engage in a process lifting up the value of everything. Not only do I self-validate, I value that which is around me. All of us are a part of the whole of reality. The systemic process of caring for and locating value in self, other, and context serves to establish a solid sense of worthness.

Virginia Satir had a clear depth of appreciation for the place of worthness in the therapeutic process. Her approach emphasized over and over that worth considerations provided the guidelines for all her work. All her interventions were made in terms of worth. Many therapists often wonder what, out of all the themes that develop in a family interview, to pick out for further examination. Satir was clear in her approach. She picked up on that which offered the best chance to get to the worth possibilities. How many times have we observed in Satir tapes the comment: "How would *you* like things to be?"; "Can you think of a time when things went well?"; or "How does it feel to tell me about something good happening in your life?"

One of the initial goals of a therapist is to help a family gain hope that positive change is possible. Bringing the worth position into the therapeutic process as quickly as possible serves to enhance the probabilities for creating an effective therapeutic atmosphere.

Respecting a client's sense of value includes providing the opportunity for the client to face his or her destructive thinking and actions.

The extent to which we are able to engage the worthness dynamic in creation of the therapeutic atmosphere is related to our differentiating capacity. A solid self enables us to sense and know that all people have value. When the therapist does not believe in the worth of the client, it is difficult to make interventions that energize the client's sense of value. Respecting a client's sense of value includes providing the opportunity for the client to face his or her destructive thinking and actions. That which has no value we will allow to self-destruct.

Virginia Satir's way of working with people provided depth for the worthness consideration. It is reported that when asked how she had the ability, often without prior identifying information, to work with people in front of large audiences in city after city and country after country, she provided a central insight into her success as a family therapist. Satir operated from a belief and a goal. She believed that each one of us possesses a part of great value within us. In other words, each person has enormous value and worth. Her belief about value is important. Without that basic belief she would not have been able to pursue her goal as a therapist. The organizing goal for all her work was the identification of that valuable part in the client. Once identified, the valuable part was energized by Satir's many treatment techniques. A simple and a profound guiding light for all that Satir did in her work was based in a sense of worthness.

Purpose

The purpose consideration addresses the intentional dimension of the therapeutic process. It is the in-order-to dynamic for both the therapist and the client. Purpose poses the fundamental question, What are we to accomplish as a result of our time together? It fills in the blank in the sentence: We are here in-order-to _____. Purpose serves as a perceptual medium that directs attention to specific aspects of reality. Purpose limits what is felt, thought, and done. In a way, it is a cognitive map that serves as a guide for the therapeutic process.

It is important to know that purpose serves as a context setter. Recall from the discussion of the human realities that the context primarily refers to the humanmade part of life. It is the frame of reference that we construct to make sense of life; context provides meaning for behavior. The same words may have different meanings in different contexts. If you see me being brought out of the ocean by a lifeguard and I yell "I've been saved," the overall context of the event establishes the meaning of my statement. I have just been rescued by the lifeguard. On the other hand, if you see me coming out of a Baptist revival meeting and I yell "I've been saved," there is a new and different meaning to the same words. The difference in meaning comes from the context. Where does the meaning to our words come from?

We make it up by our agreements with each other as we create culture, society, and the many institutions of society. We create a context.

Purpose establishes the frame of reference or context for behaviors. If you want to make sense of what I do, or have, identify the context from which I am operating. Without knowing the overriding context, certain behavior may seem very strange. For instance, many of us have experienced a meeting of a newly formed committee. For a brief period of time, nothing that is taking place seems to make any sense. In spite of great effort by the chair to move the meeting forward, nothing can be accomplished. Finally, the light bulb comes on in our heads. We sense the hidden agenda for a small group of the committee members. When we know what their purpose is, all the things they have been doing make sense. Given the hidden agenda of certain people in the group, all of the behaviors that take place make sense. Those of you who have experienced such a group process know that for the group to move forward, the hidden agenda(s) must be identified and receive consideration.

The positive part of establishing purpose in the therapeutic process is that, once established, all transactions may be viewed in terms of their relevance to the established purpose. If the client tells me that he wants a more positive relationship with his wife and then proceeds to blame her for all of the troubles in the marriage, there is an incongruence between the client's words and his stated purpose for seeking the helping process. Clarification of purpose is in order.

Several years ago a young physician came to see me. His stated reason for seeking help was to improve his marital relationship. His unending complaints about his wife and his refusal to talk about his part in the marriage relationship seemed incongruent with his stated purpose for seeking help.

Purpose establishes the context for therapy, and context gives meaning to all that is said and done.

I asked the client to "try something that might clarify his situation." I gave him three sheets of paper and a pencil. I asked him to take the first sheet of paper and, in writing, give me (1) his reason for coming to see me. When he had finished, I asked him to take the second sheet of paper and give me (2) an opposite reason for seeing me. He wrote his answer. Then, I gave him the third sheet and asked him for (3) another reason for seeking help. When he finished writing his third response, he put the pencil down, looked me in the eye, and told me that he now knew that his reason for coming to see me was to get rid of the feelings of guilt he was experiencing. He wanted to go through the exercise of seeking help so that he could say that he tried to save his marriage. As his story developed, he had a girlfriend that he planned to marry following his divorce from his wife. After talking about his girlfriend for some extended period of time, he looked at the three sheets of paper, leaned back, and said that what he had just told me was not all of the truth. In fact, he had an elaborate plan to ditch his girlfriend in order to be free to live his own life. His girlfriend was an excuse to get rid of his wife.

As the client talked about his intentions for the future, he became congruent in his different modes of communication. His words began to make sense to me. While one may question the honesty of his plan, the client had faced himself, his intentions, and his purpose for seeking help. Before he left his session with me, he expressed his intention to level with both his wife and girlfriend.

I never saw the client again. About a year later I heard that he had divorced his wife, left his girlfriend, and became an available bachelor in his social group.

Helping to clarify a client's purpose for coming for therapy may help identify the incongruence between what is said and what actions have taken place.

It has been my observation that anxious clients tend to locate themselves at the extremes in their ability to focus on a direction in life. At one extreme, there is a narrow, rigid focus that seems to dominate all of their activities. The hidden purpose behind this narrow focus is out of their awareness because it is controlled by lower brain activities. The therapeutic purpose becomes a clear-headed examination of what they want out of the treatment process. An examination of the incongruence between what the client states he or she wants out of treatment and what he or she does in treatment is useful to the client. The purpose behind the stated purpose becomes a focus of the treatment process.

At the other extreme is a scattered sense of the purpose for seeking help. As the client attempts to express hopes for the treatment, the therapist engages in a clarifying process. The intention is to get to the in-order-to for the process of therapy. When a client is unable to clarify his or her purpose for seeking help, it is not unusual to establish a beginning purpose of discovering what is contributing to this inability. The process is a kind of examination of metapurpose. The difficulties behind the client's inability to focus on what the end point of treatment will look like becomes a focus of the treatment process. A kind of meta-purpose process is developed. The client ends up dealing with why he or she cannot figure out what is wanted from therapy. In the entire process it is the client who is required to reveal, in his or her own words, the purpose of seeking therapy. In some situations, the establishment of a clear purpose for the therapeutic process moves the treatment process forward in a kind of quantum leap. Dealing with the fears around what the "real" problem might be may reduce the level of anxiety and consequently allow for a more nonanxious and rapid examination of family concerns.

In family situations, each family member has his or her own inner pictures about what will happen as a result of the treatment process. Looking at the individual purposes that guide each person in a family group is both revealing and likely to move the treatment process forward. Individual family members do not have to agree on specific purposes, but clear distinctions between common family purposes and individual purposes are important to the process. Again, the incongruence between what clients say they want and the actions they take becomes an area of examination.

Specific purposes shift and change during the process of therapy. Our alertness to a shift in a dominant purpose by the client comes from our own intention to be sensitive to changes in purpose. Clarifying a shift in the purpose of therapy for the client is essential if communication is to make sense. The surest sign of a shift in purpose takes place when what the client is talking about makes no sense from the perspective of the established purpose.

The rule-of-three probably adheres for this dynamic. When the incongruence in communication takes place the first time, there is reason to be aware of a possible change in client's purposes. When the incongruence takes place a second time, the signal for change in purpose becomes stronger. When the third instance of incongruence occurs in the client's communication patterns, it is time to explore a change in purpose by the client. A minor change in purpose may be a sign of growth by the client. On the other hand, there is also the possibility that the client has regressed. Either way, the alternate purpose needs to be addressed by the therapist.

For therapy to be effective, it is essential for the therapist and the client to maintain an awareness of the dominant purpose for the therapy.

A major concern for some family therapists comes from the situations in which agency responsibilities involve multiple purposes, some of which are contradictory. The therapist who needs specific information in order to determine if a child should be taken out of a home may find it difficult to create a safe working atmosphere for the client. The family will sense the difference in the administrative direction and the type of relationship required for a therapeutic alliance. There are times when our purpose is to gain information only. At other times our transactions with clients are purely for therapeutic purposes. When there is a blend of purposes, the dual purpose requires clarification. For instance, in protective services work, the purpose of the client contacts may be to decide whether or not a child should be taken out of a home or whether or not a court order restraining the parents from seeing the child is needed. Being absolutely clear about the purposes of the therapist is a primary requirement in agency contexts that have multiple missions.

In the therapeutic context, it is useful to clarify the initial purpose from a positive perspective. Satir looked for the client's hopes and expectations from therapy. Clients are fearful of, but expect to talk about, their problems during therapy. Requiring a discussion of expectations from the treatment process initiates a reframe of the problem from the very beginning of treatment. The question is: What do you want out of the therapy process? Operating in the dynamic of purpose, we ask such questions as: "What do you hope will happen as a result of coming here?"; "How would things be if you did not need help?"; or "What would have to happen for the family to work well?"

The therapist's purpose is simple and straightforward. The therapist wants to know the direction the client is headed in the therapy process. A major factor in establishing an effective treatment atmosphere is to create a mutual understanding about what is to take place in the treatment process and why it is to take place.

"Why" is a productive approach when directed to purpose, rather than to past explanations or stories. Why are you here from the in-order-to dynamic rather than the what-caused-you-to-get-here dynamic energizes expectations, not explanations.

Within the dynamic of cause, "why" is useful if the purpose is to get to the stories that underpin the client's current activities. Within the in-order-to dynamic, "why" is a way to give room for creative considerations. Positive growth takes place within the context of possibilities. What are the possible outcomes? The direction is not old explanations, new explanations, nor even better explanations, it is the creation of new possibilities. The new possibilities include alternative ways to look at activities for the future, examine new behaviors, and create positive stories for the future.

It is prudent to be aware that emotionalized reactions are likely to involve a shift to an earlier time that involved a different purpose. Like the human in the rat-in-the-maze story, the purpose shifts from getting the cheese to being right based on past experiences. In emotionalized reactions our human cybernetic machinery does not control for here-and-now considerations. The machinery allows, even promotes, an intrusive process that automatically operates outside the present situations.

For the creation of an effective treatment atmosphere, the purpose consideration needs constant attention. Of all the necessary but not sufficient considerations, the purpose dynamic is most closely associated with a therapy process that does not squander the time of either the client or the therapist. To the extent that the emotionalized survival reactions are kept in check, there will be clear direction to the treatment process. When automatic processes take over, we forget the purpose of the particular helping process.

Finally, the purpose dynamic is active in the work of the therapist. When the treatment is not following the purpose, the therapy process drifts. There is a lack of open communication on the part of the therapist. The therapy process takes on a ritualistic atmosphere rather than a moving, exploring, and creating atmosphere. When we spend time going through the motions of therapy rather than being on track with the purpose as a therapist, what we are doing is no longer therapy. It is something else.

Worldview

All human beings evolve a unique worldview. My worldview is simply the perspective from which I view life. As part of my worldview I hold a wide range of values, beliefs, identities, roles, self-images, labels, positions, and contexts. All of these parts of my worldview are crystallized in the language available for me, in my communications with myself and others and in my dealings in various contexts.

Recall that the self is the context for all of the "I ams" I hold as part of my worldview. The self is more than any of the mind-constructed "I ams" or positions that I hold. The self is the context for all the parts of my worldview. The self is the television screen of my life, and the self never appears on it. The self comes out of the activities of the whole brain and nervous system. It does not exist in a place and yet it is. Self is a reality, a "what is." It is the source of my "I ams."

From worldviewness, a worldview is seen for what it is, a view of the world from a particular location.

The differentiating self clearly knows the values, beliefs, and identities I hold as important at a particular time. The differentiating self maintains the distinction between self and all of the parts of my worldview. The differentiating self contains all my life contexts but does not permit any one of them to rule the self. The differentiating self can take positions and particular perspectives and not become that particular position or perspective. The differentiating self operates in worldviewness. From worldviewness, a worldview is seen for what it is, a view of the world from a particular location, nothing more and nothing less.

The differentiating self realizes who and what he or she is within a context of love, caring, and integrity *and* transcends any humanmade philosophy or formula for living. What I can do and what I have flows out of the possibilities of my being rather than an allegiance to a set formula for living. Satir often noted that in therapy there are considerations not formulas.

To the extent that I am undifferentiated, there is a strong probability that my worldview will become enmeshed with emotionalized right/wrong. The undifferentiated self operates in a survival mind state, a reactive mind. The undifferentiated self does not distinguish between the self and any thing or idea the mind regards as self. Reacting out of right/wrong survival concerns, the primitive mind regards challenges to humanmade worldviews as threatening to the survival of the self. When my primitive mind intrudes to protect what is regarded as self, psychological survival mechanisms are energized. The primitive mind functions to ensure the survival of anything regarded as self. Like a radar, the primitive mind scans the horizon for survival threats. Any part of my worldview identified as my *self* is therefore guarded by automatic psychological survival mechanisms.

The radar of the primitive mind uses resemblances to identify physical and psychological threat. Anything that resembles a threat from past pain and anxiety activates the automatic defense mechanisms. Since so many things resemble other things in this world, humans constantly stay in a state of survival anxiety. The anxiety comes from the primitive mind's way of knowing. The primitive mind works on resemblances and does not distinguish between past and present in its reactive functions. The primitive mind reacts automatically to real or perceived threat.

The automatic reactive mind does not always sense my best interests. The reactive mind cannot distinguish between real present danger and perceived threat based on the past. Under threat, the reactive mind often intrudes into the creative thinking functions of the higher brain. The power of the reactive mind is created out of an override of the higher brain (cortex) functions by the lower brain functions (limbic and reptilian). In a lower brain override, the neo-cortex may be deceived into thinking it is still in charge when in reality it is not. In such a situation, the mental functions of the higher brain have been taken over by the automatic survival functions of the lower brain to set up a reactive mind. Under threat, the reactive mind uses all means available to perpetuate my point of view as the *right* view. When there is little or no differentiation between my self and my mind, the right point of view is a matter of survival. The reactive mind acts in reference to any identity or position identified as my self. The reactive mind automatically functions to make the undifferentiating self right.

To protect the survival of my undifferentiating self, I create stories that serve to justify all my activities and therefore prove me right. When the functions of the cortex have been taken over in the service of survival, the stories are well thought out and reasonable. Reasonableness is used to defend the actions of the reactive mind. To the extent that our life stories serve to justify our activities, we remain stuck in a narrow range of activities. The baggage of the past and our obliviousness to other possibilities virtually eliminate alternative points of view.

---

*Under threat, the reactive mind uses all means available to perpetuate my point of view as the **right** view.*

Given the power of the worldviewness consideration, it is a major dynamic in the creation of the therapeutic atmosphere. Worldviewness is an active dynamic for the therapist as well as the client. The information obtained about the client system and the way it is obtained will reflect the treatment perspective held by the therapist. The meaning we derive from client activities will be filtered through our therapeutic frame of reference, or worldview.

The client will enter the therapeutic process from his or her frame of reference, or worldview. For the purposes of creating an effective therapeutic atmosphere it is critical to recognize the following. (1) In the domain of human relationships, there is *no objective reality*. For humans, that which is distinguished exists and that which is not distinguished does not exist. This means that the alcoholic who sees green Martians, sees green Martians. (2) The fact that humans agree on something does not constitute an objective reality. Remember, at one time there was agreement that the world was flat. (3) In the realm of human relationships, reality is not one; it is many. There is not a universe; there is a multiple universe. (4) There is, in the human sense, no human reality that you and your clients are trying to discover. (5) Collectives of people such as tribes, families, etc., have a kind of shared, or consensual, worldview that often is revealed in the family history. The past frames the present and the present frames the past. (6) All client systems are programmed to give attention to what fits its worldview and ignore that which contradicts its worldview.

The implications of the worldview dynamic for the therapeutic process are many. A fundamental implication for our work is found in the critical difference between seeking *the* truth in family matters and identifying alternative perspectives. One of the productive possibilities in therapy is the process of helping family members recognize alternative views and actions rather than defending its "truth." From that perspective, family therapy takes on breadth in addition to depth. Basic to the RSM is the therapist's specific co-examination of his or her worldview and the degree of congruence between client actions and his or her worldview. Needless to say, the ability of the therapist to differentiate between a personal worldview and worldviewness is essential to any in-depth look at worldviews and realities. The understanding of the difference between a worldview and worldviewness will help the therapist to remain nonanxious when the client's defensiveness emerges.

Reframing/Deframing

Closely allied with the dynamics of worldviewness are the processes of reframing or deframing.[2] All human activities take place within some kind of background or frame of reference. A frame of reference provides a particular context for activities. Context gives meaning to the communicational part of the activities.

Deframing is a process designed to create doubt about the accuracy of the definition of the context from which a person derives meaning from certain activities. Deframing is designed to create questions about ideas or perspectives that have been presented as "truth" by a client. Deframing therapist responses to information might be: "I am not sure about that," "I don't know about that one," "Are you absolutely sure about that?" or "Your comments have a different meaning to me." The comments given by the therapist are designed to raise doubts about a particular meaning made of some activity.

Reframing is a process of offering a different context from which to consider a piece of information. Given a different context, the meaning under examination may change. Some years ago just before my daughter's senior year in high school, I was informed that I would have to drive my daughter to school every day at 7:00 a.m. The carpool she had been in the previous year had dissolved, and no bus service was available. The thought that I would have to leave for work much earlier in order to drive my daughter to school displeased me very much. Additionally, I would be locked into a specific time and place every school morning. I engaged in a lot of internal complaints about my new responsibilities.

As the senior year approached, I started to think about how much I enjoyed being with my daughter. I realized that the drive to school would be a time for us to talk and get to know each other better. I also considered the fact that this would be her last year at home with us. The more I thought about the situation, the more positive the idea of the drive to school with my daughter became. Just before the first week of the school year, I started to look forward to my new opportunity.

What changed about taking my daughter to school? The only thing that changed was my frame of reference for looking at driving my daughter to school. Given the new, more positive frame, the meaning of what I was to do every school morning shifted. (Indeed, the trips to school were delightful.)

Another approach to reframing is situation based. In one context a behavior may be called stubborn and in another situation the same type of behavior may be called standing up for yourself. In the context of a parent attempting to get a daughter to do something, the refusal to do it may be labeled as stubborn. In the context of not going along with the ideas of an out-of-control group of young people, her parents may label it as standing up for what she believes. Every piece of behavior or every experience is appropriate, given some context, some frame.

Virginia Satir was a master at putting a positive frame on the intentions behind behavior. It was thought to be stretching it a bit when she framed a wife's chase after her husband with a knife as her attempt to get closer.

Both deframing and reframing symbolize a therapeutic atmosphere of discovery. The style of the therapist is: "Let's see if there are other views"; "Let's see what else we can learn from this"; and "I am intrigued by other possibilities." The discovery spirit, in creating a therapeutic atmosphere, sets the stage for future examinations of specific fragments of a client's reality. Reframing is a natural therapeutic application of the dynamics that flow out of world-viewness.

Worldviews and parts of worldviews are not given up easily under the best of therapeutic circumstances. The capacity to differentiate between perspective and truths and between worldviews and worldviewness assists in the process of considering alternative life paradigms.

Relational Communications

Humans are in constant communication with each other. Someone once defined communication as the difference that makes a difference. This means that a response or a reaction to a difference shows that a communication has taken place. Human communication is a complex process. It is a difficult process to describe and/or understand. In recent years several important characteristics of human communication have been identified.[3] Following is a discussion of communication characteristics that are relevant to the RSM.

Cannot Not Communicate–Communication provides the energy for human systems. Without communication, human relationship systems would cease to exist. Human communication takes place on both the verbal and nonverbal levels. One cannot not communicate (Watzlawick, 1964). On the verbal level, factors such as tone, loudness, quietness, intonation, etc., give clues to the meaning of the words that are spoken. On the nonverbal level, body positions, gestures, facial expressions, speed of movement, etc., provide a wealth of information that is conveyed to others.

Silence is a communication.

The existence of verbal and nonverbal modes of communication give rise to the possibility that the verbal message and the nonverbal message may be in disagreement. If I motion with my hand for you to come closer but verbalize a stay away message, it is impossible to know which message should be followed. The straightforward way to deal with conflicting messages at the verbal and nonverbal levels is to ask for clarification about what message is intended.

Silence is communication. If I speak to a friend in the hall where we work and he passes by without returning my greeting, what message has he sent me? Is he angry and not speaking to me? Did he not notice me? What did the silence convey? There is no way to know without checking with my friend. Silence is a communication.

Content and Relationship–All messages simultaneously provide content, or information, and a command as to how the message is to be received, or a relationship message. There is what I say, the report, and how I say it which implies how the message is to be received, the relationship involved. The relationship information is metainformation since it is information about the information.

Disagreement may take place over the content and or the relationship aspect. Disagreement over the content of a message is possible to resolve by looking to other sources for the answer. If I say "The time is 2:00 p.m. on the dot," you may disagree with me. However, we can find a clock to verify the accuracy or inaccuracy of my report. However, if you react to my message by saying "you seem to be implying that I am usually late," it is a relationship response. It is difficult to resolve any disagreement on the relationship level. If I respond with "I was not commenting on your timeliness," you can in turn respond with "Yes, you were." The "No, I was not; yes, you were" series of interchanges will be difficult to resolve. The disagreement is a relationship disagreement about who is right and who is wrong. It has been my observation that in human relationships any content disagreement that lasts beyond sixty seconds quickly becomes an emotionalized relationship disagreement. The main issue becomes one of how you were treating me during our disagreement. That's a relationship disagreement!

It is difficult to resolve present issues within a past emotional context.

In ongoing family systems the relationship disagreements of the present carry the baggage of past content disagreements. Present disagreements based on content quickly resemble the relationship pain of past disagreements. The atmosphere of the discussions quickly becomes negative because the past has invaded the present. A past context has been imposed on a present context. It is difficult to resolve present issues within a past emotional context. There is an incongruence of meaning because of the difference in the time contexts.

Relationship disagreements are difficult to resolve because the issue concerns how people see each other in their relationship and, by implication, how we will treat each other. We do not want to be disconfirmed by other people, especially those with whom we have an ongoing relationship. In relationship issues we can either agree, disagree, or disconfirm. To be disconfirmed is very painful to most of us. We are disconfirmed when we are ignored. The plea is: If you don't agree, at least disagree with me! One of the most powerful punishments for wrongdoing is to shun someone. To shun someone in some cultures is to act as if they do not exist. To be shunned is to be totally ignored in every way–a powerful punishment indeed.

All communicational interchanges are either symmetrical or complementary, depending on whether they are based on equality or difference. Included in both types of interchanges may be an emotionalized communication called mutual need-based communications.

Symmetrical Communications–Communications that push for equality means that there is an implication of sameness in the relationship. In this aspect, what (content) is being said is secondary to the relationship implications of equality. There is a mirroring part to symmetrical relationships in that as one does, so does the other. At its best there is freedom to be who and what I am, and my other will respect that part of me. Likewise, I will do the same for my other. The dangers of relationships organized around equality come from possible competitiveness and overconcern about continued equalness in *all* matters. For as one does and has, the other must do and have if the relationship is to be equal. Rights and duties of each partner may become the content for relationship disagreements based in symmetry.

Complementary Communication–In complementary relationships the pattern is organized around communications that reflect the acceptance and advantages of differentness. There is a fitting together of different behaviors that form a whole. For instance, the relationship of teacher-student, parent-child, therapist-client, or up-down, are examples of complementary relationships. Since the relationships complement each other, a completeness emerges from the whole. Complementary relationships function well as long as the partners continue in their individual complementary role and communicate confirmation of the arrangement. The reality is that people and circumstances change, and complementary relationships established over the years require change. Changing a rigid complementary relationship may be a threat to either or both partners involved. Stagnating in either a symmetrical or complementary relationship has a high probability of pain when relationship change is demanded.

A fundamental question for all human relationships is, "Who is going to define the nature of our relationship?" A growth-enhancing relationship is based upon communication that is geared to the continuous discovery of what fits for the people involved in the relationship. The basic ingredient for this kind of communication is people who stand solidly on their own two feet. They feel strong enough to be dependent, independent, and interdependent, depending on what fits for all the realities involved. The answer to the question, "Who is going to define the nature of our relationship?" is, "We are!" Well-differentiating people have the ability to stand on their own two feet.

Mutual Need-Based Communication–Family relationships controlled by emotional dependence, or "need"-based communications are human disasters waiting to happen. Unfortunately, this type of survival-based need is sometimes called "love." Survival fears, possession, other-validation, and dependency get mixed and are called love. Need-based communications are survival demands put into words; "I am nothing when she is not around," "I need her in my life," "If she leaves I will kill myself," and "I cannot live without her."

In mutual need-based relationships, the threat of the loss of the specific other is a psychological death issue. Both need *each* other. Need ordinarily refers to life-sustaining requirements. We need water, air, food, shelter, and other people to survive. In reality, humans need other human beings. Psychologically, we do not need a *specific* human being to survive. We may want to be with a specific human being, but we do not *need* that particular person. Over a lifelong relationship with another, we may even want to have and enjoy a need for a spouse or other family member.

For marriage, a relationship based on wanting someone and someone *wanting* us keeps the relationship on a what-fits-for-us basis. It is a relationship based on freedom and choice. The reality is that my wife does not *need* me and I do not *need* her. We want each other, and we choose to be with each other in love and caring. My wife is not forced by psychological need to stay with me. I do not *have to* meet my wife's psychological dependence need by staying with her. When our need for other people locks in on one specific person, that person holds psychological life and death in his or her hands. The relationship is fraught with fears of abandonment and loss. The level of anxiety is enormous. A sense of demand sets in for both partners. There is a sense of being burdensome. The relationship becomes a feeding process; each feels empty without the other.

In the mutual need-based relationship, the person in the one-down position acquires the power to define the relationship and who is wrong in the relationship.

When mutually needy people divorce or separate, the entire process is filled with rage and viciousness. Physical violence may be part of the separation process. The communications pattern is characterized by constant attempts to prove he or she is more needy and victimized than the other. An interesting twist in this type of relationship is the source of control for the relationship. Ordinarily, the person in the one-up position defines a relationship. Exactly who is in the one-up position may shift and change in a mature relationship. In the mutual need-based relationship, the person in the *one-down* position acquires the power to define the relationship and who is wrong in the relationship. The relationship battle becomes an effort to gain the one-down or victim position. The winner is the loser! People who serve as parasites for each other are fearful people. They are easily threatened, and they are prime candidates for abuse and violence.

The Punctuation of Events—The meaning of a sequence of events is contingent upon the punctuation of the communicational sequences between the communicants (Watzlawick, Beaven, and Jackson, 1967).[4] In other words, where, by the nature of the communications, does the sequence of events start? In one sense, communications may be regarded as a long series of messages between and among people. The meaning of a particular set of communications depends upon where the punctuation is placed. The classic example for a family is from a set of exchanges in an argument between a husband and a wife about pursuing and withdrawing. The wife says that she is critical of her husband because he withdraws from discussions with her. The husband, on the other hand, says that he withdraws from the arguments because she nags him. The interchange is a constant "I withdraw because you nag," "I nag because you withdraw," etc. What truth and what meaning can we get from this sequence of communications depends upon the punctuation imposed. If the punctuation establishes that the nagging is the result of the withdrawal, one meaning is established. If the punctuation establishes that nagging is the cause of the withdrawal, clearly another meaning is established. For the relational systems therapist, the meaning given by each partner is important from his or her perspective. How should the entire sequence be punctuated? There is no one answer. We know that the couple's cause/effect argument does not work to resolve the issue. The fact of a strong disagreement within an overall context of relationship problems with a history tells us that another way of approaching the issue may be important. A broader systemic view of how the entire sequence of events affects the marriage is an alternative way to punctuate the larger set of events. Clearly, punctuation organizes human activities. Distinguishing the different meanings that arise out of particular punctuations provides a wide-angle view of human events.

The story about the rat and psychologist is a humorous example of the meaning that comes from a particular punctuation of events. If we observed a psychologist who puts a rat in a maze that has cheese down one tube, the rat explores the various tubes and finds the cheese for the first time. If the same psychologist puts the cheese into the same tube for subsequent explorations of the maze by the same rat, the rat takes shorter periods of time to explore the maze to find the cheese and press the lever. If we ask the psychologist what he or she is doing, the psychologist will tell us the rat is being trained to find cheese in a complex maze and press the lever for the cheese. If we talk to the rat we may get a different story. The rat may tell us that he is training a psychologist: "Each time I find the cheese and press the lever, the psychologist gives me food."

Message Sent Is Not Necessarily Message Heard–All of us bring our own personal context to the communications process. When I send a message to another, I assume that the receiver of the message shares some part of my context. I may send a message out of a context of concern for the well-being of my spouse. She may hear it as a control message, telling her what to do. Her receiving context gave the impetus for a different meaning. For a family with a particular historical context with its influence on meaning, it is difficult to establish a new, more productive context. Messages sent will be referenced against the historical context. Satir's emphasis on the positive intention (context) behind messages moved people toward at least a consideration of a new context.

The Metafactor in Communications–The communication about the communication is an inherent part of the messages that we send. For instance, when I ask a question I have made a declaratory statement. When I ask "What do you hope will happen as a result of coming for treatment?" I have made several statements. For instance, I have stated that I do not know what you want from treatment; I want to know what you want from treatment; I assume that you will tell me what you want from treatment. Language is complex and language about language is even more complex. What is the relationship message when I say, "Tell me what to do?" How does one respond to the sign that says "Ignore this message" or the statement "Don't be so compliant"?

The power of communication is enormous. The client comes to the therapeutic process with an established context for family communications. The meaning of everything that is said is referenced against the context that has been fashioned out of the family history; the family is caught in the box of their own context. The family is so caught in the process of their context they cannot see all that is going on around them. It is like trying to see air or like a fish trying to see water. The family is so much a part of the context that the content is mystified by attempts of others to explain it. They want to change, but it is impossible to change when they are locked into the context of meaning that created the problems. A new context is needed—a therapeutic context that encourages new considerations. It is a context where the language of nonjudgmentalness, responsibility, worthiness, purpose, and worldviewness is spoken.

The meaning of everything that is said in a family is referenced against the context that has been fashioned out of the family history.

SUMMARY

The purpose of giving full attention to the necessary but not sufficient considerations is to create the possibility of an effective therapeutic atmosphere. The purpose is to create a special wrapper for the therapy process. It is a therapeutic wrapper that assists the client in looking for new and additional perspectives and coping skills. We are talking about the ecology of effective therapy, the conditions under which therapy may occur. For both therapist and client, it is a discovery process.

The seven necessary but not sufficient considerations form the essential ingredients for an effective treatment process. The self-differentiating capacities of the therapist set the tone for creating a powerful therapeutic atmosphere. A therapist rhythm is established. The therapist's nonanxious, self-directed presence allows him or her to clearly establish the purpose of the therapeutic process with overall attention to the positive value of the client. The differentiating therapist will not likely permit emotionalized right/wrong dynamics to gain momentum. The overall safe treatment atmosphere, in turn, energizes honesty and self-reflection in the essential client dynamics. The therapy process is in action.

NOTES

1. Peck, S. (1978). *The Road Less Traveled.* New York: Simon and Schuster, pp. 35-36.

2. For a more comprehensive discussion of this subject, see Bandler, R. and Grinder, J. (1982). *Reframing,* S. Andreas and C. Andreas (Eds.). Moab, VT: Rand People Press.

3. See especially Watzlawick, P. et al. (1967). *Pragmatics of Human Communication.* New York: Norton. Watzlawick, P. (1964). *An Anthology of Human Communication.* Palo Alto, CA: Science and Behavior Books, p. 2.

4. Watzlawick, P., Beaven, J.H., and Jackson, D.D. (1967). *Pragmatics of Human Communications: A Study of Interactions Patterns, Pathologies and Paradoxes.* New York: Norton. pp. 54-59.

CHAPTER 5

LIFE STANCES

How Life Stances Develop
Life Stances and the Realities
Life Stances and Differentiation
The Life Stances
   Affirmative Life Stance
   Responsible Life Stances
      Compliant
      Assertive
      Objective
      Distractor
      Self-Concerned
      Sensor
      Loyal
      Summary
   Life Stance Profile
   Dysfunctional Life Stances
      Submissor
      Aggressor
      Detached
      Avoider
      Demander
      Emoting
      Subservient
The Life Realities Revisited
   Facing the Realities

All human beings are required to face the vicissitudes of life. In the process of dealing with the complex nature of living, each one of us evolves a patterned approach to the human interactional side of existence. This patterned approach, or life stance, toward transactions with the world is especially prominent within one's family system.

The term life stance is used to draw attention to identifiable positions toward the realities of life and the resulting patterns of behavior. Another way to approach life stances is to notice that the activities of people are redundant; we do the same things a lot. We especially show repetitive behavior in our family context. We take a life stance in our family transactions.

HOW LIFE STANCES DEVELOP

Life stances evolve as each human being goes through the process of meeting basic survival, safety, and growth needs. As we go through our human developmental stages, all of us (1) experience transactional processes with others—primarily family members when we are very young—and (2) we observe other people in transactions with each other. Basically, we adopt behaviors that are necessary to get along with important others and behaviors that others have adopted toward us. Other people serve as teachers of behavior in both a modeling role and in forcing us to adapt to them. In our observations of and transactions with others, we learn what behaviors are possible. We know that children of abusive parents are often abusive themselves. At times young people will react to specific adult behavior by adopting behavior patterns exactly the opposite of the ones manifested by the adult.

Life stances evolve as each human being goes through the process of meeting basic survival, safety, and growth needs.

As human beings we also observe ourselves and evolve a number of "I ams." We take on self-images and begin to evolve within those images. We identify with ourselves. In the best of circumstances, we evolve into a state of beingness that provides the basis for a solid self, a self that is the container for all the "I ams" but is not any particular "I am." In the worst of circumstances, we lock in on an identity and all that goes with it, and we defend that identity to the point of physical or psychological death. Our identity becomes an emotionalized point of right/wrong.

A differentiating self continues to receive input throughout life. New information is taken into account and used for adaptive purposes. There is a sense of flexibility and openness to new experiences and ideas. There is a realization that how I deal with all the information given me in life flows out of my very beingness. One's capacity to engage the process of differentiation will influence the nature of one's life stance.

LIFE STANCES AND THE REALITIES

Implicit in the evolution of a life stance is the person's connection to each of life's realities. Each reality is! Each of these four realities–self, other, context, and the spiritual–exists. Our connection to all the realities is vital to our existence. A life stance identifies how I perceive each life reality.

Establishing a differentiating self is based on a connection to all of the realities, not part of them. Our ability to have an abundant life is a function of the extent to which we are connected to each reality. The realities exist independent of whether or not we connect to them.

It is important to note here that realities are not values or beliefs. We are talking about *what is*. We are addressing that which has been recognized as real by humans in one form or the other throughout the history of humankind. On the other hand, what is a desired value shifts and changes over time. Certain values come and go. Realities stay the same.

Realities are independent of our values. The four life realities exist in balance, tension, and synergy with each other. Remember, realities exist whether or not we connect to them. Without a balanced connection to all the realities, there is a sense that something is askew or we feel a void. Something is missing. A sense of urgency develops. Survival needs are energized. As humans we tend to attempt to fill the void with something. Oftentimes we fill the void with more attention to one of the realities to which we are already connected. To the extent that *survival needs* drive the nature of the connections to one or more of the realities, a kind of emotional lock-in takes place. We *need* the intensity of relating to that reality. There is a tendency to lose the flexibility that is available when we are connected to all of the realities.

The realities exist independent of whether or not we connect to them.

Living all of the realities brings us the abundant life we seek. The abundant life is not "me." It is not "you." It is not "the context." It is *all* of the realities in a dynamic tension and balance. We have the possibility of living in the independence, interdependence, and intradependence of all of the realities. Life in its total abundance is available to us. The realities are timeless and universal. By accounting for the realities, we connect across all categories of human life. The integrating question across cultures, races, gender religions, etc. is How does this subject or activity connect with each of the realities of life? All categories of human existence are required to deal with self, other, context, and the spiritual.

Living in the realities moves us toward the abundance we want. Living in the realities is not trying. It is not forcing. It is not focusing on values and beliefs. It is fully accounting for self, other, context, and the spiritual.

Out of fully accounting for the realities flows what we know as "a differentiating person." Virginia Satir often spoke of comparing the "Seed Model" with the "Threat and Reward Model" of life (Satir and Baldwin, 1983).[1] Living fully in the life realities means that we live in the freedom of our total being. We do not *have* to do anything (prescribe), or *not* do anything (prohibit). We engage in what fits for a person living in connection to the realities of self, other, context, and the spiritual. That is a seed model! There is no "have to" in the seed model. There is what fits.

In examining life stances, the goal is to consider the nature of the connections to each of the realities. The nature of those connections pushes us toward certain patterned activities and away from certain other activities.

LIFE STANCES AND DIFFERENTIATION

An individual's life stance is associated with his or her differentiating capacities (see Figure 5.1–Differentiation Scale). While the scale is not real, it is a vehicle that may help to understand the connection between life stances and differentiation.

You will recall that on the differentiation scale 100 is the ultimate in differentiation capacities. Zero on the scale is a total lack of capacity for differentiation. The scale shows that depending on the extent to which one has the capacity for differentiating, there is either a solid self and the ability to be in a affirmative life stance, a scattered self and the ability to occupy a responsible tendency, or a pseudo-self and exist in one of the dysfunctional stances.

FIGURE 5.1. Differentiation Scale

	100	
Solid self	**75**	Affirmative
Scattered self	**50**	Responsible
Pseudo-self	**25**	Dysfunctional
	0	

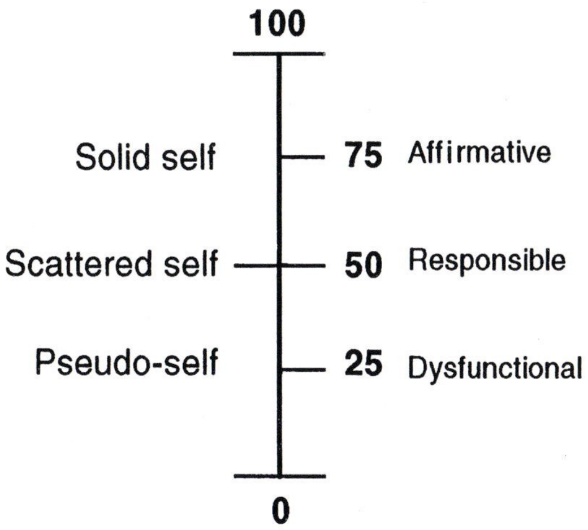

THE LIFE STANCES

Affirmative Life Stance

Affirmative people are fully connected to all four life realities. They are aware of the *self* as who and what "I am." And, this fully connected self serves as the context for all of their "I ams," roles, identifications, values, and beliefs. It is a differentiating self that is self-defined and self-regulated. Affirmative people are connected to the *other* reality. They are neither enmeshed nor cut off from important others. Affirmative people know that they have a connection to a context that has humanmade values, beliefs, and roles. They are aware that they live in a culture, a society, and a country with human-made imperatives. Affirmative people sense the spiritual as the ultimate context of their existence. They know that the spiritual is the most personal of all the realities. It is their connection to the ultimate power of the universe, God. Out of their connections to the four realities flow the following tendencies.

1. Affirmative people have a mind-set that actively seeks the appropriate response to life events. An appropriate response simultaneously promotes the growth potential in all of the realities. The connection to the spiritual provides the link to that which is ultimate, nonchanging, and secure. The defining characteristic of affirmative people is their use of all the realities to reach their full life potential. The organizing personal context for the affirmative person is one of love, caring, and integrity in his or her connections to the realities.

Affirmative people are fully connected to all four life realities.

---

2. Symbols of value and worth as defining references mean very little to affirmative people. They may enjoy fine clothes, houses, cars, or other items of material wealth, but these items do not define them. Power, prestige, and position are used to make life more abundant for everyone involved, not to foster self-narcissism. Affirmative people have the ability to enjoy the "finer things" in life, but they do not *need* them.

3. Affirmative people are not caught up in the HAVE, DO = BE process of life. They do not have *to have* a big car, an advanced degree, or wealth or *to do* certain things in order *to be* something great or worthwhile. Being affirmative means that what they have or do flows out of their being, not vice-versa.

4. Pain and frustration in life have a particular meaning to affirmative people. Primarily, they do not bring pain and frustration on themselves. But, when painful and frustrating events occur, they look for the growth opportunities in the events. It is more than a positive mental attitude; it is a stance that is geared to finding the growth opportunity in all of life.

5. Affirmative people are honest people. They speak the truth as they know it. They walk their talk. They are congruent people. They are what they say they are, and they do what they say they will do. They have the capacity to speak from the I-position.

Affirmative people are honest people. They speak the truth as they know it. They walk their talk. They are congruent people.

---

6. Affirmative people are not always ready to blame others. Affirmative people own their own experiences They do not attack others. They have learned that *what you attack runs your life*. Affirmative people have acquired a fundamental law of life. They know that the time, effort, and energy you give to attacking others puts others in charge of you and your life. Affirmative people also know that when you attack something, or someone, there is a high probability that you will energize exactly what you attack.

7. Affirmative people are self-validating people. While they appreciate support from other people, they have an internal validation process. Their self-validation process enables them to fully connect to themselves, other people, their context, and their spiritual side.

8. Operating with their neocortex in control, affirmative people are very creative. They occupy the top levels of the differentiation scale. They often do not fit the status conscious "societal mold" promoted by Madison Avenue. The crucial factor in their not fitting the mold is that they are not rebelling against something. Affirmative people know who and what they are and do what fits for them. What fits for them comes from the solid self.

Affirmative people do not attack others or their ideas.

9. Affirmative people are poised to add to the substance of life. They are always ready to promote growth and potential. They are other-validating people. They extend the abundance that life holds.

10. There are very few fully affirmative people. The world is not friendly to affirmative people. While they do not attack people or their ideas, their attention to reality may seem like an "attack" to some people.

11. Affirmative people come in many forms, styles, and circumstances. If and when you meet an affirmative person, you will know it. It is to the extent that you are a differentiating person that you will appreciate an affirmative person. To the extent that you are not a differentiating person, you are not likely enjoy the presence of an affirmative person. The lack of enjoyment will come from you and not from any intrusive actions on the part of the affirmative person.

In your role as a therapist you are not likely to see many affirmative people. They have a remarkable capacity to cope. However, the events of life have the ability to overwhelm anyone. An affirmative person will seek help if needed. And, an affirmative person will make excellent use of a differentiating therapist.

The use of the term *affirmative* as a life stance may convey a static quality that is not intended. The term "affirming" may more correctly convey the action or behavior that flows from the affirmative process. However, the term affirmative does capture the positive part of the connection to the life realities and the resulting abundance that flows from accounting for all realities.

Responsible Life Stances

As experiences accumulate, each person is drawn to a certain mode of interacting with the life realities. This level of comfort with certain relational patterns may be called responsible tendencies. In the responsible stance, the individual tends toward a certain mode of patterned activities and has available to him or her a variety of relational responses. This relative flexibility in transacting with the human realities is associated with the capacity for self-differentiating.

In the responsible stance, the individual prefers a certain mode of patterned activities and has available to him or her a variety of relational responses.

People who tend to occupy the responsible stance show a varying capacity to be differentiating. In using the differentiation scale to demonstrate responsible tendencies, responsible people may be thought of as occupying the middle part of the scale. There are times when a responsible person demonstrates many of the capacities of a differentiating person and other times when he or she may have trouble with self-definitions and self-regulation. The defining characteristic of the responsible person is the constant struggle to find the values and beliefs to serve as the internal guide for facing the human realities. There is an overall tendency to do certain things and to have certain things in order to occupy an "acceptable" role or safe place in the social scheme of things.

We are at our best when we sense a strong connection to all of the realities, including the spiritual reality. Virginia Satir said, "When people forget their spiritual dimensions, they feel lost because they have no connection with the life force or universal mind (Satir and Baldwin, 1983).[2] Left to their own devices, humans seek to create a safe place from which to struggle with the human realities of self, other, and context.

The people occupying the responsible stance may be thought of as the "good normal neurotics" of our society. Most of us fit somewhere in that broad category. We have our moments of peak differentiating experiences but often spend our lives struggling to connect with the human realities.

Indeed, it is the pattern of playing down, or diminishing, one or more of the human realities of self, other, and context that gives life to each of the seven responsible tendencies within the responsible stance. When a human reality or combination of human realities is diminished or highlighted, we demonstrate specific patterns of interactions. It should be noted that any one of the responsible tendencies are appropriate at a given time and/or place. The following is a discussion of the seven responsible tendencies that make up the responsible stance.

Compliant

The *compliant* tendency is preferred by many people. It is a tendency to be helpful, agreeable, cooperative, and alert to the opinions of others and the expectations of the context. It is a positive tendency. Compliant people are "yes" people (see Figure 5.2). They start interactions from the "yes" position. They believe that people can make it best in life by being nice. They are willing to be second in the scheme of things. They play down the self and highlight others and the context. Many people are very comfortable in the compliant tendency. There are times, places, and situations when being compliant is appropriate for all of us.

FIGURE 5.2. Compliant Tendency

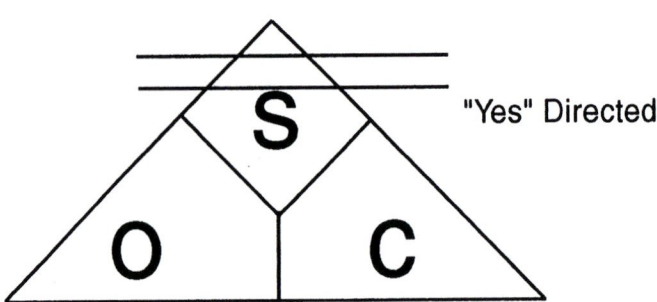

Compliants start interactions from the "yes" position. They believe that people can make it best in life by being nice.

Assertive

The *assertive* tendency is a comfortable mode of interacting for many of us. It is a tendency to be a take-charge person, to be alert to what the expectations of the context are, and to assert personal wishes within that context. Assertive people have no trouble being first or expressing their opinion about how something should be accomplished (see Figure 5.3). They believe people win by stepping forward and taking control of the situation. The assertive people play down the other reality and highlight the self and context. There are times, places, and situations that need assertive people. All of us will find ourselves in situations where it is appropriate to be in the assertive tendency.

FIGURE 5.3. Assertive Tendency

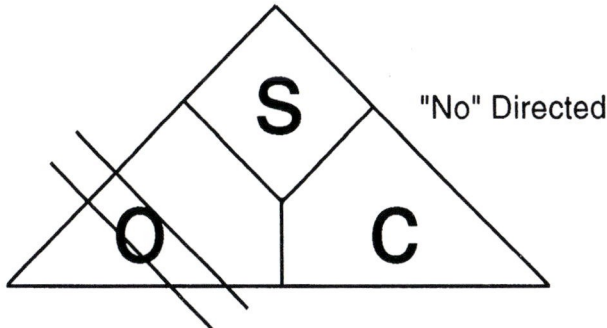

Objective

The *objective* tendency is the preferred mode for a number of us. People who prefer the objective tendency tend to be rational, analytical, fact-finding, and systematic in their approach to interactions. They rely on rules, regulations, logic, and expectations to organize their lives. They give excellent critiques and are finely attuned to the logical (see Figure 5.4). The world needs people who prefer to live within the assertive tendency, yet there are situations when it is appropriate to be objective in our mode of interacting. The objective-tendency person highlights the context reality and plays down the realities of self and other. As can be surmised from the realities that are played down, the objective person tends to avoid personal connections.

FIGURE 5.4. Objective Tendency

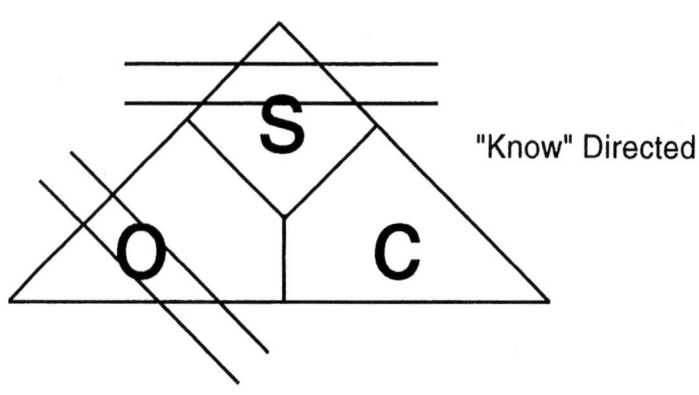

"Know" Directed

People in the objective tendency rely on rules, regulations, logic, and expectations to organize their lives.

Distractor

The *distractor* tendency is a mode of interacting that plays down all of the realities. People who prefer the distractor tendency are distanced from the ordinary considerations of self, other, and context. They tend to be seen as creative, active people with a "different" idea about events and people (see Figure 5.5). They seem to always be out of the flow of the events that are taking place. Distracting people often serve the purpose of breaking the tension in an emotionally heavy situation. They crack a joke that is completely off-the-wall or do something that changes the direction of an event. The world needs distractors. Their lack of connection to any of the realities often makes them appear to have a short attention span or to be people who always miss the point. A close consideration of their distracting mode will reveal that they are very comfortable in their way of interacting. They feel great satisfaction in the responses they get from others or the context. On the other hand, their inability to focus on anything or complete goals or projects is distracting to others and their context.

FIGURE 5.5. Distractor Tendency

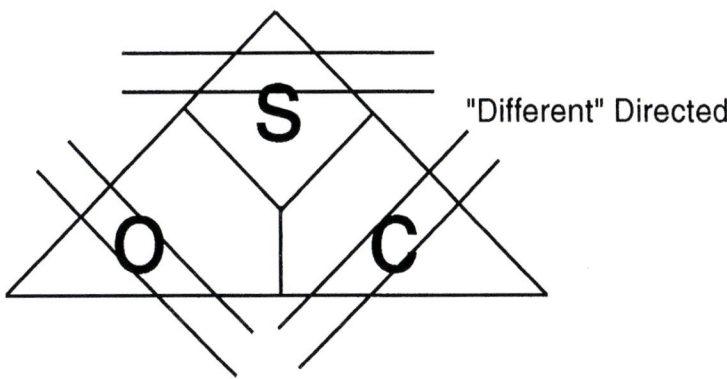

"Different" Directed

Self-Concerned

The *self-concerned* tendency seems to be a mode of interaction that is currently gaining popularity. Self-concerned people highlight the self reality and diminish the realities of the other and the context (see Figure 5.6). At its best, the self-concerned tendency is fun-loving, action-oriented, and spontaneous. At their worst, self-concerned people can come across as self-centered and impulsive. There are times, places, and situations when the self-concerned

FIGURE 5.6. Self-Concerned Tendency

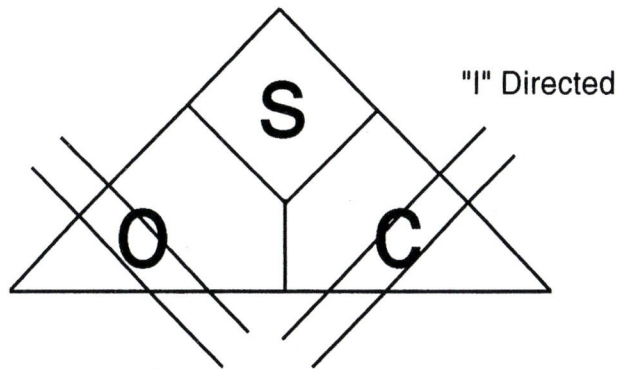

"I" Directed

tendency is needed. There are events where the most appropriate behavior is to look after one's self.

Sensor

The *sensor* tendency is a people-directed mode of interacting. At their best, people in the sensory tendency are sensitive and empathetic to the personal part of life. Sensors highlight the self and other realities and diminish the context reality. To the sensor, the feelings and wishes of people are much more important than rules and expectations (see Figure 5.7). The personal human side of life demands their attention. The world needs people who are open to the inner feelings, wishes, and hopes of themselves and others. There are times when the sensor tendency is needed. Sometimes sensors may come across as too emotional and sensitive. Yet, what would the world be like without the emotional side of life? Emotions make us real people.

For people occupying the sensor tendency, the feelings and wishes of people are more important than rules and expectations.

FIGURE 5.7. Sensor Tendency

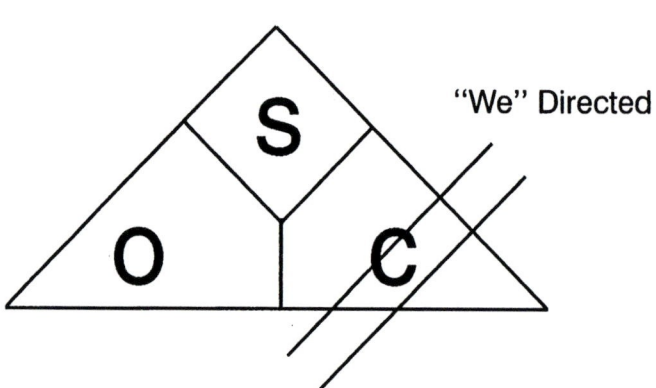

Loyal

Some people are very comfortable in the *loyal* tendency. These are people who find great satisfaction and comfort in giving their full commitment to another within the agreements made with the other person. Loyal people want to be devoted to a specific other. The loyal tendency plays down the self and the context and highlights the other (see Figure 5.8).

There is a need for people who have the ability to occupy the loyal tendency. Great accomplishments have been achieved through the loyalty tendencies of people in many relationship forms. Loyalty in work relationships and loyalty in family relationships are the most obvious places for this tendency to emerge. The world needs loyal people.

FIGURE 5.8. Loyal Tendency

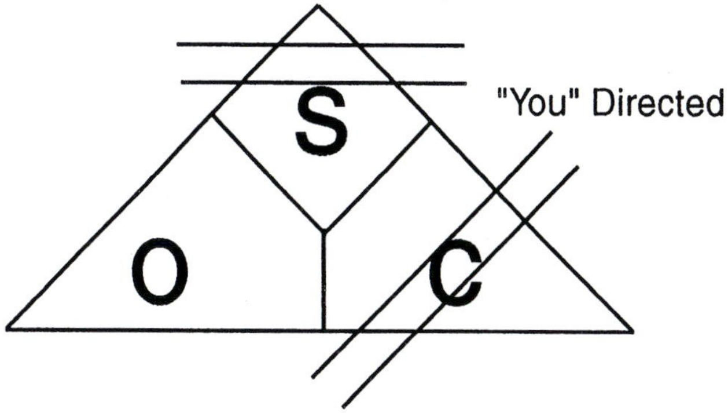

Summary

The seven responsible tendencies show the various combinations of highlighting and diminishing the three human realities. People in the responsible stance tend to be most comfortable in one or two of the tendencies. At the same time, they seem to pattern themselves more prominently in one or sometimes two of the responsible tendencies.

The responsible tendencies can be seen in living, changing, and moving people. The tendencies are not discrete categories or bounded off clusters of behavior. There is much overlap between and among the tendencies as people vary their connections to the life realities. A person's differentiating capacity is not static. Our behavior patterns vary as we show our capacity, or lack of capacity, to be self-defining and self-regulated.

The effective family therapist will be aware of his or her own patterns of interacting in family situations. Through the process of assessing the client's stance situation, the therapist will recognize those personal tendencies that need attention in himself or herself. The process of strengthening what is weak or putting in what is missing is a basic part of enhancing one's differentiating capacities.

Life Stance Profile

The process of constructing a personal life stance profile provides a view of our own assessment of which, and to what extent, we prefer particular responsible tendencies. The vertical line is the percentage of time spent in a particular context such as the family, a marriage, at work, or life in general. Bar graphs are placed on the horizontal line to indicate the amount of time spent in each responsible tendency. For example in Figure 5.9, the client sees himself as compliant most of the time. He also sees himself as interacting in an objective mode much of the time. The degree to which he occupies the other tendencies is indicated in the life stance profile by reading from left to right. A life stance profile provides a glimpse of the areas the therapist may need to examine in the process of therapy.

For beginning therapists, constructing a personal life stance profile may provide directions about areas of self-awareness and self-development. For one young therapist/intern, the life stance profile revealed a strong preference to be nice and nonconfronting. When his clinical work was reviewed on videotape, his compliant tendency toward clients confirmed an overall problem in dealing with demanding clients. The earlier life stance profile exercise served to enable the therapist/intern to become aware of his patterns in the treatment situation.[3]

Dysfunctional Life Stances

The seven dysfunctional stances reflect an extremely low capacity for self-differentiating. Dysfunctional stances cluster in the lower fourth of the differentiation scale.

FIGURE 5.9. Life Stance Profile

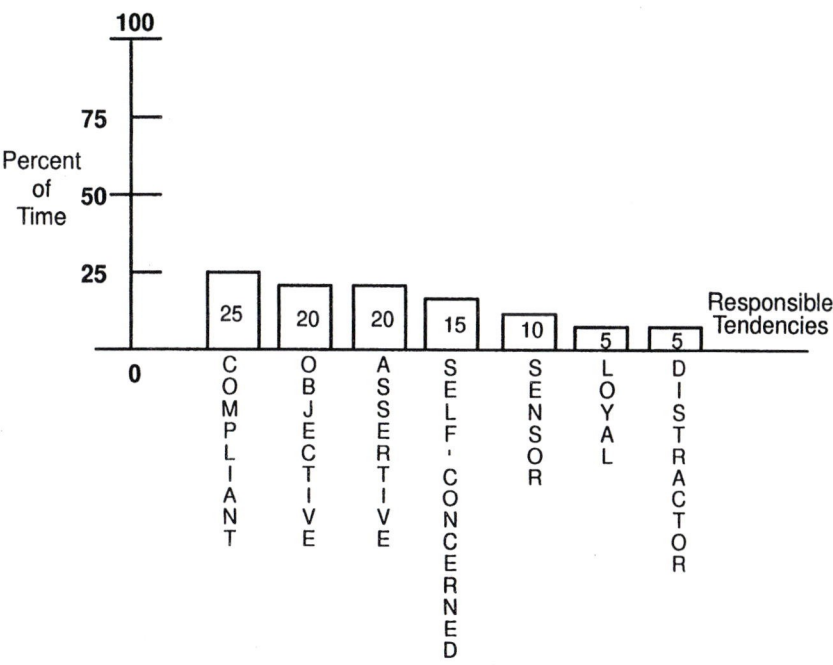

People in a dysfunctional stance are basically anxious people who are predominately ruled by lower brain functions. They have an inflexible approach to human interactions. Much of what they do seems to be directed toward setting up life situations that confirm their stance as the "right" way to live. The manipulative nature of their activities brings with it a high probability of being self-destructive. A defining characteristic of the dysfunctional stance is the survival directedness that pervades all activities. People in a dysfunctional stance seem stuck in survival efforts that require the elimination of, or disconnection from, one or more of the life realities. People in dysfunctional stances play out their life drama in a repetitive pattern that uses other people as "bit players" in their predetermined life story. As a group, they avoid personal responsibility, are stuck in emotionalized right/wrong, seek validation from others or the world, have a low sense of worth, and have only a vague sense of a purpose in life.

Since they function without a substantial connection to one or more of the human realities, their survival efforts are based on lack of full information about themselves, others, and the world around them. Their activities are predominantly destructive to themselves and often injurious to others. Dominated by lower brain functions, their survival activities tend to be automatic, emotionalized, and forced.

A word of caution is in order here. A person stuck in a dysfunction stance tends to become an "expert" in the ways of his or her stance. The client will have life stories and defensive-based justifications for being in the stance he or she occupies.

One other important consideration is in order here. Except in extreme cases, no reality is completely eliminated. The activity characteristics described in each stance are associated with *the extent to which* the realities or reality is eliminated, distorted, or over-highlighted. No dysfunctional stance exists as an entity. The dysfunctional stances are ways to approach certain overdetermined "stuckness" in repetitive patterned behaviors. The following is a discussion of the dysfunctional stances of the human realities.

Submissor

The person "stuck" in the *submissor* stance eliminates direct connections to the reality of self (Figure 5.10). The survival conclusion of the submissor is that it is dangerous to manifest a self in human

FIGURE 5.10. Submissor Stance

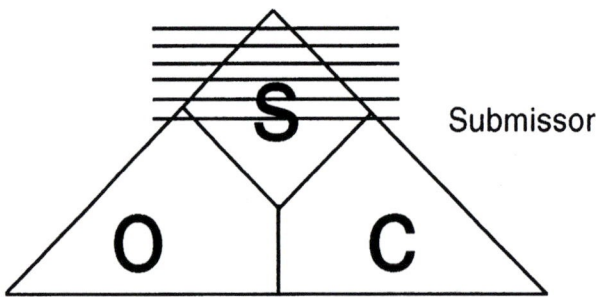

interactions. The submissor lives in a world that is strongly connected to the realities of other and context. Perception is directed "out there" to the demands of other people and the rules and demands of the context. There is extreme concern about activities that are "right" in the eyes of the world. (How am I doing with you in this context?) Their validation for living comes from others and the context.

Within the submissor stance, we find the "true victim" in interpersonal transactions. These are the people who somehow end up being wrong, at fault, or put down in almost all situations. The submissor "wins" by proving how victimized he or she is in life. There is a sense that the submissor believes that if I hurt bad enough and long enough, someone will care.

In the therapy situation the submissor presents story after story that shows him or her to be the loser or victim. If the therapy moves to enable the client to face his or her part in the stories, the client often becomes the metavictim by pointing out how victimized he or she is by the victim pattern. ("You are right. I am so bad at what I do. I don't know what to do.")

If the therapist does not move to enable the client to face his or her part in life transactions, the victim role often gets worse. At some point the client is brought face to face with the stance he or she has taken. Again, the client becomes the metavictim. It is a difficult stance to deal with in the therapy context as well as in life's family relationships. The words employed by the submissing person are concerns about the "out there" of pleasing others and the context. The words hide the self-centered survival *needs* of the submissor. The submissor chooses the flight reaction to threat.

The manipulative nature of the submissor stance brings with it a high probability of energizing anger in human relationships. The anger then serves to demonstrate to the submissor just how "unworthy" he or she is in life–a victim again. The extreme for the submissor stance is suicide, the ultimate elimination of the self.

Aggressor

The person "stuck" in the *aggressor* stance eliminates or disconnects from the other reality and highlights the realities of self and context (Figure 5.11). They deal with life from power and strength. The survival conclusion is that to make it in life I must be first; I must

FIGURE 5.11. Aggressor Stance

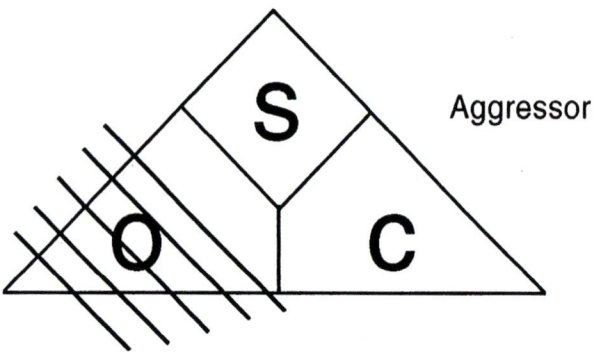

be in charge. There is a strong blame component to the aggressor stance. One way to stay one-up on other people is to find their faults and blame them for any shortcomings they may have. The life rule for human interactions is to discount other people to the greatest extent possible.

Aggressors are very focused people. They are focused on what they need and how to use the context to get what they need. They are quite aware of the context and how to use it to obtain their demands.

In the fight or flight reaction to threat, the aggressor is immediately ready to fight. The "forced" nature of this stance prevents the person from seeing the effect on the person who is the target of the aggressive action. The reality of the other is not available for consideration; it is blocked out. The ruthlessness of an aggressor will likely be measured by the constraints of the context. The aggressive person is connected to the expectations of the relevant context. The context also provides the rules and expectations that serve to "justify" whatever activity has been initiated by the aggressive person. The context expectations and rules will be twisted and stretched to serve the survival needs of the aggressor. The felt needs of the aggressor are covered over by the words of bureaucratic roles and expectations. The extreme for the aggressor stance is a carefully planned murder of an other.

Detached

People who are stuck in the *detached* stance eliminate the realities of self and other and highlight the context reality (Figure 5.12). They ignore human factors and organize their life and the rules and regulations of a context. Facts and logic carry the day with a detached person. They are driven by demands of routine and organization. They are detached from the human part of existence. They are excellent role players because they know exactly what is expected of a particular role. For instance, a person in the detached stance plays the role of the teacher, the physician, the lawyer, the psychotherapist, the nurse, or whatever to perfection. They know the role very well. The problem is that a detached person is not, in essence, a physician or a nurse. He or she plays the role but he or she is not real. Anyone who has experienced the difference between a real physician and a person in the role of a physician can understand the subtle but deep difference.

The detached stance enables a person to avoid connections to his or her own feelings or desires. Their wants are there somewhere but not available to the detached person. Likewise, closeness to another living, feeling person is not possible because the other person is essentially eliminated from consideration. The communication style of the detached individual is devoid of attention to the warm, caring part of relationships between and among humans. In the fight or flight reaction to threat, the detached person seeks intellectual compromise.

FIGURE 5.12. Detached Stance

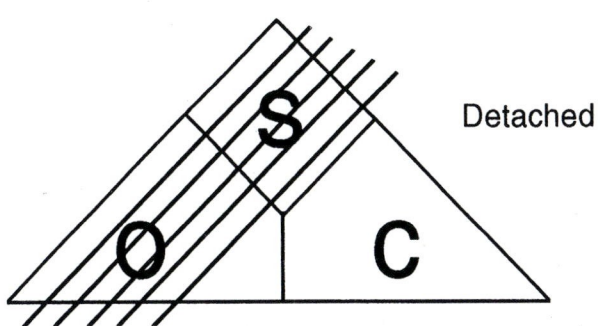

Avoider

The *avoider* eliminates all of the realities by disconnecting from all of them (Figure 5.13). It is as if the avoider has a thick screen over any point of connection to the realities of life. The organizing factor for people in the avoider stance is survival threat. They see other people, the context, and themselves as dangerous and unreliable. Their view of life is that you cannot trust other people; avoiders have stories to justify the mistrust. For the avoider, you cannot trust any context. The church, the government, society, etc. do not have the survival interests of the avoider in mind. There are numerous examples of the threat to people that come from the context. The avoider does not find a part of himself or herself that can comfort survival fears. They do not see themselves as reliable or possessing integrity. Their body breaks down; feelings seem out of control; and thinking is scattered. The self cannot be relied upon.

The survival conclusion is that since all is dangerous and threatening, do not rely on or connect with any of the life realities. The person in the avoider stance hides and stays on the move. Relationships, jobs, locations, and commitments are temporary. Basic survival is the need experienced by the avoider. The anxious words of the avoider illustrate the lack of connection to the realities of life. The looseness of thought and actions show no anchor to self, other, or context. The extreme result of avoiding is psychosis.

FIGURE 5.13. Avoider Stance

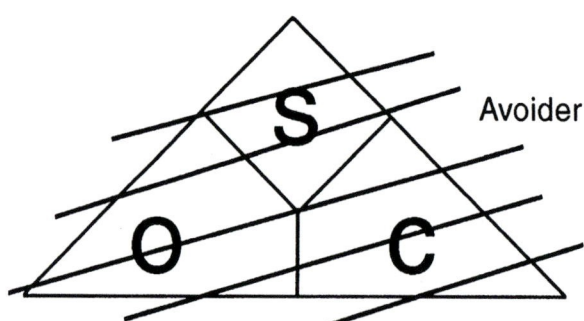

Demander

The *demanding* person eliminates the human realities of other and context (Figure 5.14). For the demanding person, the guiding philosophy seems to be "grab what you want when you want it." They often come across as impulsive and driven. Most often they are action-oriented and obviously self-centered. They may use clothing, cars, and behavior to draw attention to themselves.

When asked why they have done something, a common reply is, "I don't know." In fact, they do not know why they do things. Life is simply a *stimulus-reaction* world; no reasons are necessary. They are out of control with minimum input from higher brain functions. Any thinking that takes place is in the service of lower brain activities. Thus, their planning and thinking go into getting what they want. Their survival needs are so intense they feel "exposed" to the world. Demanders ordinarily cover their needs with deceptions of extreme bravado or a kind of scheming passiveness. It is a form of deceptive behavior seen in reptiles. Reason and logic cannot be used to provide alternative behaviors. Have you ever reasoned with a lizard?

The demanders' lack of connection to the context leaves them vulnerable to getting in trouble with the law or other regulatory officials. Lack of considerations about the law or social expectations raise the probability of running into trouble with some agency of society. In contrast to the aggressive person who accounts for the expectations of a context, the demander has trouble with rules and regulations. Rules and regulations are not part of their realities. Their activities are con-

FIGURE 5.14. Demander Stance

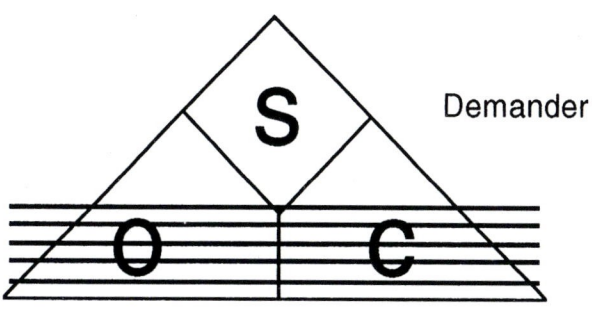

Demander

gruent with a view of the world that excludes other and context considerations.

The demanders' stories about "how life is" and their communication style reflect the self-directed survival nature of their beings. One
demander, when asked why he shot a person he was attempting to rob,
replied, "Why not? He [the man he robbed and shot] had no money.
He took up my time." About the act of robbing someone, the young
man replied, "They have more than they need. I need it to do my
thing." The communication was conveyed in a serious matter-of-fact
manner. Survival-based activities of the lower brain are in control for
the demander; thus, the reaction to threat is to fight.

Emoting

The person locked into the *emoting* stance eliminates the reality of
the context (Figure 5.15). This means that rules, roles, regulations, and
expectations are ignored and emotions take center stage. The reaction
to life seems to be, "Let emotions rule. If I let my feelings show long
enough and strong enough, my needs will be met." The focus on the
feelings side of life heightens the sensitivity to the inner emotions of
people. Emoting people develop a keen awareness of their own feelings and those of others. They become experts on empathy. They read
survival feelings down to their depth. They form emotional attachments very quickly. The problem is that the attention to emotions is in
the service of survival. Emotions are anchored in need. Their lives are

FIGURE 5.15. Emoter Stance

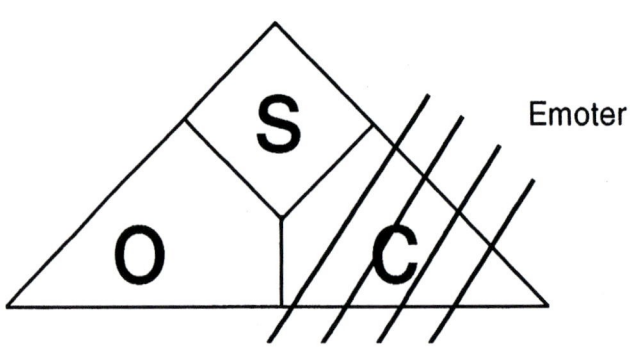

driven by the demand to have their emotional needs met. It is a matter of survival. Relationships with emotionally needy people often take on the sense of a slippery slope. The closer one gets to an emoting person, the stronger the demand for closeness gets. The slide toward total emotional engulfment with the emoting person gets faster as the relationship continues. There is a demanding quality about the communications of an emoting person. The demand is to affirm and meet *my* emotional needs. Because the demand comes from the lower brain functions, the reason and logic of a context does not enter the relationship.

Subservient

Individuals stuck in the *subservient* stance eliminate the human realities of self and context (Figure 5.16). For the subservient person, the ordinary rules and expectations of life and one's own personal wishes and desires are not taken into consideration in a relationship to a specific other. The whole of one's being is attached and enmeshed with one other person. The desires, wishes, and demands of that person are foremost in the considerations of life. The survival conclusion for subservient people is that "in order to make it in life I need to attach myself to one other person." Any logic and reason that emerges is used in the service of the survival need to be attached to another.

It is not unusual for the subservient stance to show up in gang activity, where a charismatic leader demands and gets total obedience

FIGURE 5.16. Subservient Stance

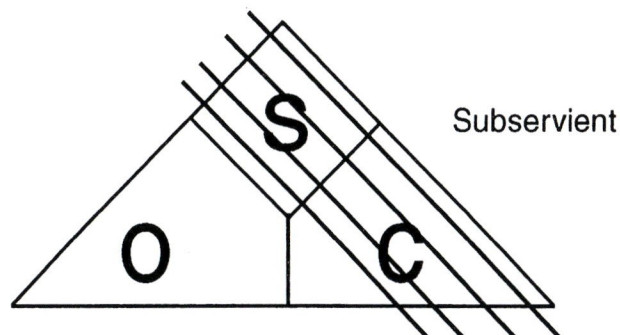

from his or her followers. The drivenness of the primitive herd instinct empowers both the charismatic leader and the obedient follower. In such a situation, the "leader" offers to meet all the basic survival needs of the person in the subservient stance.

The communication of the subservient person contains no considerations of the ordinary expectations of society or one's family. The wants, wishes, and desires of the subservient person are secondary to another. Subservient people show up in a variety of relationship configurations such as marriages, live-in relationships, groupie aggregates, and cults. Many people who attempt to relate to the subservient are often shocked when logic and reason have absolutely no effect on the subservient's stance. It is well to remember that thinking is not a function of lower brain activity.

THE LIFE REALITIES REVISITED

How a person develops a life stance is associated with the extent to which specific life realities are eliminated, distorted, or highlighted. There are no pure life stances, but there are expectable patterns and clusters of activities that emerge when certain realities are not given full consideration in human transactions. Making one's way through life without access to the information and power available in each of the realities of life means that the full abundance of life is not engaged in the process of living. It is like a boxer who enters the ring with one hand tied behind him. It is like having the power of the whole brain available for growth and full living and largely ignoring the part of the brain that provides thinking, language, creativity, caring, intimacy, playfulness, insights, reflection, and self-awareness. Uncontrolled anxiety does exactly that to us as human beings. The old statement, "That's a half-brained idea!" is true when the full power of life realities are not available.

The well-differentiating person has the antidote for overpowering anxiety. Knowing who and what we are provides the pathway to our personal integrity. A higher brain activity is available to us. Facing what is missing in our considerations of life's realities is not easy. It contains both the pain and the power of growth that is available as we encounter all of reality. Being a nonanxious presence in the presence of anxious others is the basic requirement for a family therapist. The differentiating therapist has the capacity to deal with the power of anxiety. The differentiating process contains the power for growth and an abundant life.

Facing the Realities

The realities of life serve as a beautiful four-piece mirror for reflections of who and what I am. When I look into the entire mirror, I get a full view of the essence of my being. Just as the mirror, the realities tell me what is. Similar to the way we may use a four-piece mirror, it is possible to look only at certain parts of reality. It is possible to blot out or hide parts of the reflection of the mirror. I may concentrate on one or more sections of the mirror, or I can put a covering over parts of the mirror. If I skew the size, angle, or concaveness of the mirror, I will get a distorted view of who and what I am. Some people do that with the realities of life.

How and to what extent I connect to each of the life realities gives me a particular life perspective. In my fearfulness, I screen out certain realities. I do not want to see what is there because of a fearfulness or sense of threat to my survival. The important dynamic in my hiding maneuver is that the purpose of such an activity is to seek validation for part of what I am doing rather than to seek to fully know what is. A shift in purpose is crucial. For the purpose of other-directed validation, I take part of reality and act as if it is all of reality. To perform such a maneuver is to live in illusion. It is an attempt to cheat life. Yet, life is as it is. Alignment with the realities of our universe provides a solid basis on which to face all of our relationships.

How and to what extent I connect to each of the life realities gives me a particular life perspective.

How I face the life realities provides a window into who and what I am as a human being. The human inclination is to hide, distort, or eliminate parts of reality when threatened. The process of examining how I connect to the realities gives me an entré point for bringing my life into alignment with the laws of the universe. The first law of the universe is that what is, is. A failure to account for what is (reality) means to live in illusion. The history of humankind clearly tells us that is not easy for any one person or group of people to face the brokenness of their connections to any of the life realities. It is easier to go *around* our broken connections to illusion reality than to experience the pain of facing ourselves in relation to each reality. Growth and maturity is painful. Change is painful. Change is likely to make me anxious. When I do not want to be anxious, I may try quick fixes in order to get immediate relief. I may get stuck in a life stance largely based on illusion.

The issue is whether or not I can maintain my integrity in the face of strong survival anxiety. Fear is painful. The reality is that to grow and mature I am required to regulate the powerful activities of my lower brain functioning. It is not easy to face them head-on. It means that I must face anxiety and work through it and not devise ways to go around it.

I am required to face personal integrity issues every day. Do I do what I say I will do? Am I what I imply that I am? Do I fully know who and what I am? These are integrity issues. To deal with them I am required to face myself; I am required to be honest. I have to face my relationships with others. How do I handle the closeness/distance issues in my family? Sometimes it is easier to go around the relationship issues by whining, blaming, "rising above it all," or running from the issue. Life requires that I face my connections to various life contexts. Have I kept my agreements with me concerning the nature of my participation with my family, my marriage, my work, my profession, or my community? The nature of the mirror I choose to look into is my own decision.

It is said that in war the first thing to go is the truth. As in war, the psychological survival battle quickly generates attempts to hide, distort, or eliminate truth. The pain of what is may be too intense. In my survival mentality I *need* to blame others or something for my problems. Yet, the growth need is to trust myself. How do I gain self trust? The answer: I *choose* to trust me. I choose to be honest. I make choices to get to my integrity. To hold onto my identity is my integrity–to be honest. The goal is to get to my differentiation process. To examine my connections to the realities is the requirement of integrity. The requirement is to know how I make sense in an emotional world. It is not easy to face reality. The prospect of change is painful. Putting in what is missing in our connections to the life realities is likely to make me anxious. Consider the following case situations.

It is said that in war the first thing to go is the truth. As in war, the psychological survival battle quickly generates attempts to hide, distort, or eliminate the truth.

Dr. T was referred to me from the Department of Psychiatry of a large medical center. The department chair did not think that Dr. T should be treated by any one of his peers in the psychiatry department. The chair suggested to Dr. T that he call me.

Dr. T was a young psychiatrist who had an IQ of over 160. He was experiencing major problems in all his relationships, both professional and personal. The pain of several disastrous relationships with girlfriends and the possibility of being dismissed from the psychiatry staff at his hospital led him to seek help.

He quickly demonstrated that he was stuck in two dysfunctional stances. Most often he initiated relationships from the *emoting* stance, and at some point he would become an intensely *demanding* person. He was driven by a fear of being wrong in any encounter with other people or in any context. With an IQ of over 160 he could intellectually defend himself very well from being wrong. He enjoyed talking about confrontations with others in which he always "won," or he was proved to be "right."

Dr. T came into one treatment session angry and frustrated with his girlfriend. On the previous night he had become involved in an argument with her. He had proved her wrong and could not understand why his girlfriend was upset and distant for the rest of the evening. Some time was spent with him in analyzing what was present but missed in his interchange with his girlfriend. It was very difficult for him to connect with his girlfriend on a level that allowed him to see that while he may be right in his arguments with her, he was "wrong" on the relationship level. Over a period of time he learned that when he won an argument with her he was a "loser" on the relationship level. The anxiety of being wrong is in all human beings. A key to understanding Dr. T was that in both the *demander* and *emoter* stances the reality of context is distorted or eliminated. Dr. T had trouble bringing the expectations of a particular context into his awareness.

When he was asked to teach a specific seminar for the psychiatry residents, he did not find out anything about the expectations for the seminar. In reality, the particular seminar he was asked to teach had a unusual history within the teaching curriculum. He did not find out that over the years the informal expectations in the seminar were that little information would be presented during the seminar. In fact, the seminar traditionally had been a time of discussion of personal issues. Dr. T entered the process demanding that the residents listen to and study his lectures. The residents' complaints were so strong that the Chief of the Department of Psychiatry had to intervene. The length of the seminar was shortened and Dr. T was not asked to teach it a second time.

During social occasions, Dr. T often singled out a particular female to engage in an "open emotional" discussion. Typically, after "opening his heart" to her, he would ask the female to tell him about herself. When an "emoting" response was not forthcoming from the female, he would shift into his demanding response with *demands* that she tell him about herself.

Dr. T said, "What I now realize is that before I join a game being played in the street, I need to watch a while so I can learn what the game is all about." He recognized the need to face the reality context in his own way.

Partly, his learning to face the context reality involved homework that consisted of going to social occasions and discovering what the explicit and implicit expectations were for the particular event. Increased connections with the context reality and the other reality did not come easily. After a particular confrontive and painful session with Dr. T, his developing awareness of the context reality was demonstrated by a comment that was couched in his urban background. Dr. T said, "What I now realize is that before I join a game being played in the street, I need to watch a while so I can learn what the game is all about." He recognized the need to face the reality context in his own way. *His journey into the pain* of facing the realities was on its way.

In another case, the 'Ws,' a sixty-two-year-old man and his sixty-year-old wife, were referred to me from a medical ward. The wife had been hospitalized for an unsuccessful suicide attempt. When the family issues emerged as a precipitating factor, they ended up in my office.

The husband was a retired Army colonel. His wife had spent her entire life in the home. They had two adult daughters who lived in the home with them. I later learned that the daughters had stayed at home to "preserve the family."

The husband was stuck in the detached stance. He was not connected to human feelings, either his own or those of others. He worked for the Internal Revenue Service. He knew the tax code item by item and line by line. He was strongly connected to the reality context with its rules and regulations. The wife was stuck in the submissive stance. She was not connected to her own wants and desires. The reality of self was eliminated from consideration. Mrs. W often occupied the victim role to the fullest.

The story of her unsuccessful suicide attempt revealed the stance dynamics for both of the Ws. On the evening of Mrs. W's hospitalization, one of the daughters rushed into Mr. W's office yelling that Mrs. W had overdosed, was dying, and the rescue service needed to be called. Mr. W calmly put his newspaper aside and told his daughter to calm down so that they could carefully plan a reasonable response to the problem. Mr. W came up with the following plan. They would call the rescue service. They would ask the rescue service to come to their house without their sirens on. The ambulance driver was instructed to quietly come up the alley behind the W's house. The rescue service did as instructed. Mrs. W was quietly taken out of the home, put into the ambulance, and taken to the hospital. While in the hospital, the couple's marital problems were revealed to the ward social worker.

The Ws agreed to come in for weekly interviews to work on their marriage problems. The task of connecting them to their missing realities began. Mrs. W was locked into a pattern in which she simply was not connected to her own wishes and desires. She looked to others for guidance and validation. Mrs. W played the victim part to the fullest.

Almost every sequence of events between her and others resulted in Mrs. W being wrong for something she did or did not do. As her "victim" pattern emerged in the interview sessions, she took on the nickname "Mrs. Poor Me." As therapy progressed, she would catch herself establishing her victim position and say "I am Mrs. Poor Me right now."

Nicknames caught on in their sessions. Mr. W soon acquired the name "Mr. Right." His major purpose in interactions was to establish his rightness. Often, he went to great lengths to establish that he was right. As he developed some awareness of his rightness anxiety, he joined his wife in the nickname game. He called himself "Mr. Right."

The therapy process was not easy for this couple. Their entire lifestyle, including that of their daughters, was organized to preserve the stances in which each family member was stuck. Connecting with who and what I am is painful. For Mr. W the pattern of not experiencing his feelings or those of others around him was not satisfactory to him, but it was safe. It was difficult to allow feelings in his sphere of awareness. The change process moved forward slowly. Mrs. W eventually took the initial step in a connection with herself and her wants and desires.

The two grown daughters each sought treatment for themselves. As the relationship between their parents changed, the daughters had to face their part in the overall family dynamics. About six months after Mrs. W's failed suicide attempt, both of the daughters had moved into an apartment of their own.

The therapy process was not easy for this couple. Their entire lifestyle, including that of their daughters, was organized to preserve the stances in which each family member was stuck.

Individual change is fearful. The problem is not that we do not want to change but that it is scary to go into places where we have never been before. The presence of the therapist offers possibilities for exploring those fearful places in the unknown. Assisting in the process of putting in what is missing means that our client takes a few steps and examines the question "Does it fit for me?" The purpose of the therapeutic process is to see more clearly what is right in front of us. To be who and what I am eventually means I am required to connect with my inner wisdom. The process of my looking inside me to find my integrity is not a nonsensical journey. It is a journey to truth. And, it is not easy to seek inner wisdom about me for the purpose of honesty and truth. The therapist, however, can help to provide the atmosphere for the journey to self.

Providing a person with the opportunity to choose to move into a fuller awareness of his or her integrity is a major purpose of therapy. Connection, or lack of, to the life realities is the window for the therapeutic process. It is not easy to open the window to the life realities. An open window means that I face who and what I am. Often it is easier to live in the illusions of a socially sanctioned, emotionally driven, nonthinking, unaware mammalian model for life. For many, the thinking, self-aware, human model for life is fearful.

The differentiation process is the vehicle that can deal with the anxiety issues all humans experience. The starting question for all our individual activities is: How does what I do show for who and what I am? It is not a question that looks for our narcissistic self; it looks for our honest self. A clearminded focus on the integrity question eventually brings us face to face with ourselves; this is called the process of differentiation.

The Appendix of this book has a complete exercise based on the material presented in Chapter 5.

NOTES

1. Satir, V. and Baldwin, M. (1983). *Satir Step by Step*. Palo Alto, CA: Science and Behavior Books.

2. Ibid, p. 160.

3. For a paper and pencil, nonresearch-based life stance and tendency procedure, see the Relational Systems Model Stance Tendency Recording located in the Appendix.

We live in relationships with other people. Other people are a "what is." They are real! Since human beings are social creatures, other people are necessary for our physical and psychological survival, safety, and growth.

Beginning in infancy we have basic food and protection needs that require other people. In the process of meeting our basic human needs, we weave a complex network of human relationships. "We experience the existence of ourselves and others primarily and immediately in terms of relationship and not of observations" (Watzlawick, 1964).[1] Even the hermit lives his or her life in relation to other people. In living this lifestyle, the hermit simply chooses to be isolated from others. Even when we are not in the physical presence of others, we carry images in our mind of how other humans are and what they will do or say in a given situation. The question is not, "Do we have a relationship to others?" We are already in relationships with others. The question *is,* "In what relationship are we with others?"

In one sense, the shifting and changing human relationships make up the essence of human existence. For example, relationships between parent and child change; the husband and wife relationship changes over time; and relationships between and among siblings modify throughout the family life cycle. Relationships with friends, co-workers, and acquaintances shift and change according to circumstances. Given the interdependence of people in various social aggregates, a change in one set of relationships will effect changes in other relationships.

Every human being must account for other people. The manner in which we connect to others is the arena of concern in consideration of the reality of other. The RSM directs itself to family concerns as a beginning point for an individual's connections to the reality of others.

LIFE STANCES AND RELATIONSHIPS

Each one of us carries our life stances into every interpersonal transaction. Thus, we approach interpersonal situations from the particular perspective implied in a life stance. Our voice, body, position, facial expression, and body movements all combine to indicate the particular life stance from which we operate. In the marriage and family context, a patterned way of interacting among family members develops over time.

Even in the initial encounters with other people, we work to create the "right" atmosphere in which to validate our preferred stance. It is more than accidental that submissive people who play a head game of "poor me" consistently find themselves in transactions where they experience injustice.

Each of us carries our life stances into every interpersonal transaction.

The observation that some people approach human relationships in ways that have a high probability of experiencing injustice is in no way a "blaming the victim" dynamic. It is a bringing into awareness behavior patterns that have a high probability of specific outcomes. We train people how to treat us in social situations. To avoid observing what is present and noticeable is to live in illusion. It is interesting to note that aggressive people constantly "find themselves" in situations where blaming others or putting others down is "required." No matter which of the stances we occupy, we find ourselves in circumstances where our particular stance is "justified." The push to be right organizes our life. We seek our validations any way we can get them. All of us attempt to create a set of circumstances that validate our own life stance.

Over time all close human relationships exhibit patterned transactions. These patterned relationships are most apparent in family relationships. For instance, spouses quickly establish a particular way of relating to each other. In marriage, life stances and cultural forces merge to form the uniqueness of each marital relationship.

THE MARITAL RELATIONSHIP

For the purposes of this discussion, the marital relationship will be considered in its traditional sense. Ordinarily, we begin our existence in a family or family-like configuration.[2] In some cultures it may appear more tribe-like than family-like. Marriage is an emotional relationship between a male and female who are committed to a life together. They have formalized that commitment through a socially sanctioned marriage ceremony. At a minimum, it takes a male and a female to provide the continuation of the life process. The sperm of a male and the egg of a female are necessary. Papero (1990) says that the family process begins with a breeding pair.[3] From that perspective, a family is a system that exhibits patterns of emotional and social functioning.

Clearly, there are marriage-like relationships that do not fit the traditional view of marriage. To the extent that such relationships are like the traditional marriage, the emotional, systemic dynamics will adhere in their evolving pattern of interactions. To the extent that a two-person relationship is more like a close relationship between two unmarried adults, the dynamics of close two-person relationships will adhere.

The dynamics of human relationships are universal in nature and, therefore, except for the uniqueness inherent in each close human relationship, the relational systems model cuts across race, gender, culture, religious, or other sociocultural groupings. All human relations are a combination of the personal, emotional, and social forces that prevail in the relevant contexts.

Marriage may be thought of as part of the unfolding developmental processes of individuals. It is a phase in the maturity process for all humans. A major developmental issue of adulthood has to do with intimacy. Intimacy is the process of being who and what I am in a close, enduring relationship with another.

Intimacy in marriage involves both risk and growth. The growth emerges from the sense of integrity that comes from being in touch with oneself in the presence of a distinct other. There is self-awareness and other awareness and a joining of realities. It is the total sense of fully being with and joining another in both the erotic and nonerotic dimensions of an evolving, changing, and growing relationship.

Intimacy in marriage signifies both an advanced stage of individual development and the beginning stage of the life cycle in a family. Marriage from this perspective is an integral part of both personal development and the developmental stages of the family.

Marriage may be thought of as part of the unfolding developmental processes of individuals. It is a phase in the maturity process of all humans.

By its very nature, the marriage relationship energizes powerful emotional dynamics that always exist between and among people. Humans are driven by two opposing needs: the need to be separate from others and the need to be close to another. The emotional forces of separateness and closeness are constant and pervasive. They always stand in tension. For growth to flourish, they demand an appropriate balance. We deal with the separate/close forces all our lives. The risk in marriage comes from an inability to keep the two forces in balance. The intensity of the marital relationship brings the separate/close emotional forces to life.

Each marital partner comes into the process of marriage with an evolved level or capacity for differentiating. Bowen's theory (and others) suggests that marital partners have similar levels of differentiation and undifferentiation (Papero, 1990).[4] The process of marriage provides a place to enjoy the intimacy of the self-other relationship *and* maintain the integrity of the self. The basic growth and maturity question of marriage is, Do I have the capacity to be a strong self and be in an enduring intimate relationship with another? The reality of other in the marriage has its own unique dynamics.

At one level marriage deals with the paradox of the giving of oneself in order to complete one's self—to give in order to receive. To gain one must give, not bargain. For instance, when I toss a ball up into the air, I can think of tossing the ball away from me. Holistically, I am also tossing the ball to me. In order to receive the ball I must toss it away. Marriage is a test of maturity. To experience intimacy I must give intimacy. In order to be a self, I must give of myself. In order to give to me, I must give to another.

In an open society, such as exists in the United States of America, the selection of a marital mate is not a random process. Satir often said in her many workshops that we know more than we know. We just don't know we know it. There are understandable reasons we select a particular husband or wife. The straightforward reason we select a particular person for a mate comes from the attraction we have for people who have located a level of differentiation that is similar to our own. While we may differ with our spouse in many ways, we seek out and marry someone who is similar to ourselves in emotional maturity.

Marriage is not the only area where emotional likes assemble. People who are similar in their emotional maturity level tend to find each other. If you want an accurate view of your emotional maturity level, look at your spouse, friends, and other associates.

Over time the level of differentiation or maturity may shift and change more for one spouse than the other. The anxiety of emerging discrepancy in emotional level does not send a differentiating spouse running to the extremes of emotion fusion or an emotional cutoff. People at the higher levels of differentiation seem to handle the shifts by engaging in activities designed to encourage mutual growth in differentiation capacities.

In the O case the couple had married in their early twenties. From the discussions in the interviews, it appeared that at the time of the marriage both of the Os were in the mid-range on the differentiation scale. As time passed Mrs. O continued to grow in her level of maturity. Mr. O's initial reaction was to regard Mrs. O's growth as an invalidation of him and his place in the marriage. He became more self-concerned and, at times, passively demanding in the marital relationship. Mrs. O's increasing capacity in her differentiating process widened the gap between their maturity levels. At an early point in their relationship problems, they sought professional help.

People who are similar in their emotional maturity level tend to find each other. If you want an accurate view of your maturity level, look at your spouse, friends, and other associates.

As with many couples who are mid-range in their differentiating capacities, the Os used the therapy to engage in a mutual examination of who they were as individuals and as a couple. Part of the process of marital intimacy is the capacity to self-disclose in the presence of one's spouse. The purpose of personal disclosure is not to seek validation from one's spouse but rather to more closely define who and what *I am*. With the help of an effective therapeutic atmosphere, the Os re-established their connection to each other. Mr. and Mrs. O each used the process to increase their differentiating capacities. Their areas of mutual interest and concern also provided part of the glue that enabled each one of the partners to pursue individual interests. The therapy process provided the place for Mr. and Mrs. O to make the choice to establish a satisfactory balance on the separate/closeness continuum.

To the extent that a couple is located on the lower part of the differentiation scale, the self/other connection will be subject to dysfunction. In times of stress these couples have trouble maintaining a balance in the separate/closeness forces. "In the closeness of an intense relationship the emotional selves of each blend or fuse together into a common self, a 'we-ness'" (Papero, 1990).[5] The marital partners become very dependent on each other for emotional validation. Each partner feels a *need* for the other. They form an intense need-based interaction between them.

Marriage relationships based on dependence, "need," or other-validation are human relationship disasters waiting to happen. Need-based dependency is sometimes called love. Possession and dependency get mixed together and are called "love."

Humans need water, air, food, warmth, and other human beings for survival and growth purposes. Adult humans do not have a psychological need for any one specific person.

Individuals at the lower level of the differentiation scale become mutually dependent on each other. They fuse with each other on a need basis. Need implies survival so that without the other person, fears for survival are energized. "I can't get along without him," "I would die if something happened to her," "My life would be over if I lost her," and "I feel I am nothing without him," are all common reactions to the threat of loss of a "needed" person. Each partner feels empty without the other. It is like a feeding process. A burdensomeness often sets in. When the fusion gets too intense, they tend to fight as a distancing maneuver. Immediately after the fighting ceases, they start an enmeshment process over again. It's a porcupine-like relationship. They stick each other when they get too close, and once separated, they move toward each other once again.

A common pattern in these "needy" relationships is an effort by a partner to prove that he or she is the more needy of the two. Activities designed to establish the most needy position are characteristic of couples locked in a fight to be the deprived one in the relationship. It is important to note that the winner in the battle is the loser. The most needy is the "winner." In ordinary relationships the person in the one-up position defines the relationship. The one-up person defines who is right and who is wrong in their transaction. In the needy relationship the person in the one-down position defines the relationship. The battle is to be in the loser's position. The loser is the winner!

A common pattern in needy relationships is an effort by a partner to prove that he or she is the more needy of the two.

People who have lived in a need-based relationship may develop a deep sense of rage toward themselves and their partners. The sense of rage overwhelms the parts of the marriage that keep them in their relationship. When these couples divorce or separate, the disengagement process is filled with anger and viciousness. Physical violence may be part of both the marriage and the separation. It is important to remember that survival-based need reactions are automatic. Thinking and choice are not in control of the process.

Choice is the defining dynamic in intimacy-based relationships. What a growth enhancing sense I get when I realize that my wife chooses me for a spouse. She has no need for me. She is free to choose me or not choose me, and she chooses me. There is no sense of *have to* or burdensome feeling in our relationship. There is the freedom for both of us to grow and mature as individuals and as a couple. As a differentiating couple we have anxiety and stress in our marriage, and we face the stress head on. When we are in a low point in our differentiation process, we tend to attempt to avoid dealing with the problem directly. We may blame, ignore issues, and go around a problem for a while, but the problem always circles back on us, usually in a stronger form. A problem ignored gains power until it is faced and dealt with fully.

It is important to remember that survival-based need reactions are automatic. Thinking and choice are not in control of the process.

FOUR WAYS OF DEALING WITH ANXIETY

Papero (1990) suggests that there are four basic patterns that families use as ways to deal with anxieties that may inhabit the marital relationship.[6] As stress builds in the marital relationship, the couple makes moves to relieve the stress. One way to relieve stress is for the marital partners to pull away from each other. They draw back like porcupines whose quills have stuck each other. Moderate movements back and forth between closeness and separateness are characteristics of all enduring relationships. The distancing provides some relief from the intensity of the relationship. The closeness provides the possibilities for the intimacy process. Kerr (1981) points out that the distancing is a way of avoiding one's discomfort or reactivity to another.[7] The problem is that we tend to blame the other for our own reactivity.

Gottman (1994) identifies stonewalling, or distancing by withdrawal, as one of the major destructive patterns in a marriage relationship.[8] In his studies, men are identified as the withdrawer and women the pursuer in about 85 percent of the distancing processes. It is well to remember that both partners are dealing with their own reactivity to the other. They avoid the issues in the marriage by stepping around the conflict. In the process they do not deal with their relationship concerns. Couples in a distancing-type relationship pattern may not achieve a sense of intimacy with each other, but depending on their differentiation levels, they may stay together in the marriage.

A second way to handle the stress in a marital relationship is to fight. Closeness and distance issues are handled by a volatile fighting-type relationship. The fighting keeps them at an acceptable distance while also keeping them in contact with each other. Ordinarily, the emotions are intense in the volatile fighting-type relationship. When such couples are passionate with each other, they are extremely passionate. When they are negative with each other, they are extremely negative. The struggle for each partner is one of managing reactivity to survival fears of self-regulation and self-definition. For them it is less painful to fight than to face one's own part in the marriage relationship.

Therapists who work with this type of marital relationship learn to be nonreactive to the extremes of fighting and loving presented by these couples. It is during the time of negativity that the fighting may get out of hand and damage the relationship permanently. As long as the loving part of the continuum is five times stronger than the fighting part of the same continuum, these couples may stay together (Gottman, 1994).[9] If the couple is able to address the differentiation process, the extremes in the marriage become unnecessary.

The third way of handling stress in a marital relationship is to join in an unconscious collusion to displace the stress of the problems onto a child. The anxiety in the relationship between the parents directly relates to the involvement of a child. A low level of differentiation influences the ability of both parents to look at themselves or their children as separate distinct persons. To avoid the pain of looking at themselves and their relationships, they become concerned about one or more of the children. The attention to the child serves to distance each spouse from each other emotionally. Simultaneously, the child's problem brings the parents together over some mutual concern.

Basically, anxiety in a parent is expressed in sensitively and reactivity to a child (Papero, 1990).[10] The independent functioning of both the parents and the child becomes impaired. The overconcern about the child links parents and child in a dependent enmeshing type of relationship, which involves a younger generation in the problems of an older generation. As the parent-child relationship becomes closer, the child becomes a "willing" participant in the enmeshment process with the parent. The emotional immaturity of both the parents and the child runs the relationship. As the child grows older, the push toward independence is likely to be met with a stronger effort by the parent to control the adult "child."

The human tendency for any two people to involve a third person when they cannot get along is called triangling. When the anxiety level reaches a certain point in one or the other of a pair, one of them will move to involve a significant third person (Papero, 1990).[11] All humans engage in the triangling process. It is so common in our life we hardly notice our involvement in the process. In its broadest sense, anything can be used as a triangling object. Sports, work, causes, and intellectual pursuits are examples of things that may be used as "triangled" objects. In one troubled relationship, the family dog was triangled. Concern and care for the dog replaced dealing with the troubled relationship. The spouse who avoids the anxiety in marriage by overworking has triangled his or her work. The triangling process often has the effect of calming things down.

When the anxiety between a marital pair is great, a web of interlocking triangles may involve all of the family members. Different family members may be used as the "triangled" person in different situations. Brothers, sisters, parents, and uncles all may serve the triangling process.

The human tendency of any two people to involve a third person when they cannot get along is called triangling.

The concept of the triangle describes the automatic predictable behavior of two people who are experiencing difficulty controlling their relationship anxiety. The two-person relationship is very unstable when under stress. One or the other of the two will automatically move to the triangle–a third person or a significant something in the environment. At any one time all of us will serve as the triangled person. At other times, we may move to triangle another person. The purpose of triangling is to calm relationship anxiety down to a tolerable level. Our tendency to get stuck in a triangling process will be associated with the deficits in our differentiating capacities.

The special problem associated with involving a child in the emotional processes of parents is that the child quickly develops an increased sensitivity to the emotional forces in the family. When the anxiety level between parents increases, the child unknowingly will tend to become entangled in the marital relationship. This heightened emotionality between the parents and child further increases the vulnerability of the child to the triangling processes.

The predictability of the triangling process has led to the development of sophisticated family therapy methods designed to address the complex issues that are part of intergenerational triangling.[12]

The fourth way of handling stress in a marital relationship concerns the level of functioning of each spouse. In the marriage relationship, one spouse becomes the overfunctioning one and the other spouse becomes the underfunctioning partner. In situations involving spouses at the middle or higher levels of differentiation, there may be considerable variation in which partner is underfunctioning or overfunctioning at a specific time or specific situation.

In marriage at the lower levels of the differentiation process, the overfunctioning/underfunctioning pattern can become extreme and fixed. Over time, the pattern adopted to avoid the stress of intimacy may become a source of anxiety itself. The underfunctioning partner may feel victimized by constant criticisms and contempt of the overfunctioning partner. The overfunctioning partner may feel a righteousness anger and contempt toward the inadequate partner. If the feelings overwhelm the higher brain functioning, the partners feel flooded by their negative feelings.[13] Emotions take over and the ability to bring cognitive processes into the relationship becomes limited.

Under conditions of sustained chronic anxiety, the low functioning individual may develop a physical, emotional, or social dysfunction (Papero, 1990). The physical or emotional illness absorbs the relationship stress that would otherwise need to be faced by the couple. Illness "requires" the compassion and care of the overadequate partner. Social dysfunction such as trouble with the law or other governmental bureaucracies "requires" the expected support and attention of one's spouse.

Casual observation of a number of couples who have maintained their relationship in the face of considerable relationship stress will show that the overfunctioning/underfunctioning pattern has served to keep them together. The illnesses and social problems take all their energy and time. The pattern seems to work as long as the generalized anger and disagreement between them does not regress into contempt and personal criticism.

When the marital conflict reaches a point of physical reactiveness, cognitive processes are no longer used to sustain the relationship. The negative interactions create a complex feedback loop between the spouses that involves physiological arousal. The anxiety of the relationship is part of the physiology of each spouse and as such is not under the willful control of the higher brain. The relationship comes under the domination of the reactive brain. Reason and logic do not work in these situations. The marriage has reached a critical reactive level. Insight is not likely to be a part of the process. The trauma of the marriage for each spouse requires attention. It is time for each marital partner to look himself or herself squarely in the eye. Carefully facing how I account for the reality of others in the marital relationship is not easy. Holding onto one's self *and* accounting for another in anxious situations is the key to relationship growth.

Married couples that stay together seem to use a combination of the four ways of managing marital stress. For married couples that endure, there is some sense that each partner is unique and that the marriage itself is valuable in its own way. This combination of individual uniqueness and mutual valuableness shows most strongly in the many positive transactions between the couple. At a minimum positive interactions exceed negative interactions by more than a five-to-one ratio.

MARRIAGE AND CONTEMPORARY SOCIETY

In today's world there is another pattern that many use to deal with the stress that is a part of the marital relationship. Over half of all first marriages end in divorce. Sixty percent of second marriages end in divorce. This means that when stress emerges in the marriage, at least half of today's couples terminate the marriage.

Clearly, some marriages should not continue to exist, but the high percentage of divorce among second marriages raises serious concern. Marriage is an emotional process. What conclusions about the general state of emotional maturity of our citizens are to be drawn from the divorce statistics?

The moment of crisis in our life often contains the elements for growth. Divorce is a crisis. Following a divorce, work on one's capacity for differentiating would seem to be in order. Facing one's personal integrity issues following a divorce is a choice point for engaging the maturity process at what is an opportune time for growth for many.

The moment of crisis in our life often contains the elements for growth. Divorce is a crisis.

It is difficult to go against the tide of the surrounding cultural system. Systems theory tells us that a strong social system will always outperform an effective individual. It is especially difficult to be a nonanxious presence when the surrounding anxious society has set forth, and strongly supports, a mammalian model for marital relationships rather than a human model for marriage. It is well to remember that the characteristics a society manifests depend on which part of the brain is running the cultural show. Consider this: The current behavior model supported by our society and all forms of the media connects to the herd, sexual, and aggressive instincts of people–functions that are located in the reptilian and limbic brains. Movies, sitcoms, and talk shows are prime examples of the attention given to the mid- and lower brain functions. The energy provided by the media to the sexual and aggressive parts of our brain is powerful.

The mammalian model is a seductive model because it hides its flaws. It does not allow for the capacity to think clearly about and reflect upon behavior. The mammalian model, by its nature, seeks to hide any hint that certain behaviors may be wrong. Thus, the mammalian model provides no mechanisms for identifying activities that are destructive to any or all of the life realities. A society in a regressed state is an out-of-control context.

The reality is that humans have a cortex. We have survival reactions, emotions, and the capacity to use our cognitive processes to protect ourselves and to reach our innate potential. In the mammalian model, humans are under the direction of the lower brain and use the cortex in the service of survival and limbic functions. Controlled by the lower brain, humans engage in frantic efforts to not be wrong. Self-destructive and other destructive behaviors are redefined as morally acceptable. The pain of dealing with self-regulation cannot be faced in the mammalian model.

An anxious society promotes the herd instinct. The pressure for conformity is powerful in our society. The power of the media to instill conformity is enormous. The mammalian model promotes control by the majority. If the majority of the people do it, it is OK.

The dynamics of our social context are mentioned here because therapy takes place within a specific society. The anxiety of our current society is part of the general context in which we apply the dynamics of the therapy process. Providing the atmosphere for enabling a marital pair to engage the differentiation process is a responsibility the therapist owns.

The mammalian model promotes control by the majority. If the majority of the people do it, it is OK.

DIFFERENTIATION AND SOCIETY

The differentiation process enables a marital pair to go beyond the socially induced anxiety of our time. The capacity to fully connect to another is related to our capacity to fully connect with our self while at the same time remaining fully engaged with the relational realities. On the other hand, the mammalian model for self is powered by the forces of narcissism, not by integrity. The human model for connections to the self and others is organized by the choice to seek self-integrity. Knowing who and what I am involves being fully connected to self, other, context, and the spiritual. Our current social context provides a strong challenge to the differentiation process. For the human model to emerge, the neocortical functions must be in control. The therapeutic atmosphere is a place to find our personal integrity. It is a place where the higher brain can gain control of the whole brain.

Putting in what is missing at the interpersonal level in a family addresses the realities of self and other. The power of the marriage relationship in the family is far-reaching. The marriage sets the emotional tone for almost all that transpires in a family unit. The power of the marital relationship may abate some during the latter years of the family life cycle. However, it remains the pivot around which the nuclear and extended families revolve. Enhancing the differentiation process in the marital relationship will have a strong positive influence on the entire family unit, possibly for generations.

DIFFERENTIATION AND THE MARITAL PAIR

In marriage the relationship goal is to be a self and connect fully with one's spouse. The intent is not to *use* my spouse to validate me. If I need my wife to validate me, the growth of our relationship cannot move forward until I get all the validation I *need* from my wife. In such a relationship, validation becomes a fix I need to make it through the marital day. This is not to say that I do not enjoy, want, and value my wife's support and caring. I experience her support and caring as a pleasure for me but I do not *need* it to survive. I am pleased that she chooses to support me and challenge me on occasion.

In the differentiating process my communication is from an I-position. The I-position is my way of letting others know where I stand at a moment in time. At my best, my messages are clear and congruent on all levels. There are no hidden demands in my communication. I am not communicating to another in order to run his or her life. I communicate to the other for my integrity. I want you to know where I stand as information to me and to you. While I may want you to do a certain thing for me, I fully respect your choice in the matter. I account for me, you, the context, and my spiritual being by the nature of my communication.

The differentiation process engages the dynamics of human boundaries. Growth-producing relationships may be close, but they are not invasive; the boundaries of self and others are respected. The human emotion forces of separateness and togetherness play out their tension in the arena of human boundaries.

One of the primary elements of the differentiating process is the capacity to manage the tension between the emotional forces of separateness and the forces of togetherness in situations of extreme anxiety. From the perspective of the life realities, the concern centers on the nature of one's connectedness between self and other. Overly intense connections lead to fusion between people. The kind of boundary needed for self-definition breaks down both in the fusion and triangling processes. At the other extreme of emotional attachment is a lack of connection to another. An emotional cut-off is a reactive distancing from another. The person who "runs away" from a spouse without facing the relationship issues is as emotionally connected to the other as a person who is fused with another person. The elimination of the other reality through emotional cut-offs with people to whom one is emotionally attached comes from lower brain intrusiveness into the realm of human relationships.

The nature and the degree to which the other reality is accounted for in stressful situations will affect the quality of the relationships experienced by people in both brief and enduring encounters. For example, Mr. and Mrs. Q ordinarily get along with each other quite well. They occupy the mid-range on the differentiation scale. Mr. Q prefers the compliant tendency within the responsible stance. This means that he highlights the realities of others and context and diminishes the self reality. Mrs. Q prefers the objective tendency within the responsible stance (see Figure 6.1). She highlights the reality of context and diminishes self and other. In evaluating the relationship, Mrs. Q usually assumes the leadership role through the use of logic and organization. Mr. Q is regarded by others as a "nice," affable person. Between the two of them, the reality of self gets diminished. In social situations the Qs often go along with the wishes of other people or other couples. Over the recent past, the Qs have become more aware of their combined tendency to be too

FIGURE 6.1

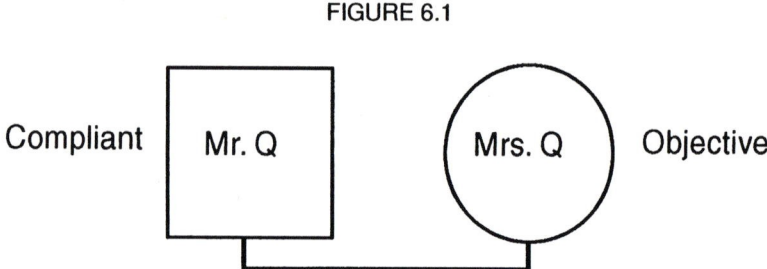

agreeable in their social relationships. The process of self-awareness for the purposes of integrity led to enhancing the reality of self.

The process of differentiating continues throughout one's entire life. Self-awareness for the purposes of integrity includes attention to our connection to the reality of others. Engaging the process of differentiation enables one to connect with all the realities with an increased sense of clarity.

FAMILY LIFE-SPACE DIAGRAMMING

A treatment technique that provides an opportunity for a family to examine the nature of the internal family boundaries is called family life-space diagramming. Using life-space diagrams draws attention to, and enhances the awareness level in, the arena of personal boundaries.

In the life-space diagram exercise, the clients are asked to use rectangles drawn on a piece of paper to represent their family relationships. Ordinarily, they each are given a pencil and two pieces of paper. They are asked to use the size, shape, angle, length, tilt, and distance from one another on one sheet of paper to represent the relationship between and among the members of their family. They are asked to give a family member name to each rectangle. Then they are asked to use the same procedures in their rectangles on the second sheet of paper. The second paper is used to represent how they would like for their family to be, *ideally*. The family is told that there are no right or wrong ways to draw the rectangle. Their individual drawings will only reflect how they see their family as it is and how they might want it to be. Each family member draws his or her rectangles without help from any other person.

When each family member has completed his or her drawings, the family is seated in a circle and each drawing is viewed one at a time. The family life-space diagrams depicting how it is now are presented to the rest of the family by each family member. Ordinarily, one of the most differentiated family members is asked to go first.

Generally, it is a good idea to avoid selecting the most invasive person to present first. The critical point for the process is to let the family know that there is no *right* drawing and there is no *wrong* drawing. It may be useful to give everyone the idea that this is the opportunity for the curious part of each person to emerge. Open discussion and disagreement is given a strong "OK" by the therapist during the process of reviewing the diagrams. Each life-space diagram is presented to other family members for their comments. After everyone but the presenter has commented on a diagram the presenter may explain what he or she intended to show in the particular drawing. The presenter may choose to give only a general idea of the meaning of the drawing. The primary goal is not to do the life-space diagramming process properly; the goal is to use the process to get a view of how family members play out their personal boundary issues.

After everyone has presented their representation of the family as it is, each person is given the opportunity to present their ideal family drawing. The differences between what is and the ideal are subjects for discussion. The therapist directs the questions toward using the process to allow each family member to look carefully at himself or herself in relation to other family members. There are no *right* conclusions to be drawn from the process. The relationships are taken where they are and examined from that point.

Although it is not likely, if a family has a problem with the idea of life-space diagramming, the members are encouraged to talk about their concerns. There is no pressure to convince a family member to change his or her mind about participating. There is a move to energize the curious part of each family participant. The family should be strongly encouraged to explore their reactions to the life-space diagramming exercise. Life-space diagrams may be used at anytime during the treatment process, and they may be used several times with the same family. It is informative to observe how the diagrams represent the family as it is changes over time.

The R family came for help when the 12-year-old son (S1) took some money from his teacher's desk drawer. The stealing incident capped a year of low grades and trouble getting along with class-mates. S1 presented the drawing in Figure 6.2 during the life-space diagram exercise. The parents were surprised to see that S1 regarded himself as completely "submerged" in the relationship between the parents. Using the drawing as a reference point, S1 was able, for the first time, to express his feelings about his relationship with his parents and his lack of a close relationship with his younger brother. For this family, the life-space diagram process gave the family permission to examine the boundary characteristics between and among all the family members. The process provided a vehicle for approaching strongly held feelings about how the family related with itself. For the R family, the task of facing their relationships in the family had just begun.

FIGURE 6.2. The R Family

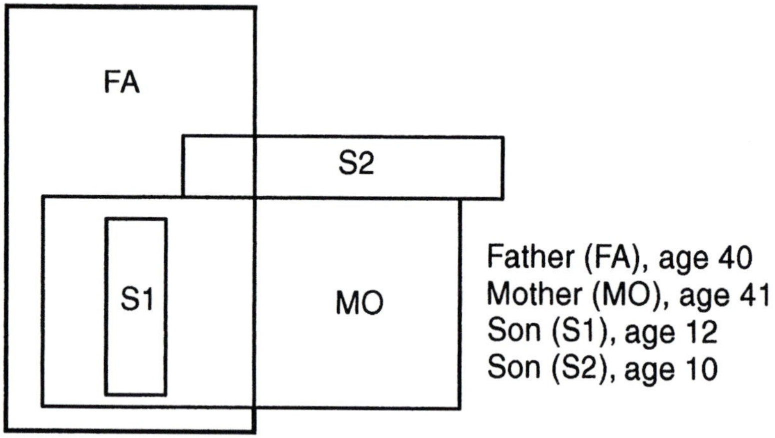

Father (FA), age 40
Mother (MO), age 41
Son (S1), age 12
Son (S2), age 10

NOTES

1. Watzlawick, P. (1964). *An Anthology of Human Communication.* Palo Alto, CA: Science and Behavior Books, Inc., p. 2.

2. In our society there is an ever increasing number of infants who begin life in a single-parent-present family configuration. The increase in single-parent-present families does not diminish the fact that it still takes a male and a female to conceive a child.

3. Papero, D. (1990). *Bowen Family Systems Theory.* Boston, MA: Allyn and Bacon, p. 28.

4. Papero, p. 51.

5. Papero, p. 51.

6. Papero, pp. 51-57.

7. Kerr, M.E. (1981). "Family Systems Theory and Therapy," in A. Gurman and P. Kniskern (Eds.). *Handbook of Family Therapy,* New York: Knopf, pp. 226-264.

8. Gottman, J. (1994). *Why Marriages Succeed or Fail.* New York: Simon and Schuster, pp. 68-102.

9. Gottman, pp. 68-102.

10. Papero, p. 55.

11. Papero, p. 49.

12. See for instance Minuchin, S. (1974). *Families and Family Therapy,* Cambridge, MA: Howard University Press; Satir, V. et al. (1991). *The Satir Model.* Palo Alto, CA: Science and Behavior Books; Papero, D. (1990). *Bowen Family Systems Theory.* Boston, MA: Allyn and Bacon.

13. See Gottman, J. (1994). *Why Marriages Succeed or Fail.* New York: Simon and Schuster and Notarius, C. and Markman, H. (1993). *We Can Work It Out.* New York: Perigee Books.

CHAPTER 7

CONTEXT: THE FAMILY–AN EMOTIONAL SYSTEM

The family is the context where the nature of our connections to all of the life realities shows up quite dramatically. Additionally, my life-stance configuration within the family reveals my unique personal approach to each of the life realities. As a family member I am a distinct individual. My interpersonal transactions within the family address the ways in which I connect to the reality of others.

The family unit is a naturally occurring human context. It provides us with a view of (1) the complex web of connections and influences of close multiple human relationships, (2) the family aggregate of parents and children, (3) the developmental stages of the ongoing family aggregate, and (4) transgenerational family transactions. The family also provides us with the opportunity to observe and experience the context that ordinarily is quite influential to our connection to the spiritual reality. The young members of a family are likely to be influenced by the nature of their particular family's spiritual journey.

As a context reality, the family is an agreement reality. The culture in which a family unit exists determines its general framework. A family's uniqueness emerges out of its personal and cultural history of transactions.

The family unit has a force of its own that transcends its individual or interpersonal constituent parts. We can't see a family context but it exists. It has the power to serve as a frame of reference for making meaning out of events. Indeed, the worldview of our family of origin ordinarily is the first context from which we make meaning of all that goes on around us. Part of our personal life filter comes from our family unit's view of life.

DIFFERENT PERSPECTIVES ON THE FAMILY UNIT

As with all contexts, the family unit may be examined from different perspectives. For instance, it may be viewed as an economic unit, a political unit, a sociological unit, or an anthropological unit.

The political nature of the family unit in the contemporary cultural climate became important during the 1980s and 1990s. Varying political interest groups in our society fought to use the family to their advantage. One of the issues that has emerged is the definition of "family." It is not unusual for a policy discussion of the family to get bogged down in disagreements about the definition of the family.

The political nature of the family in the contemporary cultural climate became important in the 1980s and 1990s.

For our purposes there are two possible approaches to the definition of the family. For reasons that will be obvious if the following suggestion is used, it is important to employ each approach to defining the family in the sequence suggested. In any event, the definition that will be useful depends upon the purpose for which it is to be used.

List Based

First, take a pencil and a piece of paper. From a quiet, reflective perspective, list the members of your family on the sheet of paper. Write the specific names of the members of your family. It is a straightforward exercise that provides for you your list of family members. You may want to complete the exercise before reading on.

The list of names will be those you think of without prior suggestions about how inclusive or exclusive to be with your list. Some people list members of their nuclear family only. Others list the nuclear and extended families. It is not unusual for the family pet to be included on the list. There is no right or wrong way to complete your list. Please make your list of family members before reading any further.

Definition Based

Second, take a few moments to write your definition of the family. Again, the definition you give is your view of how the family is defined. Take a moment to write your definition before you read any further.

Some people give a broad definition such as any aggregate of people who think of themselves as family. Some people say that the family is a mother and a father and their children. The range of definitions for the family is unlimited.

Almost always, the first approach to the definition of the family results in a transgenerational-kinship-based list of people. When asked to *list* members of your family, the thoughts and feelings that come to mind frequently reflect early childhood experiences and/or current kinship based family relationships. When asked to give your *definition* of the family, thoughts most always go to culturally derived thoughts about the family. The definition-based approach to considering the family is congruent with a political context where the purpose for activities is policy considerations.

The list-based and the definition-based approaches to the family are valuable to our considerations about how people connect to the life realities and the place of differentiating in the process of dealing with the functions of the triune brain. For the purposes of the relational systems model, the basic family unit is seen as a naturally occurring *social/emotion* system of mother, father, and children over the life cycle.

Papero (1990) notes that humans have apparently always formed parent-and-offspring units that start with a breeding pair: "one is tempted to call the breeding pair the emotional nucleus of the family."[1] The basic nuclear *family* structure is initiated when a child is produced by the breeding pair. Different aggregates of people evolve out of that basic unit, such as a single parent present unit (there is *always* a mother and a father from which a child is given life), blended family configurations of many types, adoptive families, or a single person living alone. In the RSM approach, one is always a member of a family. A single person living hundreds of miles away from the nuclear family unit *is* a family member.

THE FAMILY
AS A SOCIAL/EMOTIONAL SYSTEM

The family acts like an emotional system. Each human being in the family is subject to the emotional activity that characterizes human life. All of us have to deal with the survival and safety reactions of our lower brain. Additionally, all of us must deal with the push for growth that comes from our neocortex. To understand the family as an emotional system we look to the work of Murray Bowen and those who have expanded his work.[2]

Families demonstrate the characteristics of an emotionally influenced social system.

Additionally, the family acts like a social system. It follows the themes and principles of other social systems. At the very minimum, families show some form of organized activities, evolve a boundary, and have patterned internal communications procesess. Like other systems, the family is an organization or assemblage of people in which what affects one part of the assemblage affects the other parts. Such is the definition of a system. Families demonstrate the characteristics of an emotionally influenced social system.

THE FAMILY EMOTIONAL SYSTEM

The human brain, with its myriad of connections to the rest of the human body, appears to be the center of a highly evolved guidance system–possibly the most complex ever to evolve (Papero, 1990).[3] As presented earlier, the thinking functions of this guidance system are located in the neocortex. Part of the human guidance center is based in the emotional functions of the reptilian and limbic systems. Bowen (1966) points out that the emotional mechanisms of the reptilian and limbic systems are "as automatic as a reflex and that they occur as predictably as the force that causes the sunflower to keep its face toward the sun."[4] Given the reality that the family unit acts like an emotional system, certain family behaviors are predictable. This predictability gives the therapist clues about the emotional maturity level of the family unit, the dyadic relationships, and the individual members of the family.

All family units are attuned to survival, safety, and growth issues. The management of the anxiety created by survival issues will be a part of the dynamics of the family unit. Anxiety is contagious, especially intense anxiety. When anxiety is high, it is quite likely that the involved family members will react automatically. Predictably, family members become reciprocally reactive or responsive to each other. The nature of one member's reactions or responses affects the entire family unit. The fundamental question for each member of a family system is, "What is the nature of my own emotional reactivity in the family or in other social situations?" In the counseling situation, the role of the therapist as a nonanxious presence may serve to calm things down. The calm atmosphere may assist a person to engage the differentiation process.

Family members form relationships with each other. The nature of these relationships differs between and among the various family members. The management of the tension between the focus of separateness and togetherness is played out in the family unit. All family members influence each other during the life cycle of the family. The quality of relationships formed by the offspring in the family will be directly related to differentiation level occupied by the parental pair.

The Two-Person System

A two-person system is basically unstable. Under stress it will seek to encompass an outsider. When the two-person system is calm, it is a twosome plus an outsider. When stress enters the relationship, the outsider may be brought into the relationship. For instance, if two people have trouble handling their relationship, they may talk about a third person. This scenario is played out time after time in families. I cannot deal with my relationship with my mother. So, when I am with her, I talk about my brother. At that point my mother and I are fine. The problem is that my mother now may see my brother from a more negative perspective. My mother and brother now have trouble talking to each other about each other. My brother talks to our mother about our sister. The discomfort has changed to another triangle again. My brother and mother are fine but now our sister is the outsider and so on. When the third person to be triangled is an offspring, the tension between parents is calmed but the tension has been transmitted across generations. The child has become involved in a transgenerational transmission process.

Family Triangles

The family unit is made up of a series of interlocking triangles. The triangling process is predictable. In a three-person family there are three interlocking triangles. In a four-person family there are four triangles; with five people there are nine triangles; with six people there are fifteen triangles.

In the triangling process, the most uncomfortable of the twosome is the one that will make the move to triangle a third person. It is not unusual for the more comfortable one of the two to express surprise at the discomfort of the partner. The triangling process will rotate among the different members of the family. Again, the degree of emotional intensity of involvement in the various triads is directly related to the differentiation capacities of the parents.

Differentiation Capacities of the Parents

The differentiation capacities of the parents are crucial to the survival, safety, and growth of the offspring. The path of the family life cycle is related to every family member's ability to engage the differentiating process. Under the guidance of the neocortex and involving the entire brain and nervous system, each offspring has a developmental need to grow toward self-definition and self-regulation. The direction toward maturity is increased self-responsibility. The young person's intellect and cognitive processes are used to govern his or her activities.

Papero (1990) addresses the crucial developmental issues when he says, "To the degree that responsibility for self is not attained, the need for another is established. This need for another governs the degree to which the individual attaches to others throughout life. This set of relationships . . . established in the primary triangle, becomes a template for future relationships of equal intensity, generally with mate and offspring."[5]

The capacity to engage the differentiation process is crucial to the emotional system of a family. The ability to know who and what I am and use that knowledge as the basis for my family activities is the antidote for my lower-brain-based tendencies. Two dynamics are relevant at this point. First, there is the possibility of choosing an overall cluster of life stances dominated by the *need* for others to validate me. The lower brain activity that accompanies such a stance relegates the family to living on automatic reactions rather than choice-based responses. My relationships become need based rather than choice based. Second, in the lower levels of the differentiation scale, people organize around the emotionalized fear of being wrong. Their worldview sets in motion a supersensitivity toward avoidance and being wrong. The avoidance of being wrong emotionalizes relationships even further, thus making it difficult to break the cycle of dysfunction. Engaging the differentiation process is a way to bring neocortical functioning into the governing process for the family unit.

The capacity to engage the differentiation process is crucial to the emotional system of a family.

Human emotional behavior is predictable. What emerges from knowing about the way humans are in the family unit is that each nuclear family is the endpoint of the nuclear families before it. The family's ability to engage the differentiation process is a product of past generations and the ongoing work of the current family unit. The current family's emotional system will influence future generations of offspring. That is the way human emotional systems operate.

Predictable Human Emotional Behavior

There is a high level of predictability in the emotionally based behaviors of human beings. For instance, interactions between two relatively well-differentiating marital partners has a different quality compared to the interactions between a relatively undifferentiating marital pair. The differentiating pair can tolerate separateness and closeness as well as differentness and sameness. They have the capacity to deal with such areas as the dynamics of right/wrong, responsivity, worth, and purpose. While close to their families of origin, they are not attached to their families of the past. There is a sense of autonomy and a sense of closeness to the family in their interactions.

Any marital pair is inextricably bound to the quality of the relationships in their families of origin. The ability of current parents to function in a positive differentiating process is related to their relationships to their parents and the relationship between their parents.

The successful negotiation of the process of differentiating in the family of origin will likely lead to a strong sense of self-differentiation in the offspring. The failure to achieve a relatively strong self-differentiation process means that it is likely that the marital partner will remain emotionally attached to their family of origin. Issues relating to right/wrong, worth, and responsibility are easily energized in relatively undifferentiating parents.

There is a high level of predictability in the emotionally based behavior of human beings.

The push to full human potential is found in the functions of the higher brain. The thinking, planning, and language needed to creatively seek higher human levels of family interactions come from the entire brain working under the direction of the neocortical part of the brain and nervous system. The push toward realizing full potential in one's family unit is strong. The functions of the neocortex are energized by the motivation to be connected to my family *and* to be who and what I am at the highest levels of my unique humanity. If located at a high level on the differentiation scale, the family member will be able to deal directly with each other family member.

When the neocortex is in charge, an individual can live in a highly emotionally charged atmosphere, remain connected to the people involved, and maintain a clear headed sense of integrity. That is the essence of being self-regulated and self-defined. That is the way the fully functional family emotional system is designed to operate. The cognitive *and* the emotional capacities function under the direction of the higher brain. In such an emotional atmosphere, human growth is highly predictable.

NOTES

1. Papero, D. (1990). *Bowen Family Systems Theory.* Boston, MA: Allyn and Bacon, p. 28.

2. See Bowen, M. (1978). *Family Therapy In Clinical Practice.* New York: Jason Aronson; Friedman, E. (1985). *Generation to Generation.* New York: Guil-

ford Press; Papero, D. (1990). *Bowen Family Systems Theory*. Boston, MA: Allyn and Bacon; and Schnarch, D. (1991). *Constructing the Sexual Crucible*. New York: Norton. Families demonstrate the characteristics of an emotionally influenced social system.

3. Papero, p. 40.

4. Bowen, M. (1966). "The use of theory in clinical practice," *Comprehensive Psychiatry, 7*, p. 366.

5. Papero, p. 34.

CHAPTER 8

CONTEXT: THE FAMILY–A SOCIAL SYSTEM

THE FAMILY SOCIAL SYSTEM

The family unit acts like a social system. As a social system the family is an abstraction. As is often said about social systems, they are not something you can see or touch because they are abstractions; you can't kiss a social system. Yet, our life experiences tell us that the power of a social system is real. The power of the family social system is active in our life, all our life.

As in the family emotional system, the dynamics of the family social system are highly predictable. All social systems have a boundary to distinguish what is internal and what is external to the system. Every family unit evolves some kind of boundary for the purpose of system definition. Just as individuals, families are required to deal with the forces of separateness and togetherness. All social systems are organized. It is the nature of a social system that the interaction and interdependency among the parts of the system take place in some form of organization that has boundary. Every family creates a sense of organizational style to meet the requirements of system self-regulation. There is a need to keep the process of the family system and the processes of its constituent parts in a functional tension with each other. Finally, every social system creates an information system to communicate to itself how it is doing in relation to its existence as a functional unit. It is an information system that informs itself about itself. Every family system develops its own unique communication process. Out of the nature of the family patterns of communication emerges the family's capacity for systemic differentiation. The feedback process provides for system self-awareness. Out of self-awareness emerges the family's ability to deal with systemic integrity. The family itself evolves into a unit that tends to have either a high level of system differentiation or a low level of system differentiation. Like the individual differentiation process, the systemic differentiation process establishes some level of integrity for the family unit. Who and what a particular family unit is flows out of its boundary and its organizational and communications characteristics. Life demands that a family unit answer the question, Who and what are we as a family?

Like the family emotional system, the dynamics of the family social system are highly predictable.

Social systems tend to maintain the same, or similar, organizational boundaries and communication patterns over time. Like all social systems, the family system uses the family's communications process to maintain a steady state. Any change in any part of the system is automatically met with a compensatory change in another part of the system. The maintenance of system sameness or similarity in a family is the equivalent of the body's tendency toward a steady state. For instance, the loss of sight is likely to result in enhanced functioning for another of the senses such as hearing or touch. Loss of one arm is likely to result in increased strength in the other arm. Similarly, a change in a part of the family will likely induce compensatory activity by other family members. If a mother is hospitalized, the other family members will respond in ways to keep the family functioning in its usual way. Thus, the system dynamic says that what affects one family member affects other family members. The integrity of the family system is maintained as it is.

Knowing who and what it is as a family unit provides the capacity to account for the needs of each individual, each dyad and triad, and the family unit as a whole. There is a kind of systemic we-position that ensures that the family unit will not be ruled by the forces of the greater society or by the individual demands of one or more of its members parts. The systemic differentiation process provides an inner integrity that grows on the complementarity of its parts. In such a system all the parts of the unit are vital and have value. All of the parts are free to do what they are designed to do.

THE FAMILY GRID

Several years ago I was teaching graduate students about the characteristics of family boundary, family organizational style, and family communications. Several students proposed the idea that family systems thinking could be demonstrated through a grid drawing. It was proposed that the vertical line in the grid would depict a family's organizational style and the horizontal line would show the nature of the family boundary. Out of that particular graduate class emerged the Family Grid. The Family Grid simply provides a unique way to organize and talk about some of the family dynamics that are important in the process of understanding what a particular family is like.

Family Organization

Family organizational style may be examined along a bipolar continuum from rigid to loose (see Figure 8.1). Organization refers to the quality of a coherent unit or functioning as a whole.

A 100 on the vertical scale means that the family is extremely rigidly organized. Family rules and regulations are intense and pervasive. There is a lack of accounting for individual or dyadic concerns. The family system power is dominant and rigidly enforced; order and fixity prevail in the family unit.

Generally, the more rigid the family organization the more there is a fixed pattern of rules for the interdependency of family members. The rules are in the service of the family system. Through an elaborate configuration of system characteristics, there is a forceful static quality that demands adherence to the family system.

Imagine a smooth magnetic grid with steel balls in it. If the magnetic pull is strong, the steel balls maneuver around very little.

FIGURE 8.1

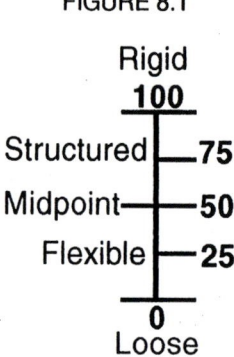

The holding power comes from the pull toward the grid by the magnetic current.

The family grid is simply a way to organize and talk about important family system dynamics.

In a rigid family, the powerful pull on family members comes from the family unit. Family control is powerful. There is a pull for members of the family to be fixed and constant in their assigned roles. A sense of sameness, fixity, and unmoveableness exists.

At the other extreme of the scale is a loose organizational style. With this style a strong tendency toward instability with large, rapid movements prevails. A zero on the vertical scale depicts a loosely organized family system with little or no power or influence on the individual family members.

In such a situation the magnetic grid is extremely weak. The steel balls roll around at random on the grid. For a loosely organized family, the family system exerts no force on the member parts of the system. Family members have no anchoring place for stabilization when needed. There is no discernable family frame of reference to discern meaning from life events. At this extreme, the grouping of people displays characteristics more similar to an aggregate of people than to a family.

The systems characteristic shows itself in what seems to be a contradiction. Loosely organized family systems resist change in their overall style as strongly as rigidly organized families. The process of the steady state exists at the random unstable extreme. A state of organized disorganization exists because systems do require some type of organization.

The midpoint on the vertical scale reflects an organizational balance in the natural tension among the realities of self, other, and context. Families in the mid-range (25 to 75) on the scale locate between a flexible and structured style of systemic organization. Families in the mid-range on the scale have developed some relative systemic regulation of their internal activities. The activities establish the integrity of the family unit, dyadic and triadic relationships, and the individual family members. The necessary tension among the three human realities is recognized and honored within the functioning whole.

Like a magnetic grid with moderate electrical pull, there is both freedom for individual movement and an atmosphere that provides a frame of reference or anchoring place. The family patterns reflect an organizational style somewhere between flexible and structured. Family organization style establishes the self-regulating process for the family unit.

Family Boundary

All systems have a boundary to distinguish what is external and what is internal to the particular system. Some boundaries are more obvious than others. The physical boundary of a person is quite apparent: the skin makes a recognizable demarcation between person and nonperson.

Conceptual boundaries, such as a family boundary, are not so easily identified. In a sense, a family boundary is a psychological boundary that divides we–family–from they–not family.

The family boundary establishes the self-defining process for the family unit. It is the quality of the family boundary that addresses the universal forces of separateness and togetherness. The family unit is not exempt from the life requirement to manage the tension between the opposing forces of separateness and togetherness.

In our current cultural climate, the nature of the family boundary has become a vital factor in the integrity of the family unit. The rapidly changing place of the family unit in the organizational style of our modern society has put enormous stress on the family as a viable social system. The intrusiveness of social forces into the family unit has been extensive. Music, television, movies, economic forces, and the government have combined to pull family members into various realms of influence. The values and beliefs of society have broken the family boundaries largely through the mechanisms of modern media. The pull away from the family unit by powerful economic forces has various members of the family working out of the home at odd hours as well as at various distances from the location of the family home. In the past, the social institutions of church and community served as mediating forces for family integrity.

The family boundary establishes the self-defining process for a family.

The horizontal line in the grid in Figure 8.2 depicts the family boundary. At the lower end of the boundary scale (0-25), the distinction between the family unit and society is relatively amorphous. Information and people flow in and out of the family-like unit, relatively unhampered by any social system dynamics with functional integrity.

At the other extreme is a solid boundary (100-75). A family at the higher level on the boundary scale is relatively isolated from the influences of society. There is little feedback from the social system of which they are a part. Family attempts to establish and maintain a position at the higher levels of the boundary scale are under enormous stress in our society. The outside distractions of economic forces, the media, and the government made it difficult to maintain a family boundary at the mid- to upper range on the boundary scale. The source of the stress on these families becomes apparent in the therapeutic context.

Families tending toward the midpoint on the boundary scale (25-75) have evolved boundary dynamics that allow for relative family integrity. Families in the mid-range move from an open boundary to a permeable boundary. The permeable boundary allows for information interchange with the wider social systems, and maintains a strong sense of we, family. The family tending toward the open boundary expects and encourages interchanges with the

FIGURE 8.2. Family Boundary

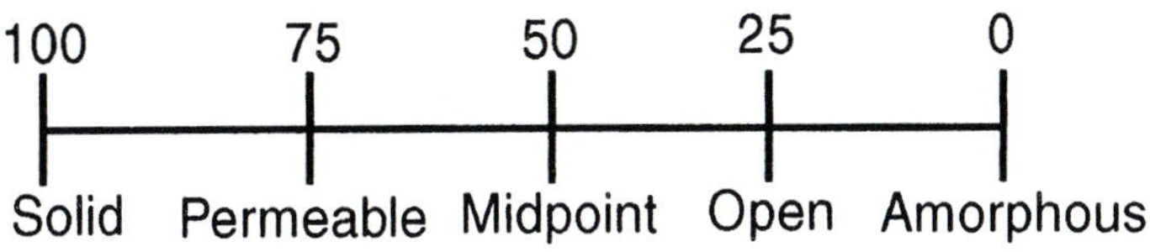

100	75	50	25	0
Solid	Permeable	Midpoint	Open	Amorphous

wider social systems, and there is enough "we-ness" to promote the integrity of the family system.

Families that locate on midpoint or slightly higher on the scale tend to establish a strong sense of identity as a functioning unit. No social system can survive well without a balance between the connections to the wider social system of which it is a part and its own sense of separateness as a functioning unit. The systemic integrity process requires the mechanisms for self-definition and self-regulation. The delicate balance among the life realities rests on boundaries that provide system integrity and intrasystems communication interchange.

Family Communications Patterns

The energy of every social system flows throughout a particular unit on its communications patterns. For the purposes of the family grid, communications patterns are examined for the extent to which they support the systemic differentiation process. A family unit exists for the survival, safety, and growth purposes of the family system and its member parts. Family system communications engage the differentiation process when they account for all of the life realities from the perspectives of the family. Thus, all communications are examined for the extent to which all the human realities are part of message patterns of the family.

The energy of every family system flows throughout a particular unit on its communications patterns.

The family grid offers a way of thinking and a tool for discovering how a family unit defines and regulates itself to meet the multisystemic demands inherent in a family social system.

Family-grid thinking proposes that the integrity of the family system is important for the family unit and its member parts. The organizational style, the nature of the family boundary, and the family communications patterns are systemic dynamics that create the overall nature of a family system. Generally, the extremes of the systemic dynamics just mentioned are dysfunctional. At the low end and high end of the boundary scale, a system will have trouble surviving as an entity with integrity. The basic flow of the boundary extremes is that the system is either flooded with outside information and people, or it is choked off from needed people and information from the wider social system. If there is too much organization or too little organization, the system either exists to control its members or its members overrun the needed family organizational process.

While grid thinking posits that extremes generally are dysfunctional, it is possible that given certain circumstances, locating at the extreme of any one or both grid scales may be necessary to create the differentiating process in a particular family. One need only imagine the need to move toward a more solid boundary if wider social system circumstances put a family unit in a dangerous situation. To survive as an individual or as a family unit, the boundary may have to be tightened.

The family grid offers a systems way of thinking and a tool for discovering how a family unit defines and regulates itself.

Generally, the extremes of almost anything are dysfunctional. Too much water or no water, too much food or no food, too much communication or no communication, or too much closeness or no closeness all are likely to create dysfunctional situations.

FAMILY GRID QUADRANTS

When the horizontal boundary scale and the vertical organizations scales are combined, a grid is formed. By plotting the boundary dynamics and organizational dynamics and drawing intersecting lines, it is possible to see the grid dynamics in terms of their consequences for the family system. The family grid contains eight quadrants. Depending on where the family falls on both the organization and boundary scales, it will locate in one of the eight quadrants (see Figure 8.3). Families at the extremes of one or both of the scales

FIGURE 8.3. Family Grid

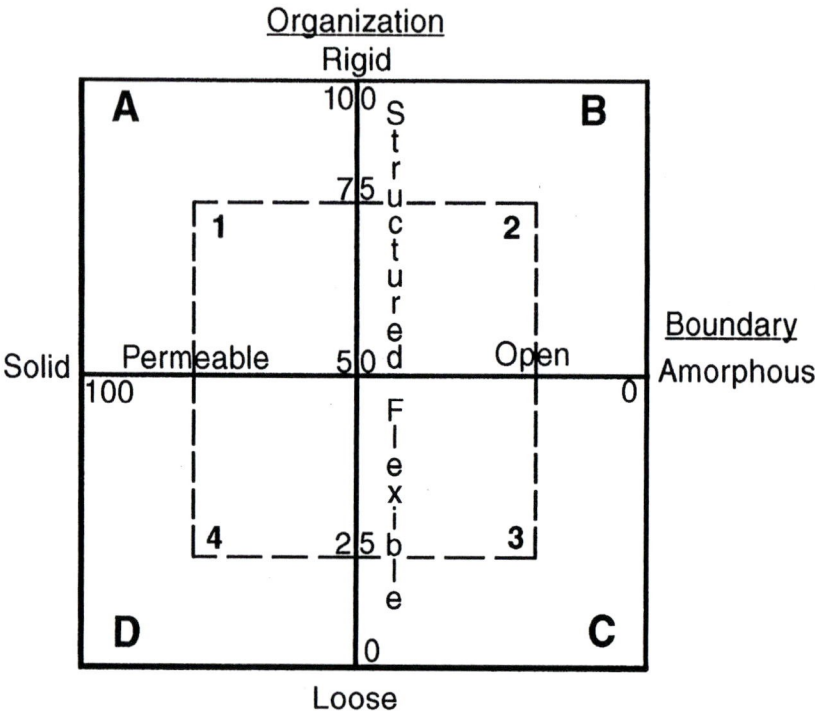

will locate in either quadrant A, B, C, or D. Families that locate in the mid-range of both scales will fall in either quadrant 1, 2, 3, or 4.

The four outer quadrants are rigid-amorphous, amorphous-loose, loose-solid, and solid-rigid. These four quadrant styles reflect a tendency to be extreme on one or both of the grid scales. The four inner quadrants are structured-open, open-flexible, flexible-permeable, and permeable-structured. The inner quadrants reflect a mid-point tendency on both the grid scales. In general, families that locate in one of the mid-range quadrants—one, two, three, or four—have a high potential for engaging the systemic differentiation process.

The quadrant in which a family locates will depend on the particular clustering of organizations and boundary dynamics displayed by the particular family. A quadrant-A family will tend to display a clustering of attributes associated with a rigidly-organized, amorphously-bounded social system. The family atmosphere in one quadrant will differ from that of families in any of the other quadrants. For instance, a quadrant 3 family that locates near the central part of the grid will provide a family atmosphere that differs vastly from that of an extreme quadrant-A family.

The process of engaging the life realities and the system differentiation process will differ from quadrant to quadrant. There are conceptual and practical reasons to posit that the nature of the individual differentiating process, especially in young family members, will tend to differ from quadrant to quadrant. Practice observation confirms over and over that the nature of dysfunctioning activities in young family offspring tend to reflect the dynamics inherent in the atmosphere of a particular family quadrant. Life experiences, research, and conceptual modeling provide rich sources for an examination of the association between the activities of young family offspring and the particular family systems style identified in each of the grid quadrants.[1]

The capacity to address the possible connection between the activities of all family members and the systemic dynamics of a family grid quadrant is made possible by the thinking that undergirds the family grid. In that sense, the family grid is a way of thinking and a tool for addressing the relationship between the systemic dynamics of a family and the differentiating processes of its members.

The eight family grid quadrants emerge out of the clustering of organizational, boundary, and communications dynamics in the family system. It is well to remember that the family grid is not real. The systemic quadrants that are identified through the grid process are abstractions that rest on a particular process of taking information and making meaning about the functioning of a family unit.

The quadrant in which a family locates will depend upon a particular clustering of organizational and boundary dynamics displayed by a particular family.

ASSESSING FAMILY GRID DYNAMICS

Given the predictable nature of family systems, an examination of specific systemic attributes has been found useful in making an assessment about family functioning on the organization and boundary scales.

All the attributes on each scale may be viewed as a cluster of impressions about a family. Ten systemic attributes have been found helpful in making an assessment about the family organizational dynamics. The attributes address the dynamics of space, control, time, emotion, recreation, meaning, discipline, roles, rules, and feedback as they relate to the domain of organization. Feedback is a pervasive factor in both the organizational and boundary domain.

Seven systemic attributes have been found useful in making assessments about family boundary dynamics. They are time, space, friends, recreation, values, territory, and feedback as viewed from the domain of boundary. Again, feedback processes are a vital and pervasive part of the clustering of boundary dynamics. The attributes that have been selected for examination on both scales are those that are sensitive items of concern for families from various socioeconomic, racial, and religious categories.

The judgments about each of the attributes reflect the opinion of the person doing the assessment. The goal of the family grid process is not to find *the truth* about any attribute under consideration. The goal is to engage the family dynamics at points of systemic relevance to the family.

Organizational Attributes

The ten attributes used to assess where a family is located on the vertical organizational scale are examined along the bipolar continuum from loose to rigid. The central points designations of flexible and structured serve to identify the midpoint range on the organization scale (Figure 8.4). (For a personal consideration of the grid dynamics, see * in the NOTES.)

Space

Space refers to the systemic expectations about a family member's emotional and physical location within the family unit.

FIGURE 8.4. Organizational Dynamics

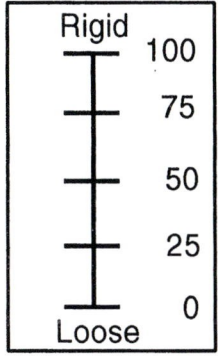

Rigidly Oriented (75-100). In a rigidly oriented family, expectations about space are fixed and constant. Family members occupy a certain point in terms of closeness and distance. There is a push toward sameness over time. In one family, the members were extremely involved with each other. Efforts to allow for some distance or even variation in the emotion and physical space patterns of the family were subtly resisted by the family as a unit. In this family, efforts by a family member to establish more time in a local youth club were resisted by the family with the reprimand that "You need to spend more time at home playing with your brother."

Space refers to the systemic expectations about a family member's emotional and physical location within the family unit.

For many families, the territory within the family is fixed as well. For instance, father has his room, his chair, and his places in the house. No one is to intrude into father's spaces–"that's the family rule." There is a strong sense of *coercion* on matters of space. There is a sense of discomfort when another family member's physical space is occupied. For instance, one simply does not stand in mother's space in the family room. Generally, there is a push toward closeness among family members in the rigidly oriented family.

Orientation of Midpoints (25-75). The midpoints on the continuum reflect a range of organizational balance in the natural balance between self, others, and context. In the mid-range, the sense of emotional and territorial coersion lessens and moves toward a sense of patterned movability at the structural level to patterned change-ability at the flexible level.

Generally, space is negotiated at the mid-range; thus, it is variable in character. Closeness and distance between and among family members are negotiated in ways that are congruent with the family unit's rules about emotional space. While family members may *usually* be found in certain physical spaces within the family territory, there are no *rules* against variations in the mid-range.

Loose Orientation (0-25). At the lower end of the organization scale, there is a sense of dispersion and indecisiveness in the emotional and physical nature of the space attribute. The predictability as to where family members are located in relation to each other is consistent only in its inconsistency. Family members may be emotionally close at one time and emotionally distant at other times. There is a sense of instability about where people are physically and emotionally. The family unit has little influence at the lower end of the scale. Individual family members "do their own thing." (Where is your family located on this attribute?)

Control

Control refers to the power of, and the process used by, the family unit to directly regulate the activities of the family members.

Rigidly Oriented (75-100). In a rigidly organized family, there is a sense of tight discipline and an authoritarian regulation process. Powerful authority rests in the hands of one or two members of the family. Family unit control, as defined by the authority figure, is strongly enforced. Rules are laid down by the family authority figure, and compliance without comment is expected. Family regulation is for the purposes of control over family members.

Orientation of Midpoints (25-75). In the mid-range, control moves from the presentation of family plans, ideas, rules, etc., to the family unit for discussion at the structured level to a consensus process for family control matters at the flexible level. Family control moves more toward an egalitarian process in the lower part of the mid-range (flexible). For the families in the lower part of the mid-range, control seems to be for the purposes of order rather than for the control of family members.

Loose Orientation (0-25). At the lower levels of the organizational scale, there is little power over family members from family system regulation. The individual family member exerts a kind of do-your-own-thing approach to the control process. Individual desires predominate with virtually no organizing frame of reference or control from the family unit. (Where is your family located on this attribute?)

Time

Time refers to how the family is oriented toward the factor of time as it relates to the family and how family time is used to schedule activities.

Rigidly Oriented (75-100). In a rigidly organized family, considerable family unit effort is given to how time is scheduled. Scheduled activities follow a predetermined course with little or no alteration in the schedule permitted. The family unit organizes time for all family members. The family clock rules the activities for everyone. Past traditions and future expectations often are used as frames of reference for organizing family activities. "We are scheduling the holidays this way because we have always done it this way." "If we are going to do X next year, we must begin planning now!"

Time refers to how the family is oriented toward the factor of time as it relates to the family and how time is used to schedule family activities.

Orientation of Midpoints (25-75). In the mid-range, a family organizes itself in terms of present demands. Plans and schedules are employed but may be altered in view of individual needs or situational requirements. In the structured range, the family is the starting point for time planning, but circumstances or family member's needs are taken into account if an alteration in the scheduling of time is needed. In the flexible range, circumstances and individual preferences are used as a starting point to formulate a family schedule.

Loose Orientation (0-25). At the lower level on the scale, families tend to live in the spontaneous present in which the individual clock rules. Very little, if any, time is organized around family unit needs. Family members do what they wish whenever they decide to do so. (Where does your family fall on this attribute?)

Emotion

Emotion refers to how and to what extent the expression of feelings are monitored within the family context.

Rigidly Oriented (75-100). In a rigidly oriented family, the expression of emotion is closely monitored by the family. The type and range of emotions displayed are restricted by the rules of the family. If too much emotion or an unacceptable emotion is expressed, "something" will happen in the family process to bring the emotion into an acceptable mode. If the emotional rules of a family unit are broken, a child may be told to "settle down" or "control" himself or herself. On the other hand, a child or adult may be told to "liven up" if too little emotion is expressed in a particular family. Rigidly oriented families keep tight control over the family emotional process.

Orientation of Midpoints (25-75). In the mid-range, emotions acceptable to the family move from responsive and measured on the structured level to authentic and wide-ranging at the flexible level. As with all the family grid attributes at the mid-range, there is a high degree of accounting for the individual and systemic realities in how emotions are regulated within the family. In reality, all emotions are appropriate in a given context and/or with certain people.

Loose Orientation (0-25). At the lower levels of the organization scale, extremeness is characteristic of the expression of emotions. There may be unexplained periods of severe sadness and unexplained raucous laughter. The expressions of emotion are whatever the individual family member feels inclined to show at that moment. (Where is your family located on this attribute?)

Recreation

Recreation refers to how the family organizes itself in the arena of fun, games, and enjoyment. All families evolve some way of dealing with recreational activities.

Rigidly Oriented (75-100). In the rigidly organized family, fun and leisure activities are regulated by the family unit. Vacations and evenings out are decided upon by the family leader(s). Little or no input on the matter is sought from family members. The family leader(s) decides and "that is that!" The dictates of the family leader ordinarily are congruent with other family unit ways of regulating family activities.

Orientation of Midpoints (25-75). The planning for recreational activities runs from being organized by the family with some input from family members at the structured level to input from the family as the basis for planning by the flexible level family. Recreational planning is a sensitive area for families with young members. Every family will evolve a distinct orientation for approaching recreational activities. Families at the mid-range on the scale evolve a pattern that to a high degree takes into account all of the life realities. Accounting for all of the life realities may be difficult in a family with its members in various stages in the individual life cycle.

Loose Orientation (0-25). Family units at the lower end of the scale, have little influence on the *what* or *how* of recreational activities. The do-your-own-thing rule for individual family members applies for these families. Fun and pleasure is a matter of individual wishes. The realities of other and the family context receive little attention. (Where is your family located on this attribute?)

Meaning

Meaning refers to the family-unit rules about how messages are conveyed between and among family members. This attribute falls within the domain of feedback. However, meaning is considered as an organization attribute because who and what regulates the meaning of messages is of critical importance to the nature of a family unit.

Rigidly Oriented (75-100). Communication in these families is extremely clear, certain, direct, and explicit. There is a strong effort to make sure that the full meaning of a message is addressed. In rigidly oriented families, the context of the meaning often is blaming and directive. Pure logic and reason may be used to make a definite point. The communications carry a controlling quality in their message character.

Orientation of Midpoints (25-75). In these families there is some toleration of ambiguity, indirectness, and inconsistency as long as the essential message is clearly conveyed. Compared to families at the extremely high level on the organization scale, there is less of a controlling quality in the communication of families near the structural part of the scale. For families firmly in the flexible range, some vagueness in meaning is acceptable. Also in the flexible range, uniqueness in personal style of communication is valued. In the mid-range it is clear that the purpose of communications is the transfer of information rather than for the purpose of controlling members of the family. For families in the mid-range, it is also clear that the interchange of information among family members is highly valued.

Loose Orientation (0-25). Families located at the lower range on the organization scale are unclear, indirect, and incongruent in their communications. Their words are often affect-laden. With these families it is difficult to get a clear sense of what has happened or what is expected to happen in the future. The exchange of information among family members has little informational value for these families. (Where is your family located on this attribute?)

Rules

Rules refer to dictates that undergird the family system. Social systems are rule-governed. The question is: What are the family's rules about rules and what is the process for changing rules?

Rigidly Oriented (75-100). A family located at the rigid end of the organization scale lives by the rules. The rules for the family system are explicit; rule changes are rare. The metarule seems to be: if a rule is needed now, it is always needed. There is little or no reason to change a rule.

The question is: What are the family's rules about rules and what is the process for changing rules?

Orientation of Midpoints (25-75). The use of rules in the mid-range moves from generally clear rules that are used to organize family activities at the structured level on the scale to rules as guiding principles for family activities at the flexible level. At the structured level, rules may be altered, but the impetus for alteration must come from family members. In a sense, a family member must negotiate a family rule change. At the flexible level, rules are altered or changed as part of the systemic process. The rules just seem to change in the life process of the family. At the mid-range, rules are used to facilitate family functioning without overly intruding on the lives of family members.

Loose Orientation (0-25). At the loosely organized end of the scale, it is difficult to identify family rules. There is little or no attention given to family-based rules. The rule is: There will be no family rules. Sometimes, whatever rules can be identified are enforced on the impulse of an individual family member. (Where is your family located on this attribute?)

Discipline

Discipline in the organizational context refers to how rules, and the violation of rules, are handled in the family unit. Special note is taken concerning the connection between misbehavior and the predictability of the disciplinary process.

Rigidly Oriented (75-100). A family located at the extremely high end of the organization scale is automatic in the application of discipline. If a family rule is violated, there will be highly predictable consequences. Ordinarily, excuses or extenuating circumstances carry no influence in the nature of the discipline. There is a sense that breaking a family rule will have negative consequences.

Orientation of Midpoints (25-75). In the mid-range, discipline moves from a point of permitting discussion about a violation of family rules at the structural level to the encouragement of discussion at the flexible level on the scale. At the structured level, the outcome is somewhat likely to be a predetermined disciplinary process. At the flexible level, the nature of the discipline is closely related to the outcome of the discussion about the violation of a family rule. The disciplinary outcome is the result of the uniqueness of the circumstances of the particular rule violation. Again, the families at the mid-range account for the life realities in the disciplinary process. Accounting for life realities is important to a family's approach to discipline because recognition of the uniqueness of life events is a differentiating process.

Loose Orientation (0-25). Families located at the loose extreme on the scale are not routinely concerned about violation of rules or any associated disciplinary actions. There is a kind of *laissez-faire* approach to discipline. The response to a breach in family rules is more related to the particular mood of an individual family member than to an organizational frame of reference. The same action may be ignored one time and strongly reacted to the next time. There is little connection between the specific event and a disciplinary outcome. The laissez-faire approach is especially confusing to young family members who are trying to establish some routine in their lives. (Where is your family located on this attribute?)

Roles

A role refers to a defined position in relation to other positions in the family. Traditional role designations are operative for family members. Changes in roles and role expectations are always in process within the family. The definition of and expectations for a particular role is part of the concern of this attribute.

Rigidly oriented (75-100). A family located at the rigid level of the scale organizes around traditional roles and role performances. The roles are clearly delineated. Role expectations govern most, if not all, decisions about who does what and when in the family unit.

Orientation of Midpoints (25-75). Families located in the structured range on the organization scale value roles and activities associated with traditional roles. These families share role responsibilities based on individual preferences.

Families in the flexible range also value roles. These families have a broader view of family roles than the traditional perspective. Individual wishes organize their view of activities appropriate to any role. There is considerable overlapping of family activities, but it is not viewed as role sharing. The sharing of activities is viewed as an extension of individual inclinations that seek expression within the family.

Loose Orientation (0-25). Families located at the loose end of the scale ignore most family role considerations. Individual wishes and desires motivate and rule family activities. In some instances, there are negative feelings about the part roles play in family systems. (Where is your family located on this attribute?)

Feedback

Feedback in the family organization domain refers to the messages that tell the system how and what it is doing in the arena of system regulation.

Rigidly Oriented (75-100). A family at the rigid end of the scale will have a communication pattern that is primarily constancy directed. The feedback process for these families quickly identifies any deviation from the established norms of the family unit. There is a strong force for morphostasis that keeps everything in an unchanging state. Feedback is used more to keep the system the same than to inform the system about the nature of its regulatory process.

Orientation of Midpoints (25-75). On a relative basis, feedback at the structured level on the organization scale is more constancy directed than variety directed. Change with caution is possible at both the structured and flexible levels. The feedback in the midpoint seeks to keep the family system in a steady state, but systemic change is expected and accommodated.

At the flexible level, the feedback is both constancy oriented and variety oriented, with the variety-oriented feedback being a bit more persistent. The feedback promotes change within broad limits for the family system.

Loose Orientation (0-25). Families located at the loose end of the scale are almost entirely variety oriented. At times the feedback seems to support little or no stability in the system. At times, it seems as if there is no family unit feedback system in operation in the family. (Where is your family located on this attribute?)

For a summary of organizational attributes, see Figure 8.5.

FIGURE 8.5. Family Organization

	100	75	50	25	0

ATTRIBUTE:	Rigid	Structured	Flexible	Loose
Space	Constant Fixed Forced	Known Predictable Not forced	Moveable and patterned Changeable	Dispersed Unpredictable
Control	Authoritarian regulations and tight discipline.	Family rules and plans are submitted for member discussing. Democratic with a leader. Individual preferences considered.	Consensus sought Egalitarian and democratic. Individual input is determinative.	Do your own thing. Little or no power from the family frame of reference.
Time	Organized and constant. Past and future-based scheduling. Family clock rules.	Organized but can be changed for "good" reasons. Considered present. Family is starting point but individual needs considered within limits.	Organized around individual and family needs. Considered present.	Individual clocks rule. Highly irregular spontaneous present.

		100	75	50	25	0

ATTRIBUTE:	Rigid	Structured	Flexible	Loose
Emotion	Closely monitored by family. Type and range restricted.	Responsible, measured	Authentic, wide ranging.	Spontaneous, extreme
Recreation	Regulated by the family.	Family planned with input from family members.	Individual input serves as the basis for family planning.	Do-your-own thing activities.
Meaning	Clear, certain, direct, explicit, controlling.	Toleration for some unclearness, indirectness, inconsistency as long as the *essential* message is clearly conveyed.	Some vagueness and unique personal style is acceptable. Communication is for the purpose of transferring information.	Largely unclear, indirect, incongruent, and inconsistent.
Rules	Explicit rules. Strong emphasis on rules, rare rule changes.	Rules are generally clear. Rules used to organize activities, rule alterations negotiated by family members.	Rules serve as guiding principles, emphasis on implicators and principles flowing out of rules. Rule changes are part of the system.	Few discernable rules. Little if any attention to rules. Existing rules en-forced impulsively.

FIGURE 8.5 (continued)

| | 100 | 75 | 50 | 25 | 0 |

ATTRIBUTE:				
	Rigid	**Structured**	**Flexible**	**Loose**
Discipline	Predetermined, autocratic.	Discussion permitted but outcome is quite predictable.	Discussion encouraged and outcome related to discussion.	Laissez-faire (whatever), little or no connection between event and outcome.
Roles	Stereotyped, determinative, bounded.	Some role sharing. Roles valued and clear, blend of roles and personal preference.	Considerable role sharing and interchange, roles valued as an extension of the individual that seeks expression.	Roles diminished. Personal considerations predominate.
Feedback	Primarily constancy directed. A sense of sameness.	More constancy directed than variety directed. Cautious change is possible through the variety feedback.	More variety directed than constancy directed messages.	Almost entirely variety directed messages. Little systemic stability is possible.

Boundary Attributes

The seven attributes used to assess where a family is located on the horizontal boundary scale are examined along the bipolar continuum from amorphous to solid (see Figure 8.6). (Again, see NOTES for a more personal consideration of this dimension.) Open and permeable designations are given to the midpoint range on the boundary scale. For a system to exist, it must have some kind of boundary to distinguish what is internal from what is external to the system. If there is no boundary, there is no systemic integrity.

The family is a subsystem of our wider sociocultural system. The family's ability to operate with integrity depends on a boundary that is (1) impermeable enough to allow internal activities to take place without interference from the greater sociocultural system and (2) permeable enough to allow for communication and other interchanges with the broader society of which the family is a part. The family self-definition processes depend upon the nature of its boundary. All of the attributes discussed in this section get their meaning from the boundary dynamics of the family system.

For a system to exist, it must have some kind of boundary to distinguish what is internal from what is external to the system.

FIGURE 8.6. Boundary Dynamics

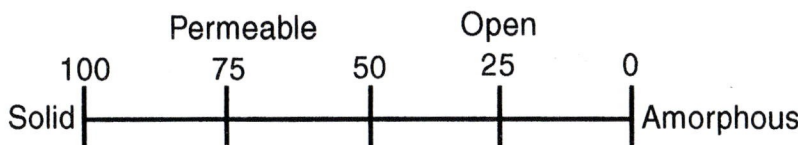

Time

The time attribute refers to the extent to which the emotional forces of individual separateness and family unit togetherness impinge on the process of a family.

Solid-Boundary (75-100). A family that locates itself on the solid boundary extreme of the scale exerts a strong pull on family members toward the family unit. These families are governed by a powerful sense that family members must spend a large amount of time with the family unit. Family emotional and physical togetherness is demanded. When separated from the family, these family members are oriented to the time when they will be back with the family.

For these families, a member's plans to be away from the family unit is likely to be questioned. ("You are not with the family enough as it is now.") One senses a kind of "family clustering" that keeps the family physically and emotionally together as much as possible.

Orientation to the Midpoints (25-75). Families located at the mid-range on the scale are either permeable or open in the nature of their boundary. Permeable boundaries support time together as a family unit as very valuable but allow for periods of individual time for *approved* reasons. Jobs, school, church, and community projects are some examples of approved reasons to be away from the family. A permeable boundary is family-unit oriented but also respects the needs and wants of individual family members.

The family located on the open part of the scale demonstrates its support for both family-unit togetherness and strong attention to individual time away from the family unit. There is no sense that the family unit needs to approve individual time involvements. The open boundary implies that the family is an organizing force in the lives of family members, and as such, specific information about individual times away from the family is provided to the family unit. As one family member said, "I want them to know where I am, not for approval but because I want to stay connected."

Amorphous Boundary (0-25). Families with amorphous boundaries exert little or no time demands on individual family members. In these families, the most of the time is spent away from the family unit. There is a strong sense of physical and emotional separateness or cut-off. Time spent with the family is not highly valued. (Where is your family located on this attribute?)

Space

Space in the boundary dynamic refers to the location within the family home that is sanctioned as acceptable for occupancy by family members. This item directly addresses an internal factor in family dynamics, but it indirectly affects the boundary domain so powerfully it is included as a boundary attribute.

Solid Boundary (75-100). A family located at the solid end of the scale has little tolerance for private space in the home. In these families, the members are expected to congregate in one room or section of the home. Houses with kitchen/family room combinations are ideal for these families. Everyone can be together in one large location. If a family member is absent from the central location for an extended period of time, efforts will be made to get the absent member into the central location. Private space is not permitted. Solidly boundaried families are likely to experience difficulties when a teenager moves to stay in his or her private room much of the time.

Orientation to the Midpoints (25-75). In a family with a permeable boundary, there is a strong emphasis on family space. Family members are expected to occupy the central family place in the house. In these families, private space is permitted, *for good reasons*. Personal care or homework are usually good reasons to occupy private space. The family pull is for family members to be together in one central space.

Families with an open boundary value both private space and family space. These families usually demonstrate a balance between the family togetherness demand and the individual separateness demand for private space. Individual developmental stages seem to be a large factor in overall space location pattern in these families. Clearly, young and older family members go through different preferences depending upon individual and family life cycle inclinations.

Amorphous Boundary (0-25). Families with an amorphous boundary place an extremely high value on individual space. Family members seldom congregate as a family group. They are "never" in the same room. They each go to their separate space in the house. There is little or no attention on family space emanating from the family system. (Where is your family located on this attribute?)

Friends

Friends refer to valued nonfamily acquaintances. While friends are important to us at all stages in our life, adolescent family members are especially attentive to the establishment of a network of friends.

Solid Boundary (75-100). A family that has located at the solid boundary end of the scale will strongly discourage individual friendships for family members. A limited number of family friendships may be pursued. That is, friendships involving my family unit and your family unit are OK. These family friendships serve to provide a family-oriented network of people. Individual friendships that are allowed ordinarily go through a rather elaborate screening process. Young family members are especially subject to the family screening process for potential friends. It is important for these families to know exactly who is in everyone's friendship network.

Orientation to the Midpoints (25-75). Families with a permeable boundary do not discourage individual friendships. They are, however, cautious about the formation of friendships. These families make a point to know all of the friends each family member associates with in various contexts. Family friendships are encouraged.

Families with open boundaries encourage individual friendships. Many of the individual friends are known by the family, but there is no effort to make sure the names of friends are known. Friends are valued and efforts are made to maintain a network of friends.

Amorphous Boundary (0-25). Families at the amorphous end of the boundary scale seek individual friendships outside the influence of the family sphere. The family has no interest in knowing about family friendship networks. Few, if any, family friendships exist. There is a strong sense of separation of individual friendships and family concerns. (Where is your family located on this attribute?)

Recreation

Recreation in the boundary dynamic refers to the pattern of participation by family members in the arena of fun, games, and enjoyment. As in the organization dynamic, the subject of recreation is especially important in families with teenagers. Recreational activity is an area of much concern to young people. With a teenager in a household, a family will be forced to address its unique rules for dealing with recreation.

Solid Boundary (75-100). A family located at the solid end of the scale will dictate that all recreational activity is a family-unit affair.

When something of a recreational nature is forthcoming, the family will be told what all of them will be doing for recreation. "We will go to Disney World this week and we will have fun." The perspective is that the only way to enjoy oneself is with the family.

Orientation to the Midpoints (25-75). A family located in the permeable range regards recreation as a family activity. However, the wishes of individual family members are sought. Based on ideas from family members, plans for a family-unit recreational activity may be altered to include the wishes of individuals. The important point is that the family is regarded as the natural unit for recreational activities, but individual wishes are heard and are factored into the plans.

Families with an open boundary encourage both individuals and family unit recreational experiences. The starting point of an open boundaried family are the wishes of the family members and establishing the possibility of family-unit fun. There is family unit interest in the recreational activity of individual family members, but there is no attempt to control the activity.

Amorphous Boundary (0-25). Families with an amorphous boundary show little or no interest in family-unit recreational activities. The individual chooses and pursues his or her own recreational interests. The family rule is "do whatever you want to do, we are not interested." (Where is your family located on this attribute?)

Values

Values refer to ideas and activities that are held by the family as important to family functioning. Values serve as guidelines for the family unit as well as individual family members.

Solid Boundary (75-100). A family located at the solid end of the scale is extremely concerned about any values that may enter the family unit from the wider social system. Various points at which outside values may enter the family system are screened. For instance, all television programs may be screened for the values they impart. The school curricula may be evaluated in terms of the values implied in certain courses. Young family members may be questioned at length about their teacher's statements relating to certain values. There is strong interest in the nature of the values to which the young members are exposed as they grow into adulthood.

It would be common for these families to prohibit exposure to certain books, movies, or television programs.

Orientation to the Midpoints (25-75). Families at the permeable range on the scale give attention to the values to which family members are exposed. The family is interested in the response of family members to a range of ideas and activities that reflect values. These families very well might watch a television special on some controversial issue. Following the special, they would have a family discussion on the subject of the television program. Adult family values in the matter would be made known to the younger family members.

Families that occupy the open range on the scale give some attention to the values to which family members are exposed. Family values are present but get overt attention only if something happens that triggers family attention to the values dimension. Family values are thought to be reflected in the actions of the adult family members. These families might spontaneously discuss the values implied in a particular event on television or reported in the newspapers.

Amorphous Boundary (0-25). There is little, if any, family attention given values at the amorphous end of the scale. Varying values flow freely into the family aggregate. The ideas and activities of different family members reflect a full range of different values. (Where is your family located on this attribute?)

Territory

Territory refers to the sense of ownership and control of property and other physical and psychological entities regarded as belonging to the family.

Solid-Boundary (75-100). A family located at the solid end of the scale is very territorial. The family sets up physical and psychological barriers that isolate the family unit from surrounding systems. Symbolically, the family yard may have a high, solid wood fence around it. For these families, it is difficult for non family members to gain entry into the family house. Even if one gets into the house, there is a strong sense that the non family person is intruding into someone else's territory. There is a strong sense of family-unit isolation.

Orientation to the Midpoints (25-75). A family located in the permeable range on the scale will show a sense of family-unit exclusivity and engagement with other people. There is a tendency toward separateness from the surrounding social systems, but a sense of connection to the surrounding social systems is present. Symbolically, these families might have a split-rail fence around their property to indicate some separateness from, and connection to, surrounding involvements. One is welcome into the home, to a limited extent, of these families. There is a sense of being welcome if you keep your distance from the private places in the house such as the kitchen, bedrooms, etc.

Families located in the open range on the scale give off a sense of separateness from, and openness to, the outer world. Symbolically, these families might have four bushes at each corner of their property. The bushes indicate a boundary, but the family is open to others. These families welcome other people into their home. There is a sense of welcomeness and openness that pervades the family territory.

Amorphous Boundary (0-25). Families located at this range on the scale have little, if any, sense of family territory or space ownership. Symbolically, there are no indicators of where the family property begins or ends. People readily move in and out of the house. One father in an amorphously bounded family complained that he often did not know who actually lived in the house. "It is like Grand Central Station." (Where is your family located on this attribute?)

Feedback

Feedback refers to the messages that tell the system how and what it is doing in the boundary process for the family unit. Boundary feedback addresses the dynamics of system definition.

Solid Boundary (75-100). A family located at the solid end of the scale will have a communication style that supports physical and psychological separateness from surrounding social systems. The feedback process is geared to identify any deviation from the family's isolated position in the systemic scheme of things. Information used by the family is filtered to fit the family norms appropriate to a solid boundary around the family unit.

Orientation to the Midpoints (25-75). The nature of the feedback at the permeable level pushes toward cautious openness to wider social system information and interchange. A family located at the open range on the scale has a feedback system that corrects for both the we-ness of the family *and* the they-ness of other systems. The character of the communication encourages openness to other systems but maintains clear boundary distinctions.

Amorphous Boundary (0-25). Feedback for families located at the amorphous end of the scale is set to receive large amounts of unscreened information from various sources outside the family. The diffuse nature of the feedback screening mechanisms supports a variable amorphous boundary of a family-like entity rather than a sense of a family unit. (Where is your family located on this attribute?)

For a summary of boundary attributes, see Figure 8.7.

FAMILY LOCATION ON THE GRID

The family grid provides a way to examine family functioning as a social/emotional system. By plotting the two dimensions of organization and boundary on their respective scales and drawing an intersecting line, it is possible to determine where a family locates on the family grid. In Figure 8.8 the T family located it self at 80 on the organization scale and 85 on the boundary scale. When the intersecting lines are drawn, the family functioning style falls in the solid-rigid quadrant-A designation.

To determine where family T located itself on each of the two grid dimensions, the family members were asked to spend some time talking about where and why their family put itself in each of the attributes in both the boundary and organization dimensions. For example, after considerable family member discussion, the T family put itself at 85 on the boundary space attribute. In the family discussions, the family became aware of the subtle but strong pull for all family members to spend time together in their recreation room. The family located in the solid or permeable areas of the scale on all of the other boundary attributes.

When the T family examined the organization attributes, they found themselves in the rigid or structured range on all but one attribute. Their score of 80 on the organization scale felt right for all the family members.

FIGURE 8.7. Family Boundaries

	100	75	50	25	0

ATTRIBUTE:

	Solid	Permeable	Open	Amorphous
Time	Pull to spend time with family unit. Togetherness is demanded.	Time together as a family unit is valued; time alone as an individual approved, for good reasons.	Support for family time. Individual time given strong attention. Family is the center for information exchange.	Most of the time is spent away from family unit. No pull from family for togetherness.
Space	Private space not permitted.	Emphasis on family space, but private space is permitted.	Family space and private space are valued.	Individual space highly sought. Family space not valued.
Friends	Outside friendships discouraged; family friendships encouraged; friends are screened.	Few individual friends; family friends encouraged. Friends are known to the family.	Individual and family friendships encouraged. Some individual friends known by the family.	Individual friendships predominate; little connection between friends and family.

FIGURE 8.7 (continued)

| | 100 | 75 | 50 | 25 | 0 |

ATTRIBUTE:	Solid	Permeable	Open	Amorphous
Recreation	Recreation shared as a family unit.	Recreation seen as a family activity but can be altered to accommodate individual interests.	Recreation activities seen as responsive to individual wishes. Family unit activities may be chosen.	Recreation seen as an individual activity separate from the family unit; little interest in the recreational pursuits of individuals.
Values	Values screened by family. Much interest in the values to which family members are exposed.	Attention given values. Values are made known to younger family members.	Slight attention to values. Values are made known through everyday activities.	Little if any concern for family values. Individual values predominate.
Territory	Very territorial. Physical and psychological barriers set up. Isolation from surrounding environment.	Sense of ownership of property. A sense of connection to and separateness from other systems.	Strong sense of openness as an overlay to factors of separateness.	Little or no sense of family boundary. Unfiltered information interchanges with surrounding system.
Feedback	Separateness–directed communications.	Cautious, openness–directed communications.	Communications directed to we-ness and they-ness.	No concern about boundary issues.

FIGURE 8.8. The Family Grid

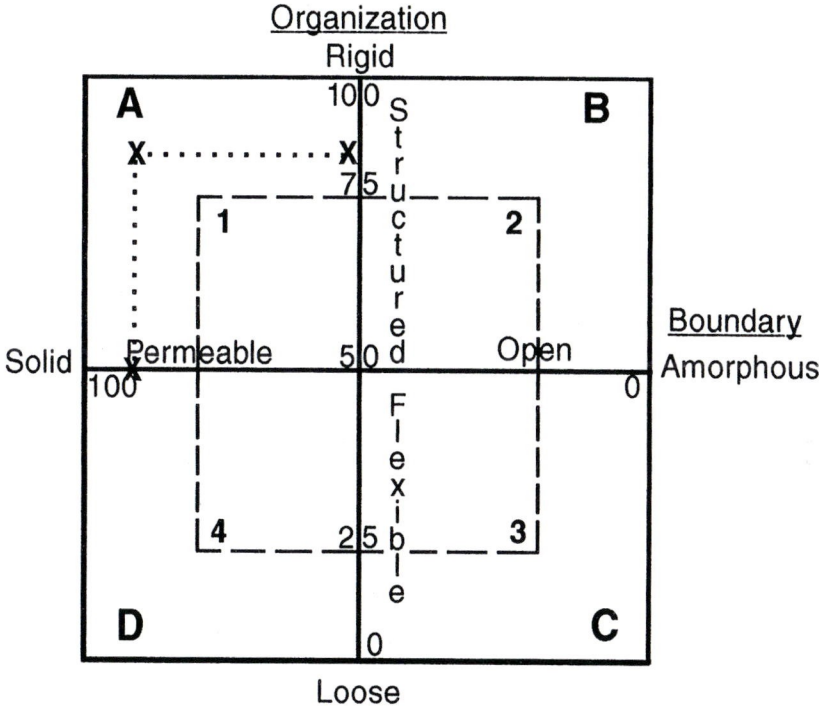

The intersecting boundary and organization lines put the family in the solid-rigid A quadrant (family grid). For the T family, the A quadrant, with its positives and negatives, felt like home for them.

The Family Grid Exercise

The process of examining the attributes for both the boundary and organization scales is enlightening for a family system. Going over each attribute one by one may take a considerable amount of time. The effort is worth it. There are not many occasions that afford a family the opportunity to look at itself for the purpose of discovering who and what it is in terms of a social unit.

While the outcome of the family-grid process is valuable, the basic purpose of the family grid is to direct thinking and attention to the family system level of consideration. For that reason, the family-grid process has remained a subjective experience for family units. How the family goes about the process of looking at itself through the grid process is a vital part of the exercise. The only directions given family members are that first, they individually determine where the family falls on each attribute; second, they are to discuss as a group where each member put his or her mark on each attribute scale; and third, they are to fully understand that there are no right or wrong places to put a mark on an attribute scale.

A family's approach to the grid exercise provides the therapist with numerous clues about the family's capacity for system-level differentiating.

In coming to a decision about where to place the mark on both the boundary and organization scales, it is useful for a family to decide which two of the scale attributes are most influential in their family and which two are least influential in their family. For example, in the T family, the boundary attributes of space and recreation were seen as most influential in the family. They had some difficulty deciding on the least two influential attributes, but finally they settled on friends and territory.

Some families cannot agree on where to put the mark on the boundary and organization scales. In such a situation, it is useful to put the different marks on the scale. In those situations where no one can agree, it may be helpful to the family to put marks on the scale to represent each family member. The point is that *how* a family conducts itself during the grid process provides much of the information needed for a therapist assessment of the family unit. It is the therapist that will help the family identify the systemic considerations that need the attention of the family.

Therapists who work with family units will benefit from going through the family-grid exercise in relation to their own family of origin as well as their current family. With the benefit of having gone through the family-grid process, therapist D came to understand how some of the influences of his past family were limiting his ability to work with certain families. Later, when his own daughter experienced some personal problems, he used the family-grid process to examine his own family. He found out, much to his surprise, that he had co-created an intense quadrant A family lifestyle. Some of his daughter's behaviors were in reaction to the dynamics of her family of origin. With some very brief family therapy, therapist D and his family were able to give up some of the dysfunctional characteristics that are part of the quadrant A family style.

There is no limit to the creative ways the family grid process may be used during family treatment. It is a tool that promotes systemic thinking and attention. It is a process-oriented exercise that works to help a family system become aware of its system-level differentiating dynamics.

FAMILY-UNIT DIFFERENTIATING PROCESS

Family-grid thinking is designed to give attention to who and what a particular family is as a social/emotional system. The attributes listed in the organization and boundary dimensions are vital dynamics in the life of a family. The attributes are places where a family co-creates who and what it is as a social/emotional system. The organizational attributes essentially address the issue of self-regulation for the family system. The boundary attributes address issues relating to family-unit self-definition. The omnipresent feedback patterns of both dimensions provide clues about the integrity level of the whole family system. The family-unit differentiation process emerges out of power of the combined organization, boundary dimensions, and feedback.

Each quadrant in the family grid represents a specific atmosphere for family members. The specific atmosphere influences the lives of all family members, especially the young members. The family atmosphere pressures family members to behave in certain ways. In a very real sense, the family atmosphere pushes its members to express their individuality in the ways made possible by the family atmosphere. In other words, specific family-system characteristics, especially those at the extremes, promote a high probability that certain member behaviors will show up in the family. Just as individuals, family systems operate in a condition called consequences. The family chooses its actions within the dimensions of boundary and organization. The family cannot choose the consequences of either an individual attribute or the clustering of all the systemic attributes. The family atmosphere, co-created by all the relevant dynamics at play in a family, is unique to that particular family. At the same time, the clustering of attributes at certain extreme points on either the boundary or organizational scale has predictable systemic results.

For example, in a *solid-rigid* quadrant-A *family,* the systemic atmosphere exerts a strong pull on family members to conform to the rules of the family unit. There is a sense of separation from the wider social/cultural systems. The reality of such a family context is intrusive on individual family members as well as the various dyads and triads that may form. The isolated, constricted family environment has an effect on all family members, especially young family members. It is not unusual for young family members to be submissive and compliant in their stances. Quadrant-A families frequently present young family members with troubled behavior in the form of passive-aggressive reactions, enuresis, school learning problems, physical symptoms, and eating disorders. Older children in quadrant-A-style families may become involved in acting out-type problems. The acting out often seems to be against the intrusiveness of the family. They act out against the family unit.

Interestingly enough, the quadrant-A-type family will likely seek therapy when a young member exhibits dysfunctional behavior. The family attitude toward therapy frequently is "fix him, give him a pill or something, but fix him." The solid boundary characteristic of this type family makes it difficult for the therapist to make an impact on the family. These families are set to extrude anyone that is seen as a threat to the established order of the family. Two strategies are important in work with quadrant-A families. First, it is important to not attack, in any way, the leader of the family. The leader has the power to take the family out of therapy, and he or she will do so if threatened. Second, the most differentiating person needs to be identified. The positive influence of the most differentiating family member will be needed as the treatment progresses.

One of the systemic goals of work with the solid-rigid quadrant-A-type family is to "disorganize them." The missing element for these families is a sense of openness and flexibility. The system is too intrusive, and the realities of self and other need to receive some attention.

Careful work that respects the boundary and organization extremes often will be successful. These families are success-oriented. They seek to make the therapy experience a positive one.

Rigid-amorphous quadrant-B-style families pose an especially unique systemic atmosphere. It is difficult to imagine a rigid regulation process with a system that has an amorphous self-defining process. The organizational atmosphere exerts strong control over the family members when they are in the house. The rule for quadrant-B families is: "When you are in this house, you will do as you are told!" The problem for the family members is that there is no pull to keep family members attached to the family household. There is no boundary that separates the sense of we-family from they-not family.

In many of the quadrant-B families, the rigid organization rules are for the purpose of parental control over other family members; on the other hand, with an amorphous boundary there is no sense of we-family. In such situations, it is not unusual for young family members to quickly establish strong loyalties outside the family. Runaways, early pregnancies, gang activity, or other outside attachments—usually negative—seem to intrude into the family system.

Single-parent families seem to set up a unique version of the quadrant-B family style. In these families, the parent struggles to maintain a sense of control over the household situation, but it is difficult to draw a family boundary around the people who are family members. There is always the question about the place of the absent family member in the family-unit dynamics. There is a dramatic loss of family control when a young person is out of the home. Influences generated outside the family seem to take over all too often.

Quadrant-B-style families do not often seek help on their own. School, police, or some other outside public agency often appear at the door with a report of problems in the community. Quadrant-B families are open to the concrete services of many outside agencies. Advice, money, housing, food, and other types of services are likely to be welcomed by quadrant-B families. Most often the services received are used to maintain the family's established style of living.

Family-level work with quadrant-B families is directed to increasing the sense of flexibility in the organizational dimension and the provision of processes for establishing a sense of we-family in the boundary dimension. Family genograms and family-grid activities with these families draw attention to the context reality called family. Positive treatment outcomes involving substantial changes in the family differentiating processes are difficult to achieve. Putting in the missing or diminished behavior is the starting point, or reason, for treatment. As with other quadrant work, identifying and working with the most differentiating family members is crucial.

Rigid-loose quadrant-C-style family-like aggregates lack both organization and boundary integrity. There is little or no family self-regulation or self-definition. These "families" display the extremes of a loose organization and an amorphous boundary on the grid scales. The young family members live in an atmosphere that exerts a minimal frame of reference from which to develop a sense of individual integrity. Someone once said, "I could hold up the whole world if I had a place to stand on." For members of these "families," there is no foundation point on which to stand. There is little, if any, family integrity on which to build a life. Often, it is difficult to think of the extremes in this quadrant as family units.

The values, demands, and enticements of the surrounding wider social systems such as gangs or cults may serve as "family" for the young members of quadrant-C-style families. Acting out behaviors are characteristic problems for the young people in this quadrant. Many of the young people in these families suffer from emotional and physical neglect. Trouble with the law or other public officials are founded in lack of family concern. With little or no family-based internal guidelines, the wider community directions exert powerful influence on the young family members. Violence on the part of males and sexual acting out on the part of the females often shows up in the young of such a "family" style.

The therapeutic goal at systemic level is to encourage the development of some family structure and an identifiable family boundary. The presence of all family members at treatment sessions may be regarded as a major positive move forward for these families.

It should be noted that quadrant-C families exist across all sociocultural and economic levels. The style of unbounded disorganization differs from demographic category to demographic category, but the basic systemic deficits for the family are the same. There is extreme looseness in the family organization dimension and extreme amorphousness for the family boundary.

Successful family work with quadrant-C families ordinarily involves the simultaneous efforts of the wider community, individually oriented intervention programs, and family-directed treatment— the overall direction of individual *and* family system integrity. The family as a differentiating organization requires language that uses the family as a behavioral referent. Therapist questions that energize family level values and directions are necessary with quadrant-C-style families.

Loose-solid quadrant-D-style families have little or no organizational integrity. It is not unusual for a sense of chaos to reign in these families. The dangerous part of quadrant-D-style families is the solid boundary that separates the family from contact with the wider community. The emotional and physical abuse that is often characteristic of the extreme of this quadrant is unknown to the wider social community. Thus, the extremes of quadrant-D families often exhibit problems involving spouse abuse, child abuse, incest, and other behaviors for which a solid boundary is required. The solid boundary keeps the flow of information about the family activities tightly concealed within the family unit.

The solid family boundary serves to keep the family from seeking outside help from appropriate agencies. The reason quadrant-D families end up in counseling often is for problems in such areas as school behavior problems, social problems such as stealing, or physical problems that require the intervention of a physician. It is not unusual for the internal family chaos to be revealed to agencies that refer the family for therapy.

The K family consisted of the parents, two daughters, ages 15 and 16, and an older son. The family came to the attention of the local mental health clinic when both daughters sought medical attention for severe neck pain. The attending physician learned of the daughters' fearfulness about the forced incestual relationships with both the father and the older son. When the family came for therapy, it was revealed that the daughters had been subjected to sex with the father and brother for over a year. The revelations about the family incest brought the activities to a halt. The court system became involved but allowed the family to remain intact if weekly family therapy sessions were held.

The family system dynamics demonstrated an isolated family with a solid boundary. The mother was not allowed to work out of the home. The daughters were not allowed to engage in any social activities outside the home. The parents had a distant husband and wife relationship. The atmosphere in the home was one of total disorganization.

Working at family-system level, the family was helped to open the family boundary. The mother took a job outside the home, and the daughters joined youth organizations both in their church and at their school. Improvement in the marital relationship helped to bring some structure to the parenting efforts. The son moved out of the house but remained in close telephone contact with the family.

The family therapy process was directed toward opening the family boundary and encouraging structure in the family organization. Prior to family therapy, the family atmosphere had been physically and emotionally threatening to all of the members of the family. The chaos had been overwhelming to the two daughters. Their only recourse was to seek outside help for reasons other than the basic family dysfunction. The physical problems both daughters suffered were the vehicle for breaking the solid family boundary. Therapy directed to the family system enabled the individual family members to deal with their relationship problems on a functional basis.

THE ASSESSMENT PROCESS

Knowing the quadrant into which a family falls provides clues about the nature of possible difficulties in forming a treatment alliance with a family. Families with solid boundaries are not likely to allow the therapist easy access to the inner life of the family unit. On the other hand, families with an amorphous boundary are likely to entice the therapist into the family dynamics quickly. In these latter types of families, the therapist's goal is to remain a distinct self who is there to help but not take over the responsibilities for solving the family problems.

The family-grid process is a way of thinking systemically, and it is an assessment tool. As a tool, it is to be used to get family dynamics into a conceptual process that the therapist may use to promote needed change in the family system. At a minimum, family-grid thinking draws attention to the systemic processes. At its best, the family-grid process helps a family define itself and gain some appropriate control over itself as a unit.

TREATMENT IMPLICATIONS: A DISCUSSION

Assisting a family system to become a functional context is a demanding and difficult task. It is in the nature of a system to attempt to stay the way it is and not change. Encountering highly developed homeostatic mechanisms in a family often has the quality of trying to flatten a partially filled balloon. At the moment you have one part of the balloon level, another part pops up.

A common therapist response to a dysfunctional family system is the abandonment of intervention at the family-system level consideration. Instead of dealing with systemic dynamics, the concentration of attention becomes either the dyadic relationships or individual issues within the family. For family members, the family may become an "it" that "I" or "we" must struggle or make tiring efforts to avoid. What is denied is that each family member is family. There is no "it" separate from the members involved. The "it" is me-extended into the context of family. Denying personal involvement in a family system does not make it so.

Consider the father who, when asked about his part in a family problem, says, "I have nothing to do with it. I stay out of it. It is between my wife and son." What he denies is that his involvement is his lack of involvement, and that kind of involvement may be a critical factor in the family system. The internal structure of a dysfunctional family unit always exhibits rather strong and obvious splits and alignments among its family members. The splits and alignments are easy to recognize and deceptive in their power to survive.

Faced with a seemingly incomprehensible family system, some therapists decide to concentrate on various subsystems within the family. Usually, the mother/father dyad is selected for clinical attention. The critical difference in therapeutic intervention is whether the parent dyad is seen as an entrance point to the total family system or, as is usually the case, the focus of the therapy shifts away from the family to the couple.

The family-system grid provides a family framework within which to direct therapeutic efforts at the personal, interpersonal, and family levels. Using the relational principle to "put in what's missing," certain clinical strategies may or may not be used depending upon the quadrant of the grid into which the family system fits. For example, families in quadrant-C may be given a homework assignment involving a bi-weekly family meeting around the kitchen table in order to organize and carry out the affairs of the family organization. It is highly unlikely that families that fit into quadrant-A would be given a homework assignment that pushes toward more organization and a more solid boundary. The solid-rigid family is likely to be given homework assignments that promote less organization and boundedness.

Clinical interventions at the level of family means that the focus of attention is on the family unit. The nature of involvement of family members in the family is where the therapeutic efforts are directed. Strategies that use other human systems levels as entrance points may be used, but the expectation is that change in the other human systems level will effect parallel changes in the family system.

NOTES

1. For a more research-based examination of many of the systems dynamics addressed in the family grid see the extensive work done on the circumplex model by David Olsen, Candyce Russell, Douglas Sprenkle (Eds.). (1989). *Circumplex Model*. Binghamton, NY: The Haworth Press.

*One way to get a deeper sense of the organizational and boundary attributes that make up the Family Grid is for the reader to use himself or herself as a learning vehicle. At the conclusion of the discussion of each attribute, think about where your family of origin and/or your current family falls on that attribute scale. For instance, where on the space attribute scale would your family fall? Each attribute scale would be evaluated in turn as you consider that part of your family's dynamics. After all of the attributes on the organizational style have been considered, look at the results of the total set of scales for organization. Use the scales to make a determination or guess about where your family falls on the organizational dimension of the family grid. Follow the same procedure for the boundary dimension of the grid. It is often enlightening to consider the systemic influences for our own family. The point of intersection on the grid for the organizational and boundary dimensions will tell you into which quadrant your family falls.

CHAPTER 9

CONTEXT: THE TRANSGENERATIONAL FAMILY

The family is a naturally occurring human context that evolves out of the history of its transactions within itself and with the wider social environment. The power of transgenerational family transactions often is not immediately apparent in current life events. Yet, a family's patterns of interaction and connections to all of life realities is a part of the evolution of a transgenerational family life paradigm. One of the tools available for a deeper understanding of the family system as a transgenerational context is the family genogram.

FAMILY GENOGRAM

A family genogram is a graphic representation of a family and its relationships over a number of generations, usually two or more. Circles, squares, triangles, connecting lines, slashes, and other markers including dates and specific letters are used to map a family's transgenerational history (see Figure 9.1). A family genogram provides a schematic picture of a family context and its patterns of functioning over time.

The genogram is a basic tool for understanding family systems.[1] It is to the family therapist what the stethoscope is to the physician. It is a starting point for understanding a client. For the family therapist, the genogram is a tangible graphic representation of a family and its history. The genogram "maps" the family structure and provides an excellent tool for updating a family situation. It is an efficient way to organize a large amount of information about

FIGURE 9.1. A Family Genogram

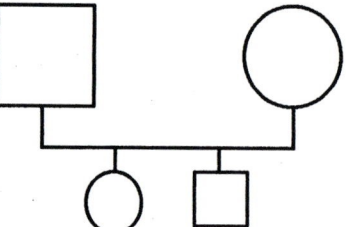

family relationships and patterns. Additionally, the genogram provides an excellent clinical summary of a family.

The mapping of interconnected family relationships over time draws attention to the systemic dynamics that act powerfully on the family unit. Not only are present relational influences apparent in genograms, but the transgenerational patterns and their connection to the here-and-now are also readily identifiable. Genograms help to clarify graphically the dynamics of family of origin. As a powerful reference group, the family of origin serves as a specific context for its members. This means that meanings and perceptions have been formulated and passed along through the generations. Family rules, values, and beliefs serve as the basis for a family's specific life paradigm.

Exactly how genogram information is used in work with a family largely depends on the specific helping setting, the theoretical orientation of the therapist, and the relevant family dynamics. The guiding purpose of the relational systems model is to identify and work with patterns of connection to the relational realities of self, other, context, and the spiritual. By its nature, genograms address the transgenerational transmission of relational patterns. Family principles and imperatives shape the nature of socially conditioned values, beliefs, and rules for a family and its members.

The family of origin, whatever its nature, serves as the co-creator of a life paradigm for family members. Understanding and dealing with our family system and our part in it serves to help clarify who and what we are as a human being. The impact of our family of origin, or early life family-like configuration, provides the basic deferring socialization dynamics for all of us.

The very construction of a genogram identifies relationships that contribute to the formation of the family identity. Just as an individual struggles with the differentiation process, a family, through its patterned relationships, evolves its own systemic identity. Knowing and dealing with who and what my family was, and is, may serve to enhance my own differentiating process. The very task of examining family relationships will reveal family values, assumptions, and stereotypes. Family-system-based areas of strength as well as emotionalized areas of conflict may surface in the genograming process.

The very construction of a genogram identifies relationships that contribute to the formation of the family identity.

The power of the family context on family members may be revealed in the examination of the transgenerational family group from which a person has descended and from which a familial sense of personhood is derived. "We Jones' " or "We Brown's" may give a person a strong identity that serves as a vital part of his or her personal life paradigm.

There are two basic levels of attention that emerge in the genogram process. First, the construction of a genogram will provide knowledge about one's family structure and relationships over time. Second, the awareness of one's family of origin, as depicted in a genogram, may remain at the conscious thought level. Intellectual awareness enables one to thoughtfully consider the implications of one's family history–whatever the shape of that history. The challenge for growth for some people is to engage both intellectual and emotional awareness of ourselves as a family being. Through facing our thinking and feeling parts, it is possible to explore how our family of origin imparted conditioning processes upon us. The genogram may serve as a tool for discovering the connections between my family dynamics and what I think, feel, and do in my life.

The relational systems model (RSM) primarily focuses on current dynamics. However, the decision to engage transgenerational dynamics through the genogram process is a family assessment issue. Generally, the principles are as follows: (1) If it is difficult to work on the current situation because of client excursions into the past family situations, the genogram may be employed as a tool for working on connections to the relational realities in general and the differentiation process specifically; and (2) if the family reality is overly diminished, genogram work may help bring the family reality into consideration. During the genograming process, the therapist engages and respects the client's personal life paradigm. The information that emerges during genogram discussions will be used to advance both the differentiation process and the client's connections to the life realities.

CONSTRUCTING
THE RELATIONAL SYSTEMS GENOGRAM

The purpose of the RSM genogram is to provide a graphic representation of a family over at least two or three generations and to provide a tool for examining a family's patterns of connection to the life realities. The emphasis and direction given the genograming process will be derived from the client-family's current situation and guiding life paradigm.

The genogram may be constructed as a homework assignment or as a part of the therapy interview process. The genogram starts with the current family and moves to the wider extended family context. The process of listing significant historical events such as marriages, divorces, deaths, separations, remarriages, etc., may be used to examine the impact of the specific event on the family. Family functioning information such as moves, job changes, illnesses, abuse, alcoholism, trouble with the law, etc., will be tracked across the generations. Family patterns develop in all areas of family events.

The purpose of the RSM genogram is to provide a graphic representation of a family over at least two or three generations and to provide a tool for examining a family's patterns of connection to the life realities.

In the RSM genogram format, an attempt is made to get ideas about the stance positions of significant family members. Starting with the client family and working toward other generations, the therapist works with the family to list the primary and secondary stances of family members. The stance information provides transgenerational information about patterns of attention to, or lack of attention to, specific relational realities.

Family Structure

Symbols are used to depict the family structure. While there are no standardized symbols to be used, the following discussion represents the symbolic structure as well as the procedures generally used to construct a genogram.[2] For gender squares and circles are used. In Figure 9.2, a square represents a thirty-year-old male and a circle represents a thirty-year-old female.

The identified patient is depicted with an inner line. For instance, Figure 9.3 shows a twenty-four-year-old identified patient.

Family members are represented by connecting lines. For marriage, the lines are connected as illustrated in Figure 9.4. The letter M followed by a date indicates the year of marriage. Two slashes on the marriage line indicate a divorce and one slash indicates a separation. Broken lines indicate a living-together relationship.

Children are depicted by lines that hang down from the marriage line. Children are depicted left to right according to age. The oldest child is on the left. Each subsequent child is listed to the right. Adopted children are connected to the parents with a broken line. Pregnancy is depicted as a triangle. Twins are depicted with the symbol shown in Figure 9.5.

Life stances for family members are depicted with the appropriate letter symbols. In couple M in Figure 9.6, the primary life stances are shown on the left and the secondary stance on the right. The husband is usually compliant with a secondary preference for being objective. The wife's primary stance is objective with a secondary preference for compliant.

FIGURE 9.2

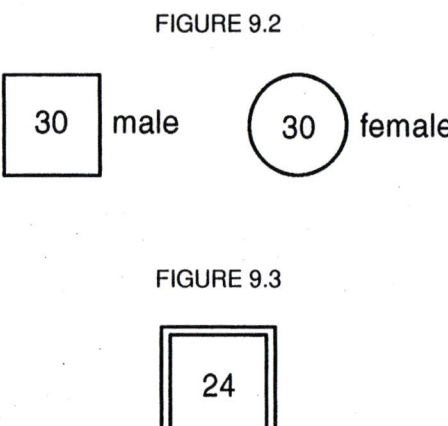

FIGURE 9.3

FIGURE 9.4

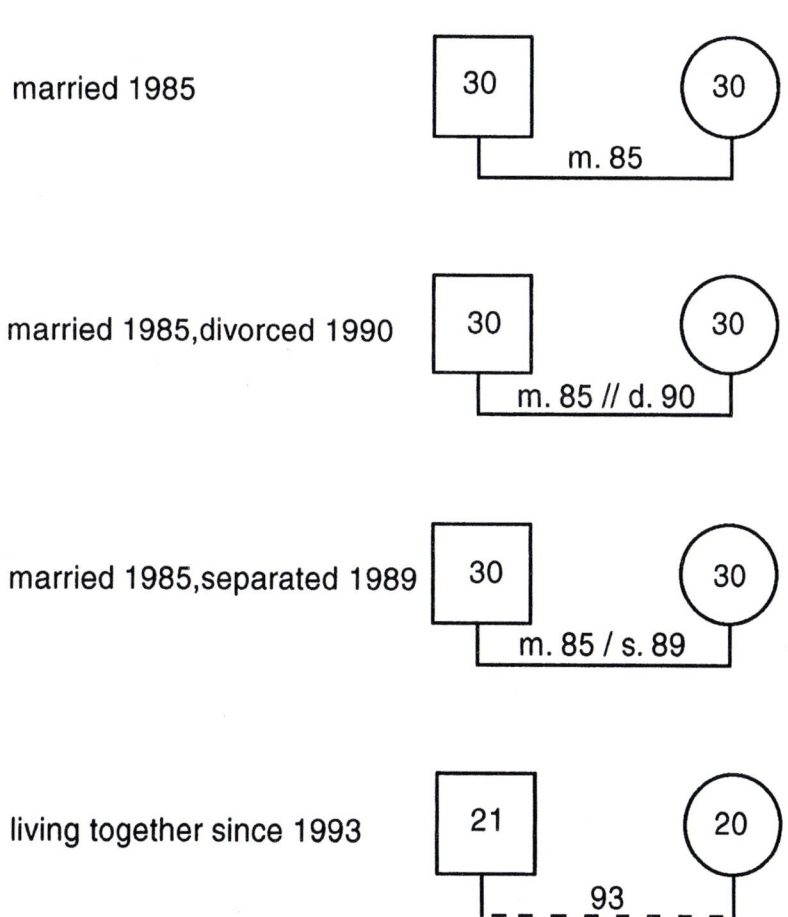

married 1985

married 1985, divorced 1990

married 1985, separated 1989

living together since 1993

Divorces and remarriages are depicted by going in order of marriages from right to left for the male and left to right for the female. For the original couple in Figure 9.7, they were married in 1978 and divorced in 1980. They had two children, a boy and a girl. Subsequently the wife has married and divorced two times. The husband married and divorced. In 1986 he married for a third time.

Unusual or complex family situations and events may be creatively depicted by the therapists and the family. An important

FIGURE 9.5

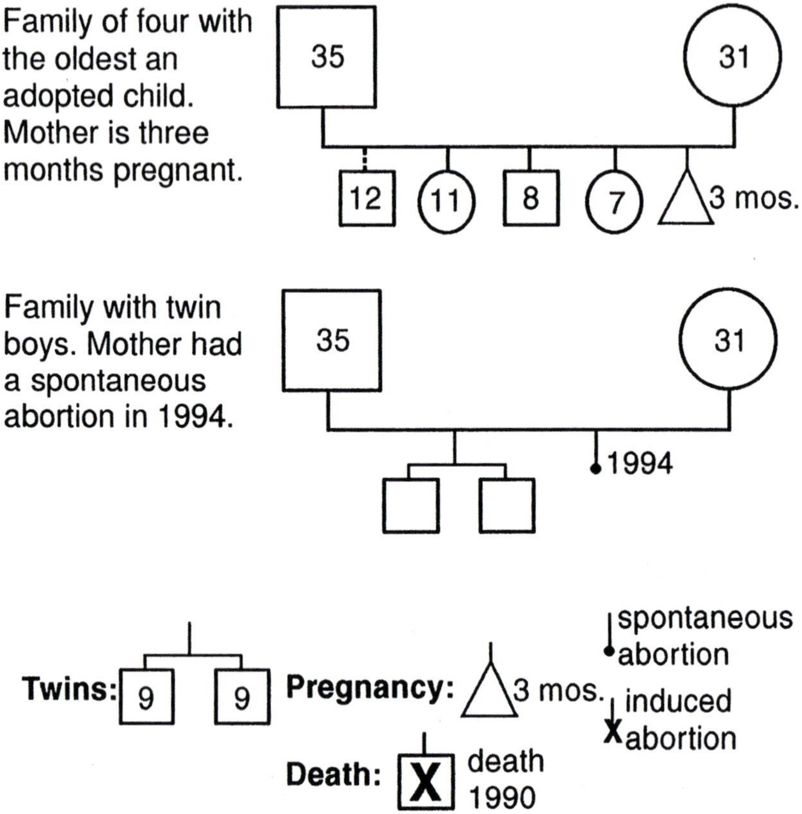

Family of four with the oldest an adopted child. Mother is three months pregnant.

35 — 31

12 11 8 7 △ 3 mos.

Family with twin boys. Mother had a spontaneous abortion in 1994.

35 — 31

1994

Twins: 9 9

Pregnancy: △ 3 mos.

Death: [X] death 1990

spontaneous abortion

induced abortion

FIGURE 9.6

C : O   O | C

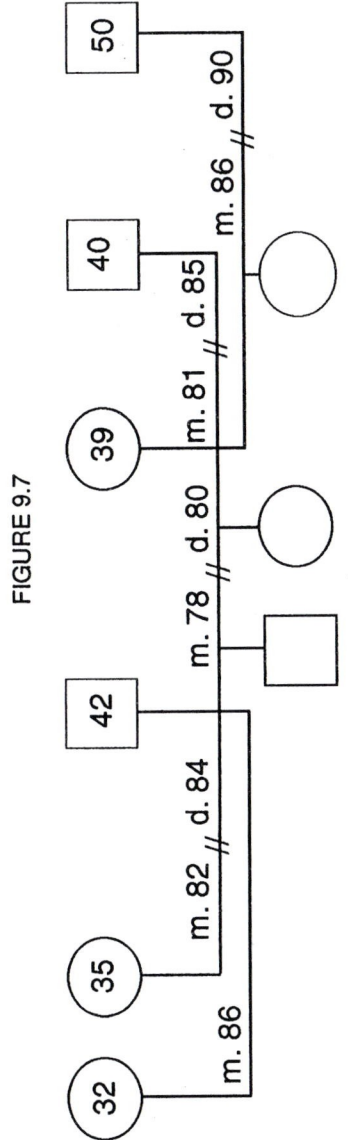

FIGURE 9.7

genogram principle is that the symbols used are consistent within the specific agency that uses the genogram information as a part of the case record.

Figure 9.8 is a RSM genogram depicting three generations. The identified patient is Ann, the nineteen-year-old daughter of Mr. and Mrs. M. Ann is a senior in college in her hometown. She referred herself to the local mental health clinic for "overwhelming feelings of inadequacy and an inability to concentrate."

The RSM genogram provides a graphic picture of the family and the life stances of the significant family members. Even at a glance, the genogram gives a lot of information about the M family. A most revealing part of the genogram is the parental and grandparental pattern of not connecting to the reality of self. The pervasive inability to self-validate was a problem. While the M case turned out to be very complex, there was a family history of low differentiation with the accompanying problems with closeness and distance in marital relationships. Ann and her entire family lived in a context, or life paradigm, designed to please others. When the demands of schooling and social relationships became too overpowering, Ann became anxious and unable to function either in her studies or her social life.

An important genogram principle is that the symbols used are consistent within the specific agency that uses the genogram information as part of the case record.

Family Narrative

The information obtained in the process of constructing the family genogram adds substance to the material available in the graphic representation. While information about the presenting problem, the current life situation, and family structure may be obtained, at the same time the context of the genogram *is* family patterns over time. Learning about the particulars of the family context can be interwoven with historical "facts" that provide a long-term view of family patterns.

The family narrative will indicate the sources of information for constructing the genogram. It is vital to identify structural and rela-

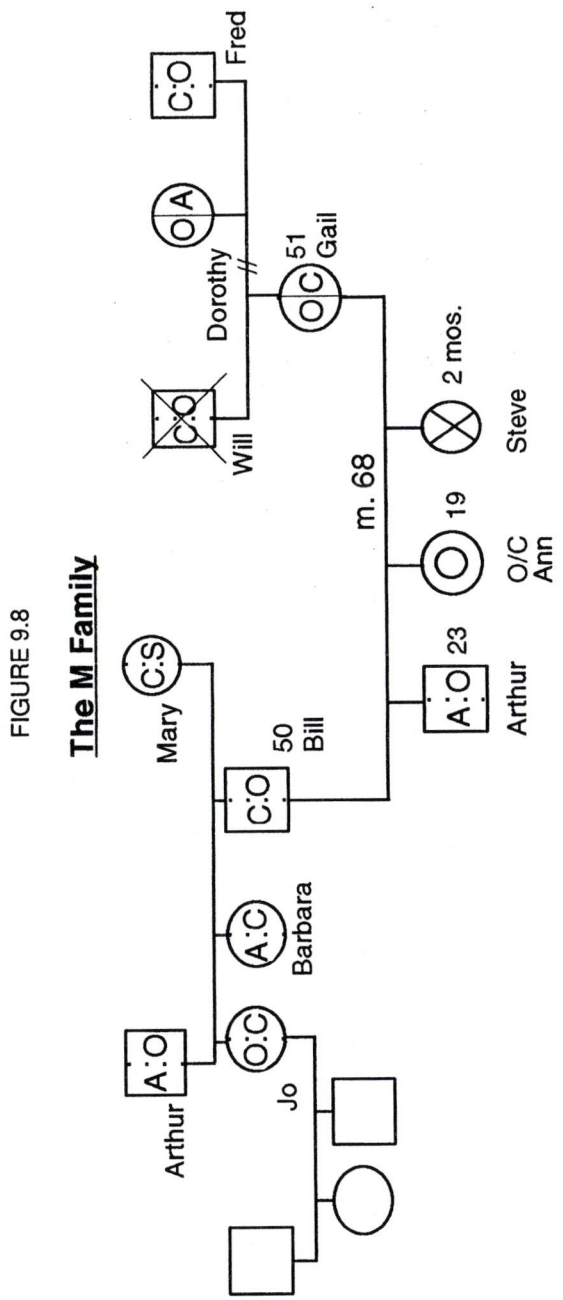

FIGURE 9.8

The M Family

213

tional patterns, patterns of decision making, how love and caring is expressed, family rules and taboos, spiritual influences, family and individual successes, family crises, and ways of resolving the crises as well as current family connections within the extended family.

Finally, the specific use of the family genogram is an assessment decision. The basic material obtained in a genogram serves to provide immediate access to family structure and relationships. In some situations, the genogram may be used as the tool for intensive family-of-origin work. For some families, the discussions in the realm of transgenerational dynamics provide the bases for dramatic individual and family change.

In the RSM the genogram is a tool for use in looking at and dealing with the relational realities. For instance, the genogram process provides the ideal opportunity to talk about the specific family situation at various times in the life of the family. Questions such as "Where was the identified patient (IP) born?" or "What was going on in the family at the time of the IP's birth?" may be addressed. Inquiries about what pressures the family was experiencing at that time are natural lines of inquiry during a genogram process. It may be of vital importance to learn about such things as stress from job loss or loss of a parent around the time of the birth of a child. The nature of the milieu during the first eighteen months of a child's life may be important to know in a specific client case. The genogram is constructed and elaborated upon within the life paradigm of the family and with an RSM overlay. Again, the family of the past is used to the extent that the client system uses the past family to frame the current problem.

NOTES

1. See McGoldrick, M. and Gerson, R. (1985). *Genograms in Family Assessments*. New York: Norton, for a more comprehensive discussion of the family genogram.
2. Ibid. The symbols generally follow the ideas of Bowen and his followers.

CHAPTER 10

CONTEXT: FAMILY DEVELOPMENTAL STAGES

Roles: The Marker for Stage Changes in the Family Life Cycle
The Multiple Life-Cycle Process
Horizontal and Vertical Stressors
Family Developmental Stages for Intact Families
    Stage I - Courtship
    Stage II - Early Marriage
    Stage III - First Child
    Stage IV - First Child in School
    Stage V - First Child into Adolescence
    Stage VI - First Child to Leave Home
    Stage VII - Last Child to Leave Home
    Stage VIII - Without Children at Home and Retirement
    Stage IX - Death
The Family Life-Cycle Process

The family unit is a naturally occurring social/emotional context that shifts and changes over time. The family unit constantly adapts to changes both within the unit and changes in the wider social environment. Each family unit has a life span that has a beginning and an end. A particular family unit has its beginning when an adult male and an adult female commit themselves to marriage. During its life, a family unit may expand through such events as the birth of children, children marrying, and the birth of grandchildren. The nuclear family unit also goes through a period of diminishing membership such as when children marry, go to school, or take employment in a new location. A particular family unit ends with the death of the original marital pair.

Each family unit has a life span that has a beginning and an end.

During the life span of a family unit, complex developmental dynamics unfold. There are average expectable phases or stages through which a family goes in its journey through life. The notion of family development stages comes from the observation that there are specific dynamics, complete with role changes and tasks to be completed, that emerge at particular transition points in the life of a family unit. This succession of predictable change points, or stages, is the essence of the concept of family developmental stages (Figure 10.1).

The reality that families grow and change over the years means that what is true for a family at one stage in life may not be true for the same family in a different family stage. My family of today is not the family of the past. While each family unit has a core identity over time, the shifting and changing demands from within and outside the family require attention.

FIGURE 10.1

Family Life Span

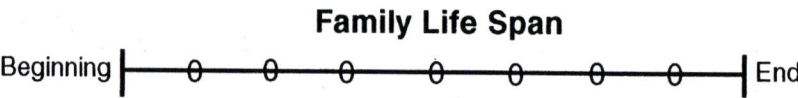

Beginning |——0——0——0——0——0——0——0——| End

The changing family provides a matrix for the differentiating process: "one differentiates within, rather than against, the family group; individual and family are not contraries, but rather cuts of reality."[1] Thus, the family group, over time, provides the context for learning to relate to the life realities. The expanding and diminishing of various roles related to the family promote relationship changes at the boundary of self, other, context, and the spiritual realities. The differentiating process is a fundamental dynamic in the life cycle of a family.

It is important to note that family developmental stages are not real. When we speak of developmental stage we have set up a "photographic still" of something that is enormously dynamic, ever changing, and complex. Viewing a family through an overlay of a developmental stage captures the general dynamics for a family at an essential point in its life span. If, as a therapist, I do not understand the developmental stage that a family is in, I do not understand much of what is going on in the family. The particular family developmental stage is the backdrop, or context, for more specific family roles, activities, and concerns.

ROLES: THE MARKER FOR STAGE CHANGES IN THE FAMILY LIFE CYCLE

In the relational systems model, shifts and changes in family role relationships are used as the marker for movement from an existing stage into a new developmental stage. Shifts in roles such as either acquiring a new role or diminishing an already existing role signals relationship changes (role = a generally agreed upon set of expectations having to do with a station in life). At their best, role alterations may be thought of as individual and group boundary changes that promote appropriate relationships with other people.

The role-change marker for stage changes in the family life cycle is somewhat arbitrary, but it captures the experience of required alterations and transitions that must take place in the life of a family unit. Shifts and changes in nodal relationship roles reverberate throughout the family system. Each stage alteration requires some family restructuring. Sometimes critical role changes are ushered in by rituals and/or ceremonies such as marriages, birthdays, or graduations. Other role changes, such as the onset of adolescence or life without a child at home, are more subtle but just as powerful in the life of a family. Role changes always bring some rearrangements of closeness and distance among family members.

The role-change marker for stage changes in the family life cycle is somewhat arbitrary.

THE MULTIPLE LIFE-CYCLE PROCESS

In order to understand family life span dynamics, there are some intervening considerations that require brief attention!

First, while each family system is going through its life cycle, each individual family member is moving through his or her own personal life cycle, complete with powerful developmental tasks and boundary adjustments that demand attention.

Second, all dyadic and triadic family subsystems are moving through their own life-cycle dynamics. The husband-wife pair, sibling pairs, the father-mother-child triad, etc., all have their own developmental tasks that will impinge on the larger family unit and the individuals within the family.

Third, each culture of which the family is a part is going through its own specific life-cycle changes. In our country, the nature of the family has been greatly influenced by cultural considerations. The place of the "family" in the entire societal scheme of things is undergoing tremendous change. The rapid movement from an agricultural society to an industrial society to an information-service society has impacted enormously on the family unit.

One of the most apparent influences on family life has been the rapid emergence of different family forms such as single parent present by choice, single parent present not by choice (death, divorce), husband/wife with no children, and blended or reconstructed families (families of divorced people who remarry and join two families into one). The unique social, emotional, and economic pressures on different family forms will create life-cycle dynamics that are different for each family form.

All of the different life-cycle processes are taking place simultaneously. It is a multivariable process that influences the family system. Each system is influencing and being influenced by each other. Additionally, the natural systemic dynamics of morphostasis (self-organizing forces that push toward equilibrium) and the forces of morphogenses (processes that push toward a new stage) are in full operation. At the extreme of morphostasis and morphogenses are absolute rigidity and absolute chaos, respectively.

HORIZONTAL AND VERTICAL STRESSORS

Relationship shifts may be associated with (1) horizontal stressors which are stress dynamics that emanate from the changes demanded by developmental movements, or (2) vertical stressors. Vertical stressors are those that come out of the blue.

Vertical stressors are unexpected immediate shocks such as illness, death, divorce, relocation, etc. In Figure 10.2 bolt-out-of-the-blue life crises are symbolized by the arrows. Vertical stressors are immediate and of the unanticipated-acute-crises nature. Developmental stressors are more incremental in nature. The circles symbolize the family life cycle changes. All families will experience vertical and horizontal stressors in their life-span journey.

FIGURE 10.2

Family Life Span

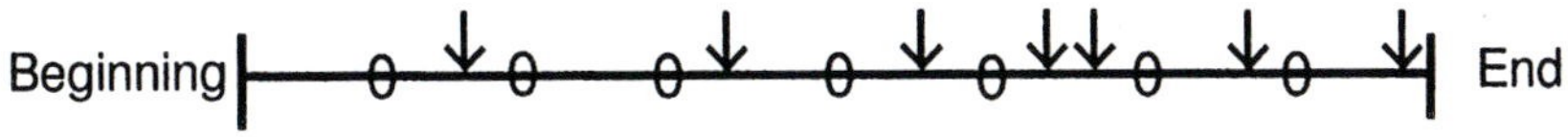

FAMILY DEVELOPMENTAL STAGES FOR INTACT FAMILIES

The following discussion addresses the average expectable developmental processes and transitions for intact families in our culture. Shifts and changes in roles serve as the marker for changes in the life cycle of the family. Given the current state of affairs for diverse lifestyles in our society, it is clear that the intact family perspective does not cover the specific dynamics for other living arrangements such as cohabitation, grandparent-headed families, single parent present families, etc. However, the dynamics relating to differentiation and connection to the life realities adhere in all family forms. Also, the use of role changes as the model marker, by implication, draws attention to changes in the family structure and functioning. Again, implicit in all the many dynamics at play in the life of every family is the vital processes of differentiation and connections to the life realities.

Stage I – Courtship

Ordinarily, a family has its beginning with a serious courtship stage involving an adult male and an adult female (Figure 10.3). It is serious in the sense that commitment to marriage is made. When a couple commits to marriage, they are drawn into a different type of relationship. It is more than a decision to be with each other for a while. It is a commitment to commit to each other through a socially sanctioned rite of marriage. It is important at this stage for each person to understand that while the commitment is to another, it is also to one's self. The integrity factor of differentiating is given its strongest test in marriage.

The serious courtship phase may be thought of as the "getting ready" time. It is period of getting ready to alter peer relationships, getting ready to alter family-of-origin relationships, getting ready to take on the role of husband or wife, and it is, ideally, getting ready to live a lifetime in a relationship with another human being.

Courtship is characterized by a lot of talking and testing of each other. Many plans, expectations, and fears are expressed during the

FIGURE 10.3

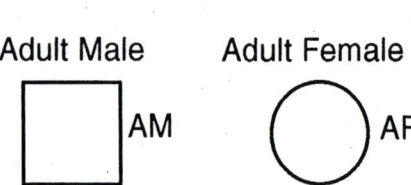

Adult Male   Adult Female

AM   AF

courtship stage. In our complex society, subjects such as where to live, financial arrangements (one checking account, two checking accounts, etc.), children (and when to have them), wedding issues, and religious issues are some of the areas that receive attention during the courtship stage.

Expectations are high during the courtship stage. Ideas about marriage based on one's own family of origin vary from "that's the kind of marriage I want" to "my marriage will not be like my parent's marriage." Included in one's expectations are observations of other current families. Many pictures are formed about what one wants and does not want in a marriage.

The high divorce rate in our culture has served to weaken the institution of marriage and the family. The picture of family life that many courting couples have from their families of origin includes divorce and the possible baggage that goes with divorce. The high divorce rate has resulted in a generation of young people with little or no experience in stable and permanent family life. Divorce-related family breakups have caused the emergence of a divorce mind-set. Couples with a divorce mind-set may not see marriage as a permanent arrangement, and they may not have the long-term commitment to marriage that is necessary to make it through the marital rough times. A divorce mind-set may also include a rigid over-determined drivenness to force the marriage to work. The natural processes of evolving a marriage that works for two unique people may be undermined. The dynamics of the courtship stage include dealing with the couple's expectations for marriage.

The high divorce rate has resulted in a generation of young people with little or no experience in stable and permanent family life.

The cultural impact on marriage instability is enormously powerful. Couples who seek premarital counseling need to have the opportunity to explore in depth where they stand in their picture of what marriage is all about. Helping couples engage the differentiating process in relation to marriage is a support to current and future generations.

Given the high divorce rate in our society, premarital counseling may provide a couple with the opportunity to explore many of the issues important to the marriage relationship. The emotional pain of divorce may be avoided by a clear look at where each courtship partner stands in relation to vital marriage dynamics. On the other hand, the premarital counseling process may reveal a depth of caring and a vision of marriage that moves the marital process in a very positive direction.

The tasks of courtship are many. The lack of cultural support for marriage and the family has imposed a challenge on the young people of our society. It is not easy to commit one's self to another when the culture supports a "me-first" orientation. Young people who consciously look at life's realities squarely and engage in the differentiating process during the courtship stage will have accomplished one of the most important tasks of courtship.

Stage II–Early Marriage

In the early marriage stage, the adult male takes on the role of husband and the adult female takes on the role of wife. The addition of the marital roles is affirmed through a socially sanctioned marriage ceremony. The ritual of the marriage ceremony publicly affirms marriage and is a visible marker of a changed relationship between the now husband and wife (Figure 10.4).

The early marriage stage initiates a lifetime test of emotional maturity. The test is this: Do I have the capacity to maintain a sense of self and be in an enduring, intense relationship with another? The question addresses the specific issues relating to the ability to give of myself *and* maintain a self. The commitment in marriage is a

FIGURE 10.4

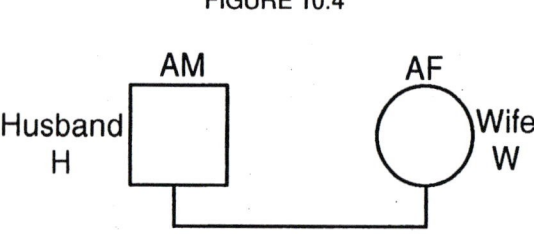

personal integrity issue *and* a relationship integrity issue. The process of maintaining a personal boundary *and* creating an intimate relationship with another is a catalyst for emotional maturity.

The early marriage stage is the time of shifting from self-interest (I-ness) to include that of mutual interest (we-ness). It is a time of relational experimentalization in which much talk is required. There are many relational tasks to engage, many of which are overlapping. The process of sharing of one's self and maintaining self-integrity is a human boundary issue. The process is never completed. It is a lifelong process.

The test of marriage is: Do I have the capacity to maintain a sense of self and be in an enduring, intense relationship with another?

Control issues–The young married couple immediately addresses the question, "Who may do what, when, where, with or without the other's permission?" In other words, who will define the nature of the relationship? The control issue cannot be ignored. In any two-party relationship, the issue of control is engaged one way or another.

Communication issues–What will be the nature of the couple's communication? Do I have permission to comment on what I think, feel, see, and hear? Do I have the ability to ask for what I want without implying that I *must* have it? Will my messages most often be I-messages or you-messages? Do I have the ability to listen? Do I understand the nature of gender differences in communications? A frequent complaint of partners in a troubled marriage is centered in communications problems. The communication pattern for the couple will be established during the early marriage stage. Will the patterns promote honesty, integrity, and openness?

Sameness and difference–A basic question for every couple is, "Is it threatening to my spouse if I differ with him or her?" Some spouses regard differentness by the other as disloyalty. Just as important is the question of sameness. Is it OK if my spouse is the same or equal to me? The issue of competitiveness arises in this area. For some, a spouse that is equal to him or her is a problem. The couple will begin to deal with this issue from the beginning of their marriage.

Family of origin–Each couple must evolve a pattern of relating to their parents. A requirement for mature functioning is the simultaneous ability to separate from one's parents and still remain connected to them. Many couples initially choose to locate at considerable physical distance from parents. Later in their married life, when there is a secure sense of separation from parents, the couple will locate closer to one set of parents.

Relationship with friends–Marriage brings alterations in one's relationships with longtime friends. The friendship associations of the past are loosened as we spend more time with our spouse. The change in friendship associations comes as a shock to some newlyweds. Relationships with friends will change. All friendships are essential to one's personal maturity. The delicate balance between no attention to friendships and extreme attention to friendship involvements is unique to each couple.

Time–The allocation of time has become one of the problem areas for modern couples. In our fast-paced, economically intense culture the time demands of work and other related activities are powerful. Simply finding the time to be together in a nonpressured situation is difficult for many fast-paced young people. Attention to this task from the beginning of the marriage is required. Time patterns will change as the family progresses through its own unique life journey.

Money–While money has always been a sensitive area for families, the two-paycheck family has added to the importance of dealing with issues related to money. Questions relating to the number of bank accounts, whose name will be on which ones, a strict budget or no budget, agreement on purchases or individual rights on any purchase, and "to save or not to save" are areas that need attention during the early stages of marriage.

Sex–In addition to problems with money and communication, sexual problems are frequently a cause for seeking marital counseling. The specifics of the evolution of the sexual relationship will, in fact, parallel the specifics of the essence of the marital relationship. Just as with the marital relationship, the sexual relationship will take time to reach its full potential. The emotional journey to depth in marital intimacy evolves over the years. It takes time, attention, and commitment. The real journey to intimacy begins with the marriage and continues throughout the life of the marriage.

Children–The question of children, whether or not to have as well as when, how many, and how they are to be cared for, are priority issues for most modern couples. The ability to plan for our offspring in our information society has brought about many questions that require a couple's agreement.

The key factor in marital success is the balance between positive and negative interactions in the marriage (Gottman).

Fighting–One of the most crucial skills necessary for a marriage is the ability to fight well. Couples will have conflict during their marriages. Marital fighting skills need to be developed from the very initial stage of marriage. There are basic fighting skills such as I-messages, responsive listening, and problem-solving processes. However, the essential ingredient for successful fighting is a marital context that gives a loud and clear message that says we may fight, but nothing is more important than our mutual commitment to and love for each other. The context of love, caring, and commitment provides a safeness within which mature fighting may take place. Fighting for the purpose of problem solving is necessary. Marital fighting within a context of personal or relationship survival is fearful and scary. The overall positive nature of the marital context requires nurturing from the beginning of a marriage. John Gottman posits that, on the basis of twenty years of practice and observations of over 2,000 couples, the key factor in marital success is the balance between positive and negative interactions in the marriage.[2] According to Gottman, the positive interactions must outweigh the negative. In other words, one of the crucial relationship skills, including fighting, is to adhere to a 5 to 1 ratio of positive times over negative times.

Validation–The dynamics of worthiness get involved in the marital relationship. Ideally, each of us is able to feel a strong sense of self-validation. Marital problems are sure to emerge if partners use each other for validation purposes. Other validation maneuvers by spouses put the relationship into a reciprocal worth process where each uses the other to feel self-worth. Ideally, marital partners support and are supported by each other most of the time. The *demand* to be other-validated by one's spouse is a relationship dynamic that does not have a place in a vital growing marriage.

How these relational tasks are resolved form the foundational dynamics for the life-cycle processes that each family must engage in its life journey. The relational tasks of the early marriage stage cannot *not* be resolved. The relational tasks *will be* addressed one way or the other. The overall patterns for engaging vital issues in a family will come from the directions set during the early marriage stage. Thus the foundation is set for the larger family system to come.

Stage III–First Child

With the arrival of the first child, the role of mother and father are added to the family context. The group of two now becomes three. Instead of a dyadic family there is a triadic family. The family unit has changed (Figure 10.5). The wife is now a mother and the husband is now a father. The routines of the family change. Time requirements change and require a different kind of planning. Relationships with friends may change for various reasons, but the time requirements of raising a child make demands on the new parents.

It is not unusual for relationships between the new parents and their own parents to be altered. The reality is that being a mother or father implies a sense of adulthood or maturity. Husband and wife roles may

FIGURE 10.5

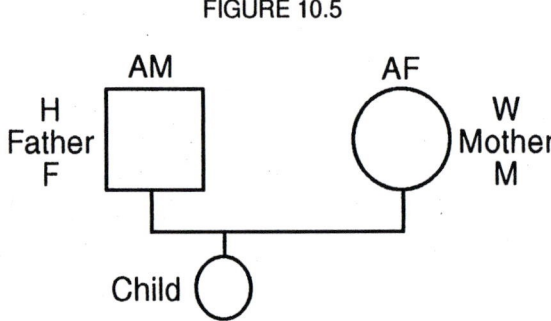

be altered in some ways. The most obvious change is the diminished time available to nurture the husband/wife relationship.

For the modern family, issues around caring for the child move to the forefront. The new mother most likely has a job. The question usually is, Does the wife/mother continue to work out of the home? On a probability basis, the answer is likely to be yes, for the time being. Child care arrangements must be made. Questions around emergencies or sickness involving the child need to be addressed. Simply put, children require time and attention. It is important to discuss who will be available, and when, to provide the care the child's needs.

If the decision is for the wife to discontinue working, the task of provider becomes larger for the husband/father. The decision to be a one-paycheck family is not taken lightly in our culture. The economic realities push for a two-paycheck family.

In one sense, the role of the child is to grow and mature physically, emotionally, and intellectually. The process of socialization begins in our childhood, and it never ends. The struggle to be our own person and to be part of a family never ends. How we deal with the closeness and distance forces in our family will likely be duplicated closely in relationships throughout our life. The nature of our family context is important throughout our life, but it is during our infancy that we learn what it is to be a maturing human being. The role of child requires a nurturing reciprocal.

The birth of additional children has an impact on the family unit (Figures 10.6 and 10.7). However, the role alterations do not involve

FIGURE 10.6

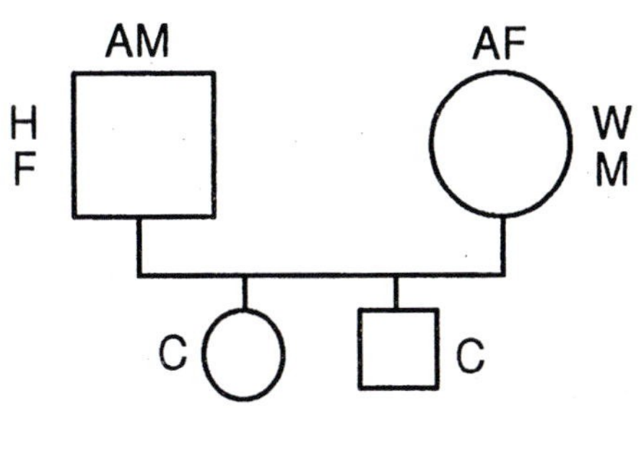

FIGURE 10.7

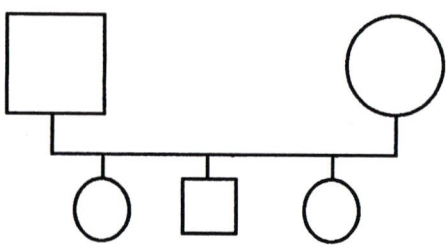

new roles but rather an intensification of the mother and father roles. For instance, with the arrival of additional children beyond the first child, the probability of the mother discontinuing her job outside the home goes up. The pressures of time and financial resources begin to weigh heavily on most families with more than one child.

Stress on the mother who stays at home may be magnified. The stay-at-home mother role may be seen as a secondary role. Her career has been put on the back burner. Modern culture's standard for success is not the stay-at-home mother or housewife. On the other hand, some women find the mother role extremely satisfying and are pleased to be stay-at-home mothers.

The social/emotional dynamics of a small family unit are as compelling and intense as a larger family. However, the larger the family unit, the more complex the structural dynamics in the family become. In a family with one child, the dyadic and triadic configurations are small. In a family of five members, the number of subsystems is multiplied enormously.

For the children in the family, the sibling relationship issues are part of the maturing process. Learning to account for my desires and wants and the desires and wants of other family members strongly influences the nature of our relationships outside the family.

Stage IV–First Child in School

When the oldest child enters school, the role of *parent* is added to the family dynamics. We become known to the school, neighbors, and wider society as our child's *parent* (Figure 10.8). As our child formally moves out of the family into the culture, the issue of

FIGURE 10.8

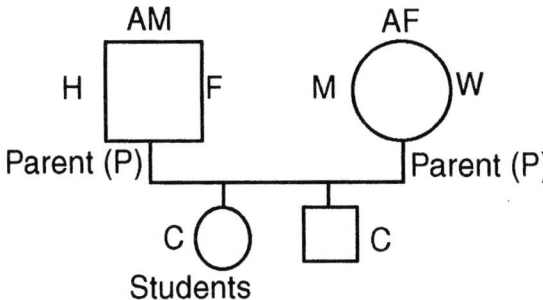

parental adequacy emerges. The child's public behavior becomes a measure of parental adequacy. Entering the formal school system is a giant move toward independence for the child. It signals what is to come later as our child becomes an adolescent and, later, an adult. As one tearful mother said as the school bus drove off with her daughter to the public school, "My little baby is growing up."

Entering the formal school system is a giant move toward independence for the child.

Having a child in school impacts our lives in other ways. For one thing, our leisure time is now controlled by the school schedule. We take vacations when school is not in session. For our child, the role of student moves him or her outside the boundary of the family unit and into the demands of the culture. The child is moved into the student role of learning about the demands of the surrounding culture and the people in that culture. The worldview of the culture is formally presented to our school child. In the best situation, the social, emotional, and intellectual growth that has taken place in the family unit prior to the school years has been adequate preparation for dealing with the role of student.

Peer pressure, while always strong, begins to assume a powerful role in the life of the student. The demand for students to conform to the subtle rules of the young in our society puts enormous stress on the need to be an individual *and* to be part of a larger group. The pressure to conform to the demands of the peer group intensify as the young person enters adolescence.

Stage V–First Child into Adolescence

When the first child moves into the individual developmental stage called adolescence, the family unit *will* change. Adolescence is the period of time in which our child moves into adulthood. In our contemporary culture, the adolescent period has been extended because of the length of time needed to prepare for financial independence and the complex nature of our economically intense society.

The presence of an adolescent in the family unit will require rapid shifts in the nature of the family system. For one thing, the parents must add the role of *person* to their repertoire of roles (Figure 10.9). The roles of parent, father, and mother remain in place but are moved into the background.

As a *person* to your adolescent, you become an adult friend to your offspring. You often relate as a good friend rather than a parent. A friend may exert influence–but not control–on someone. The major task of the parents during the adolescent period is to fully engage their offspring's emotional/maturity forward, and, sometimes backwards, in a differentiating manner. It is not easy to avoid being a parent to someone who, in reality, *needs* a differentiating person-type relationship. After all, parents have provided for the needs of their child from day one. Paradoxically, the adolescent

FIGURE 10.9

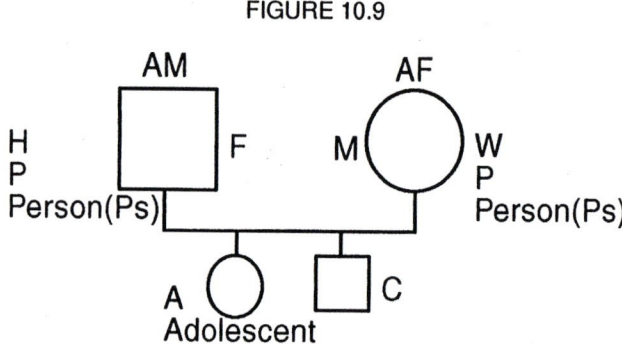

needs room to try out his or her emerging adulthood. Emerging adults make painful mistakes, and it is difficult for many parents to let their "child," now an adult, learn from mistakes. Our potential tendency to "protect" our children from all hurts requires a transformation into a reality-based support role.

The presence of an adolescent in the family will require rapid shifts in the nature of the family system.

The first child entering adolescence may put stress on the marital relationship because of parenting issues. In this family development stage, it is important to keep parent and spouse roles distinct. We may strongly disagree with our spouse about a parenting decision, but the emotionality is increased when the disagreement spreads to our marital relationship. Differentiating parent/spouses have the capacity to keep the roles distinct.

The sexuality of the adolescent may evoke sexual issues that the parent believed he or she had resolved years ago. Memories of our own adolescence may result in disciplinary patterns that are based on our own projections rather than on the actions of our offspring.

An adolescent offspring will energize parental identity issues. The adolescent will demand to know what the parent believes in and stands for as an adult. The adolescent will see the difference between what parents say versus how they act. Parental identity as an adult will likely be challenged.

As our other children enter the adolescent period, the family system will be pressed to adapt to the wants and wishes of children turning into adults. The need to assume the role of person to our adolescents will be compelling. The difficult task of not interfering with our offspring's emerging adulthood puts pressure on our own capacity to engage the differentiation process. It is difficult to know when to intervene and when not to intervene in the lives of our adolescent offspring.

Stage VI–First Child to Leave Home

When the first child leaves home, either for marriage, work, or schooling, the unavoidable realization that the family unit has initiated the downsizing process occurs. The "family" is moving toward dramatic change; our offspring has moved from infancy to child to adolescent to young adult (Figure 10.10). The person role for the parent becomes very large as we relate to our offspring on an adult-to-adult basis. As each offspring moves out of the family, the original family dynamics of husband and wife begin to emerge. The task at hand is to begin to plan for the future as a husband and wife with grown children.

For the offspring who leaves home, the tasks of adulthood begin to manifest. In the best of situations, the emerging adult will be able to regard the family as a stable, emotional resource that will not engulf him or her if support is needed. Just the awareness of a nonengulfing, supportive family presence can be a source of self-support for young family members.

Stage VII–Last Child to Leave Home

When the last child leaves home, the roles of mother, father, parent, and person change drastically. In the best of situations, the person role absorbs the various parental roles and becomes a resource role for the adult offspring (Figure 10.11). Young adults in

FIGURE 10.10

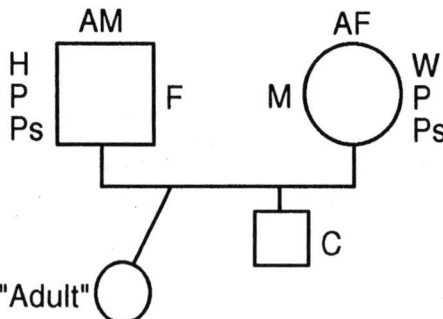

FIGURE 10.11

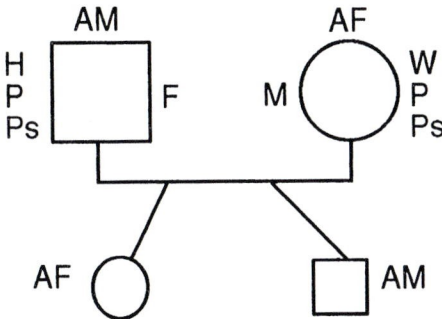

our society need the sense of emotional support a person/parent can give from the context of family. The support is caring, loving, and nonengulfing for the young adults.

Marital roles often become intensified after the children leave home. The husband and wife now have the time to develop their own relationship without the immediate distractions of children. For couples who have used the children as a buffer in their marriage, facing each other without the children present can be a daunting task. The marriage relationship may require some time in which to develop its new patterns and satisfactions. The marital tasks in this stage of family life are similar to those faced in the early marriage stage many years ago.

For the wife/mother who devoted most of her energies to the children, identity issues may emerge. The questions of "Who am I?" and "What do I do with the rest of my life?" often emerge. A late first career out of the home or a career change may be in order for some women as they work through the "last offspring to leave the home" stage.

It is not unusual for this stage to come to an abrupt end when an adult child suddenly returns home. An increasing number of young adults are returning home to live during their twenties and thirties. Families in which adult children return home to live are called boomerang families. Boomerang families proliferate because economic issues seem to be a major driving force for "children who won't leave home." Simply put, it is more economical to live at home than to rent an apartment on one's own.

An increasing number of young adults are returning home to live during their twenties and thirties.

The negotiation process for the household arrangements for an adult child who returns home is an opportunity to deal directly with the differentiation process. Setting the rules and boundaries when there are adult children at home will be a true test of levels of differentiation for both parents and the adult child. Relinquishing old roles, some with heavy emotional baggage, is not easy, but it is a growth and maturing opportunity.

Stage VIII–Without Children at Home and Retirement

As people live longer, the number of years a couple may live on their own continues to increase. In this stage of family life, the role of grandparent may emerge. In the best situation, grandparenting is a time of "loving and caring without disciplining or total responsibility." In some situations, grandparenting becomes more complicated because of divorces and remarriages for the adult offspring. Often referred to as the "sandwich generation," some couples find themselves sandwiched between caring for their own adult-children and grandchildren, as well as their own parents (Figure 10. 12).

The role of caregiver for our own elderly parents is likely to emerge during this family stage. The caregiver role for parents often

FIGURE 10.12

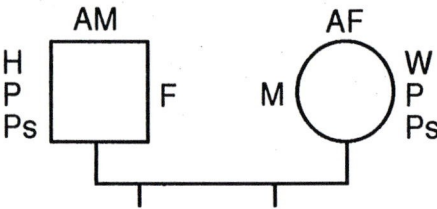

is assumed by the wife/mother. Women are most often called upon to care for parents. Issues concerning medical care, home health care, nursing home, etc., are complicated by procedures and machinery that keep people "alive" for years. Life and death issues involving "heroic medical procedures" for parents who are mentally unable to make the decisions fall upon grown children. The decisions are not easy and often require professional counseling to resolve.

Retirement in our society is an emotional process for many people. When we give up our work role, we give up a part of our identity. People are identified by the work they perform: "She is a doctor; he is a lawyer; he is a professor; she is a dentist," etc. For most people, retirement involves loss of income and loss of status. For some people, the losses of retirement are made up for by an increase in the freedom to do as one wishes.

Retirement in our society is an emotional process for many people. When we give up our work role, we give up a part of our identity.

The role changes in retirement must be addressed by both the husband and wife. Adjustment to retirement may require brief help by a counselor. It is a time of loss and emotional readjustment.

Stage IX–Death

The life cycle of a particular family ends with the death of one of the original marital pair (Figure 10.13). Based on statistical probabilities in our society, the husband is likely to die first. The role

FIGURE 10.13

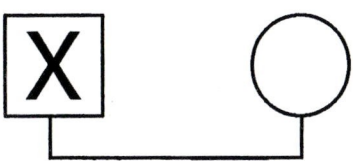

change for the remaining spouse is dramatic. The loss of a spouse ends a lifetime relationship with its many memories. In the best situation, each spouse has fully participated in the marital enterprise. An ongoing task of the later life stages of a family is preparation for death. While the personal emotional loss will be painful, the task of picking up life's pieces after the death of a spouse is easier if some prior planning has taken place. The realization that "everything is in order" is a comfort to a surviving spouse of any age.

The process of life includes death. With the passing of each generation, other generations emerge. A reality is that we have life in us and we pass that life forward in our children.

THE FAMILY LIFE-CYCLE PROCESS

In the family life cycle, many events interrupt the progressive journey. Job crises, relocation, illnesses, divorce, deaths, financial losses, and caretaking requirements are but a few of the "bolts-from-the-blue" that may strike a family at any time. As the pace of family living picks up in the ever-changing "contemporary" society in which we live, one family crisis may not be resolved before another crisis strikes. When a succession of crises occur, the level of stress on a family unit is enormous. A crisis always demands a change as part of the response to the situation. Role changes may be only one of many alterations demanded to face and address the crisis situation.

Divorce is an especially critical event in the life of a family. With almost one out of every two marriages ending in divorce, there is a fifty-fifty chance that the family life cycle will include a divorce phase. Most divorces take place early (in the first seven years of the marriage) in the life of the family. A sense of loss and blame is likely to be part of the divorce process. Whose fault was it? Who is to blame? The intense economic demands of our society add to the emotional problems that accompany divorce. The quickest way to lower one's socioeconomic level is to be female, divorced, and a single parent.

With divorce as prevalent as it is today, it is possible to identify some of the major tasks involved in a divorce stage of one's family life. Even in the best of situations of marital breakup, the divorced members will experience self-doubts, anger, and a sense of failure. Financial issues require much consideration and are stressful for both divorced members.

If children are involved, methods of co-parenting must be arranged. The task of not using the children to, in some way, "punish" the other parent requires maturity and full life reality awareness. A new co-parenting family structure will be different from the earlier one-family arrangement. The parenting issues specific to co-parenting require a sense of emotional awareness that stretch the level of differentiating for most people. The divorce stage does not pass quickly. The intense emotional part of the stage will last at least two to three years. The roles of a divorced person and/or co-parent are difficult with which to find peace.

With almost one out of every two marriages ending in divorce, there is a fifty-fifty chance that the family life cycle will include a divorce phase.

Most divorced people remarry and form a new family unit. Reconstructed or blended families, especially those with children involved, create a unique set of development dynamics. A particular blended family may be in several family life stages at one time. Simultaneous multiple life-cycle stages add to the overall stress level of the family. The newly married couple may be in the early-marriage stage, yet one partner may be in the first-child-in-the-adolescent stage and the other partner may be in the first-child-in-school-stage.

A blended family that has not carefully prepared each family member for the unique dynamics of a new family will be under considerable pressure until the negative family dynamics moderate. Role playing the joining of two family units often is a useful preparatory step for the actual journey together as a blended family. The role play provides somewhat of a "distanced" process for bringing up concerns about "living with another family."

A basic principle for working with a blended family is that attention to the early marriage stage of the family precedes work on the dynamics of the other family stages. Until the husband/wife dyad gets its relationship in order, it is difficult to get other family roles and relationships to function in growth-producing ways.

The particular family developmental stage occupied by the client/family provides a powerful defining context for all that goes on in the family. The specific impact of life-stage dynamics requires our assessment attention. Our relationship to our self, other people, our life contexts, and the spiritual dimension changes during the life journey of our family living. Simply put, we are unique and different people, depending upon the family stage with which we are dealing. Effective family work will give attention to dynamics inherent in a particular family's stage in the life-cycle process.

NOTES

1. Colapinto, J. (1991). "Structural Family Therapy," in Gurman, A. and Kniskern, D. (Eds.). *The Handbook of Family Therapy*, Vol. II. New York: Brunner/Mazel, p. 422.

2. Gottman, J. (1994). *Why Marriages Succeed or Fail*. New York: Simon and Schuster.

The relational systems model provides a particular worldview, or paradigm, for the conduct of family therapy. It is a multisystemic approach that identifies the universal dynamics that dominate human functioning. The real power of the RSM comes from the emphasis on the personal paradigm of the therapist and his or her capacity to respect client boundaries while at the same time energizing the client's growth forces. The therapist *is* the most vital factor in the therapeutic process. To put it another way, the therapist must have his or her stuff together if the therapy process is to be effective.

I think of the RSM as an additive for the larger more comprehensive treatment models in use today. The RSM encourages the therapist to be the learning vehicle for the integration of the four realities of life and the differentiating process that is necessary for human survival, safety, and growth. The power of self-consciousness that is unique to human beings gives us access to the deeper parts of self-awareness. It is the awareness of self that offers the greatest possibilities for full potential. At its best, self-awareness is used for the purpose of intellectual growth and emotional maturity rather than in the service of narcissism. Thus, while the RSM is for client growth and problem solving, the power of the model comes from the capacity of the therapist to adhere to the model's basic ideas. Following is a summary of some of the ideas that are fundamental to the RSM.

THE FOUR LIFE REALITIES

All humans exist in the universal life realities of self, other, context, and spiritual. For each of us individually, and in various aggregates of people, our time on this earth is a continuous process of dealing with the relationship dynamics inherent in each life reality. Humans cannot avoid dealing with the life realities. When one or more life realities is diminished, one or more of the other life realities is overemphasized. Our connections to the life realities become skewed. How we account for and connect to the life realities determines the very nature of our existence as human beings. The fullness of life is available only when the four life realities are given complete consideration. Our human brain provides each of us with the capacity to account for all of the life realities.

The RSM definition of differentiating gives attention to all of the life realities through an overarching context of love, caring, and integrity. In this definition, love connects to all realities in its intention to value and build up all of life. Caring means being concerned about and connected to the realities. Finally, integrity means that I am who I say I am at all levels of my being. Our spiritual part has to do with the capacity to make unique choices out of our own self-consciousness; the choice to connect or not connect with the ultimate context–God.

SELF-DIFFERENTIATION

Self-differentiation is the basic life process that addresses the human need to establish distinct socioemotional relationships with the four life realities *and* retain the capacity to function with reasonable autonomy (Papero, 1990).[1] The human differentiation process as conceptualized by Bowen and others provides us with a way to view how we manage the distinctions between emotions and thinking (self-regulation) and how we manage our distinctions and connections to the life realities (self-definition). One of the earliest recorded references to the importance of the process of self-differentiation is found in the Bible in the book of Matthew. Jesus tells his followers, "first cast out the beam out of thine own eye and then thou shalt see clearly to cast out the mote out of thy brother's eye." (Matthew, 7:5)[2] If we are to be effective in our relationships with other people, each of us needs to know who and what we are as a unique human being. The processes of self-regulation and self-definition, which are so vital to the differentiation process, enable us to use the full capacities of our brain. Knowing who and what we are is a safeguard against the inner emotional forces that sometimes hijack our thinking functions in the service of the survival and safety energies of the lower brain.

As well-differentiating therapists, we have no *need* to impose our worldview on our clients. Just as we stand on our own two feet, we respect the uniqueness of our clients. We encourage the client to examine his or her own worldview. The choice to self-reflect or not self-reflect is the client's. Thus, the requirement to be well-differentiating is especially crucial for family therapists.

Years of clinical experience with clients, teachers, graduate students, and supervising young therapists confirm the notion that the person-of-the-therapist is the crucial variable in an effective family treatment process. It is my conviction that to the extent that the therapist engages the process of differentiating both in himself or herself and as a direction for the treatment atmosphere, there is a high probability that treatment will be effective. To put it another way, the work of the therapist is limited to the extent that the therapist himself or herself is stuck at a particular level in the self-differentiation process. The emotional processes of therapy have a dramatic impact on us as family therapists. Time and time again I have observed a simple client-therapist dynamic. The process of therapy pushes the therapist to the limits of his or her emotional maturity, beyond which he or she cannot take the client. It is my thesis that while a client may have gained enormous benefit from the treatment process, when the client grows to the limit of the differentiating capacities of the therapist, the therapy will end for one reason or the other.

Differentiation is not just a concept: it is a living process. It cannot simply be taught or treated, yet it is encouraged by the process of therapy with a differentiating therapist. When in doubt about what to do in the treatment process, the answer is "differentiate" or as Virginia Satir might say, "Stand on your own two feet!"

The life requirement to engage the self-differentiating process never ends. Staying in touch with one's self for the purposes of integrity pushes the maturity process. The task of bringing the client into a deeper awareness of his or her own uniqueness and the uniqueness of others is the work of therapy. To manifest our spiritual part in our relationships to each other and our context(s) offers greater probabilities for effective work with our clients than a room full of treatment tactics and techniques would provide.

The human differentiation process allows us to examine vital boundary issues that all of us are required to navigate in our various life cycles. Inherent in looking at human boundary issues is the requirement to know and understand how a client has dealt with, and is dealing with, the powerful forces of separateness and togetherness. To the extent that there is a nonanxious presence of a well-defined, well self-regulated therapist, the client will be provided the opportunity to carefully examine his or her personal patterns of thinking and behavior. In such a process, client boundaries and perspectives are respected. At the same time, the client is encouraged to self-examine for the purpose of knowing who and what he or she is as person or aggregate of people. The client is asked to self-examine and squarely face possible inconsistencies and incongruencies between actions and stated values and beliefs.

The "facing process" is not easy. It means that I come face to face with such areas as (1) who and what I am, (2) the purpose for which I co-create who and what I am, (3) the incongruencies between what I say I am and how I act, (4) the nature of my connections to the four life realities, (5) my patterns of thinking and behaving, (6) how my past influences the present, (7) my emotionalized fears about being wrong, and (8) where I am headed in my life.

Again, the I-as-the-therapist is able to provide the "therapeutic place" only to the extent that I know who and what I am and let the client discover who and what he or she is. To provide the overlay of the RSM and not *impose* the model on the client is not easy; it is necessary. It is the paradox both of holding onto the model and of letting it go for the benefit of the client.

CORE CONSIDERATIONS

Some of the most critical dynamics of the self-differentiation process show up in the core "necessary but not sufficient considerations" (NBNS). The RSM gives full attention to the necessary but not sufficient considerations. The purpose of the attention to the NBNS is to create an atmosphere where the client is encouraged to engage in self-examination. For instance, heightened fear of being wrong–not being right–is inherent in the family therapy process. The simple question all clients have is, What have I done wrong? The fear of being wrong means that survival concerns in the lower brain are energized. Operating out of unconscious awareness, the client automatically hides from himself or herself parts of reality that are sensed as threatening to survival or safety. Bringing the missing parts of reality into awareness is the work of therapy.

Simply stated as a general operating principle, the RSM proposes that the therapist give consistent attention to the connections among client thinking, feelings, actions, and outcomes. *No* attention is given to who is right and who is wrong in relationship issues. Basically, in the right/wrong consideration, the therapist gives a congruent message that conveys, "I don't know how to deal with relationships in terms of who is right and who is wrong. Let's look at *what* happened here and see how it worked out." There is always a condition called consequences. Looking at *what* happened without right/wrong judgements may be a freeing experience.

Emotionalized right/wrong concerns generate some kind of reaction designed to cover up any hint of wrongness. Blame, or other forms of avoidance of responsibility, serves to deal with the intolerable sense of *being wrong*. A therapeutic atmosphere is one that attends to nonjudgmental responsibility. The underlying principle is straightforward. How can I deal with any behavior for which I accept no responsibility?

For the therapist, owning what is one's to own—nothing more and nothing less—is tied to his or her level of differentiation. The differentiation issue shows clearly in the therapist's ability to use the therapeutic atmosphere to encourage client self-reflection within the client's worldview and, at the same time, to avoid imposing the therapist's worldview on the client. Maintaining a nonanxious presence in the face of an anxious client who refuses to give up destructive behavior will test the differentiating capacities of any therapist. Common reactions on the part of anxious therapists are either to fail to engage in questions and procedures that move the client to self-confrontation and self-awareness or to tell the client what is *wrong* with his or her thinking and actions. Either of the above reactions avoid the therapist's responsibility to provide an atmosphere that encourages client self-awareness and responses in light of awareness.

The dignity and respect afforded the client when she or he or it is encouraged to reflectively use inner resources to resolve problems comes out of the therapist's sense of worthiness. People of worth are not permitted to avoid the realities of life. People of worth are encouraged to face problems, not go around them. The worthiness consideration addresses our never-ending yearning to sense value and worth in ourselves, others, and the world around us. Out of my respect for you, I will work to let your very best show through in your journey of life; that's a position of worthiness.

All of us evolve a personal worldview to guide us through life. The problem with a worldview is that much of it was formed while we were very young. Our worldview is the organizing frame for all that we do. It is our personal roadmap for life and carries with it the baggage of the past and the inaccuracies of the present. Yet, it is the facilitating power of our uniqueness as a human being. It is *our* worldview, and we cherish it. At its best, the process of therapy enables us to re-view our worldview for strengths and flaws. An important question for all of us is, What is the substance of our worldview *and* do we walk the talk of our stated worldview?

The very meaning of the treatment process for a client rests on the client's purpose for coming for therapy. The creation of a therapeutic atmosphere requires a clear understanding of what the client wants from therapy. It is not easy to determine what a client wants from therapy because often the client does not know what he or she wants to happen.

Clients come for therapy because of some problem that interferes with what they want. Part of the process of determining the purpose for therapy is the establishment of a clear definition of the problem. To put it in a very different way, what exists that, if it did not exist, would result in no problem? To the extent that there is clarity in what the client wants and what the problem is, the therapeutic process is enhanced. It is important to know what the problem is, who owns it, when it began, who first mentioned it, and what efforts have already been made to resolve it?

Implied in the purpose considerations is therapist attention to the connection between what the client wants and the problem. It is not enough to want to get rid of a problem. The essential dynamics are found in the relationship between the problem and what the client wants and does in relation to the problem. For instance, the problem may be the unfaithfulness of a spouse. What the client wants and does in relation to that problem is critical to the therapeutic process.

In some situations, an exacting process of examining the purpose for seeing a specific client may be all that is needed to move the therapy process to completion.

The process that keeps the treatment moving is found in the communications patterns for families. We not only communicate with others, we communicate with ourselves. We make meaning out of every bit of information with which we come into contact. A guiding principle for the communication consideration is found in the human's multilevel communications capacities. When we are incongruent in the different levels of communication, emotionality is likely to be in charge of the process.

The core necessary but not sufficient considerations provide a wrapper within which the power of the differentiation process may work. Giving attention to the core considerations is congruent with the work of a well-differentiating therapist.

MULTISYSTEM PERSPECTIVE

The human realities of self, other, and context correspond to therapeutic interventions at the personal, interpersonal, and family systems levels. As complicated as our connections to the human realities are, the human relationship to the spiritual reality is even more complicated. The spiritual reality is so very personal in the life of a human being that for some people, the spiritual reality directs their life.

In the ultimate sense, knowing who and what I am as a unique person demands that I come to grips with the source of my uniqueness. I find Sir John Eccles' comments on the source of human uniqueness very enlightening. He says:

> I am constrained to attribute the uniqueness of the self or soul to a supernatural spiritual creation. To give the explanation in theological terms: each soul is a new Divine creation which is implanted in the growing foetus at some time between conception and birth. It is the certainty of the inner core of unique individuality that necessitates the Divine creation.
>
> This conclusion is of inestimable theological significance. It strongly reinforces our belief in the human soul and its miraculous origin in a Divine creation.[3]

We exist as unique individuals in a relationship to the ultimate context, God. The question is What do we do with that reality? Our personal connection to or disconnection from God does not alter the existence of God; it does alter our relation to God.

While each person ultimately is responsible for his or her relationship to God, my own faith relationship to God through Jesus Christ has been a source of inspiration to my work with clients. My sense that each client is unique and has a divinely created soul engenders in me a deep respect for the client and the therapeutic process. Knowing the part God plays in who and what I am is a source of strength for me.

The uniqueness of all individuals shows in the nature of their connection to the life realities. The concept of life stances enables us to get a view of how an individual, on a patterned basis, connects to the self, other people, and the context. When the life stances of individual family members interact with the patterns of other family members, dyadic and triadic relationships begin to emerge. At the personal level, the extent to which one or more realities is given importance over other realities will be the degree to which dyadic, triadic, and family relationship patterns will demonstrate isomorphic imbalances. On the other hand, the importance of the sociocultural imperative of *more*—material things and personal freedoms–over interpersonal, family, and personal qualities such as love, caring, and integrity will be the degree to which families, couples, and family members demonstrate isomorphic imbalances. The parallels among the dynamics of human systems levels enable therapists to influence more than one systems level at one time.

In one sense, all of us play out a personal life script or drama based on our worldview. To the extent that we are not well-differentiating, we use other people and circumstances as bit players in our life drama. How many times have we come to realize that with certain people we are only serving as a complement to his or her leading role in a lifelong repetitive pattern of relationships? The therapy process is one place where we can enable the client to alter his or her drama of life.

Life's relationship repetitions especially show up in the lives of low-differentiating couples who *need* each other for validation. The powerful forces of separation from and closeness to another are experienced in the extreme when who and what I feel depends upon external validation. The closeness is fearful and drives us apart, and the separation is equally fearful and drives us into enmeshing relationships. In mature dyadic and triadic relationships, I am aware of my responsibility for me. My well-differentiating relationship agreements with another have to do with what I will do. An agreement is not an "*if* you do x, I will do y" arrangement: that is a contract! An agreement is an unilateral commitment with myself rather than a reciprocal contract type arrangement. It is difficult for low-differentiating people to form agreements. Yet, learning to stand on their own two feet is the therapeutic task.

The family grid is both a way of thinking about the family as a socioemotional system and a procedure for looking at the ways a system defines and regulates itself. Because of the power of the family unit in our lives, especially when we are young, the nature of the socioemotional dynamics at play in the family have a strong impact on our developing ability to engage the differentiating process. Family transgenerational and developmental issues are powerful influences in our lives. Grid thinking posits that too much family control or too little family influence seems to have its own negative impact on the life patterns developed by young family members. All of us carry unresolved family issues, or baggage, into life and our current family relationships. It is when we attempt to play out past dramas in current relationships that we pay the price of living in a personal world of unreality.

THE SOCIOCULTURAL CONTEXT

It is well for family therapists to realize that the current sociocultural forces are not marriage- or family-friendly. The contemporary cultural imperative of *more*—more money, more power, more prestige, more individual freedoms—has intruded powerfully into family life.

At one extreme, we have strong economic pressures to produce more material goods. Our economically intense society demands that all family members be economically productive. At the other extreme, we have the government taking over many of the traditional functions of the family. "The government as parent" is the battle cry for many politicians. Both of the extreme positions come together with the demand that the government provide child care for welfare mothers who "should be economically productive." The question is Where is the family in the contemporary social scheme and, even more specifically, who will take care of the children?

The loss of community that emerges out of a highly mobile, urban, and impersonal society adds to the stress on the family. Often we do not know our neighbors. We are now using money machines at the bank, voice mail in the phone system, and computer e-mail to communicate with each other. We watch sports events on television in our own home. For many people, the sociocultural context is a lonely, isolated lifestyle. The parallels of the larger social contexts show up in our personal life.

The media directs itself to the lower brain sexual and aggressive functions. Years ago, Freud proposed that humans had to deal with two primitive impulses, sex and aggression. The media has found that it is rather easy to stimulate both the aggressive and sexual impulses. Watch television commercials for one evening for proof as to which part of our brain is being addressed. Most people are intellectually aware that an impulse-driven society is likely to be self-destructive. At the same time, we are titillated by the more primitive impulses, and our reasoning power is diminished. Through sex and aggression, the media has found its own powerfully addictive drug and a way to short-circuit the full power of the human brain. The mammalian brain is much more impulsive in nature than the fully functioning human brain. For therapeutic purposes, it is well to remember that while individuals have choices, the surrounding context is enormously powerful. Encouraging well-differentiating human processes in family living is not easy in an intrusive, herd-driven society. The stress on all institutions of our contemporary society, especially the family, will affect the differentiating abilities of our clients. For a therapist to engage in a family treatment process without being aware of the enormous sociocultural pressure on the family is to ignore a powerful part of the context reality.

TREATMENT PROCEDURES

The RSM demands no specific treatment procedures. The principles that form the RSM are designed to undergird larger, more formal theoretical approaches to family therapy. Ideally, all that the therapist does in the treatment process is guided by a particular therapeutic paradigm. One of the advantages of a well-thought-out therapeutic paradigm is that it keeps us therapists fully engaged in a thoughtful approach to our clients.

The process of being well-differentiating draws attention to and encourages some "helping principles," all of which either have been covered or implied throughout this book. Following is a review of some of the treatment implications covered in the RSM:

— When someone seeks help with family problems, it is important to clarify what he or she *wants* from the treatment process.

— The client's relationship to the problem is a primary concern. Thus, the specific problem must be identified and named. (Who owns what part of the problem?)

— What are the client's actions concerning the problem? What is the outcome of efforts to deal with the problem? It is important to seek descriptive language to clarify the problem.

— There are times when it is important to "objectify" the problem. Establish the problem as something that is only a *part* of the client. Later, the problem may be relabeled as something more manageable by the client. For instance, in specific situations, anorexia eventually may be labeled a *habit* that was established years ago. A habit is something that can be worked with over time. As the destructive part of a habit is firmly identified, the client may decide to give up the specific "habit."

— Parts language may be used to identify and describe any aspect about a client that is extreme and/or emotionalized. For instance, a client who was struggling with what to do about a long-standing drug problem was helped to identify the part of him that "wants to give up drugs–that's the good part; a part we can work with." Later in the same interview, the part of the client that "fears giving up drugs" was identified and examined. Identifying polarized parts, i.e., "a part of you that wants to x and a part of you that does not want to x," may help a client deal with internal struggles (Satir, 1991)[4] (Schwartz and Grace, 1991).[5] Examining the thinking and emotions behind parts of who we are can provide valuable information. For instance, what is the self-talk that supports the submissive stance? For some clients, there is a strong "be nice" message that dominates the self-talk.

— Work within the client's life paradigm or worldview in addressing the therapy process. Be clear about exactly how the client describes everything. For example, a client who is a perfectionist in work details may be helped to see that getting away from his or her desk and establishing social networks is congruent with excellence or perfection as a worker.

— Work to create a therapeutic atmosphere that accounts for the core necessary but not sufficient considerations.

— Reflect on the client's problem, work, and worldview using the fundamental ideas in the RSM. In what is a paradox, the therapist uses the RSM worldview to seek clarification about the client's thinking, feelings, and actions. The purpose is to get a clear idea of what the client wants, the problem to be solved, the personal worldview used by the client, and the congruence between what the client says and does. There is no attempt to impose the therapist's worldview on the client. The dynamics of the *yes and no* paradox of intensely examining the client worldview from the therapist worldview provides a strong therapeutic force, albeit paradoxical, in the treatment process.

— The differentiating capacities of the therapist serve as the guiding dynamic for the entire treatment process. Much like the sign on the desk of the President of the United States that says, "the buck stops here," the therapeutic "buck" stops at the upper limit of the therapist's differentiation capacities.

— Constant reality checks for connections to the four life realities are in order. Humans under stress fight, flight, compromise, or stand firm. The life stances reflect one of the reactions or responses to stress.

— Systemic integrity is difficult to maintain in the face of stress. When a system adjusts to and patterns itself in reaction to dysfunction, the system has given up some of its integrity. Systemic responses to problems are functional as long as the ability to self-define and self-regulate remains within the system and not in constant reactiveness to the problem.

— Enormous energy for growth can be activated when the four life realities are brought into harmony. Thus, any treatment process that does not account for the whole of the life process will be limited.

— Therapeutic work at one system level, such as the family unit, can have dramatic effects on other system levels, such as individual family members or important family dyads and triads.

— The purpose of the "facing process" is multidimensional. The following are areas of life a client may need to face:

1. To distinguish between what is real and what is fantasy. In working through a break-up with a boyfriend, one client identified the difference between fantasy and reality. She became aware of a tendency to attach herself to a fantasy about a relationship and act as if the fantasy were real. She showed considerable insight when she noted that "it is impossible to hold onto something that never existed."

2. To identify unintended consequences.

3. To identify the difference between what I say and what I do.

4. To identify where I begin and end in relationships. To own what is mine; to own nothing more and nothing less.

5. To identify when I am operating out of lower or mid-brain functions rather than choice.

6. To identify my patterns and my patterns of patterns in my life.

7. To recognize that behavior based in anger is controlled by someone or something other than my choices. It took considerable work to help one client to see that her inability to let go of her anger toward her ex-husband was, in a strange way, allowing her husband to control her life. It is ironic that one of her major problems in the marriage was her husband's controlling patterns. In another situation, a client observed about himself, after a childish display of anger, "I still have a child in me. I guess you just saw him."

8. To establish the understanding that self-awareness is a unique human capacity.

9. To recognize that the family therapy process is not without pain. The resolution of family problems is different from going around family problems. To face the stress of working one's way through one's relationship to a problem is not easy. It is easier to go around it.

10. To recognize that anxiety about being wrong often results in attempts to blame others or engage in other ways of avoiding responsibility.

11. To recognize that the differentiation process is the road to the highest level of being as a unique human.

12. To identify when someone is running their life "act" on you. When I am a "bit-player" in someone else's major life drama, my only role is to play the part that complements the already determined life script of the "star."
13. To recognize that one does not *need* their spouse. Need is a survival issue and subject to lower and mid-brain functions. Relationships based on *need* have a low probability of working out well. Relationships based on choice have a high probability of working out well.
14. To recognize that part of the truth is not the whole truth. We use part of the truth to ignore other realities that may contradict our half-truths.

Finally, the concerned therapist worries about doing the "right thing" in the therapy process. The "right thing" in the RSM is to establish a therapeutic context by accounting for the necessary but not sufficient considerations. Within that context, the task is to follow the client's worldview in exacting details as he or she presents the problem and what is wanted from the treatment process. The client is helped to see the flaws and growth possibilities in his or her particular worldview. The well-differentiating therapist will continue to engage the differentiation process throughout the treatment process. In the best of situations, the client and the therapist will engage the growth processes of life together.

NOTES

1. Papero, D. (1990). *Bowen Family Systems Theory.* Boston, MA: Allyn and Bacon, p. 47.

2. Matthew, 7:5. Holy Bible, King James Version (1971). Grand Rapids, MI: Zodervan Bible Publishers.

3. Eccles, J. (1993). *Evolution of the Brain: Creation of the Self.* London and New York: Routledge, p. 237.

4. Satir, V. et al. (1990). *The Satir Model.* Palo Alto, CA: Science and Behavior Books, Inc.

5. Schwartz, R. and Grace, P. "The Systemic Treatment of Bulemia," in P. Tolan (Ed.). Multi-Systemic Intervention for Child and Adolescent Behavior Problems (1990). Binghamton, NY: The Haworth Press, p. 89-106.

APPENDIX

**STANCE TENDENCY
EXERCISE PACKET**

THE RELATIONAL SYSTEMS MODEL
Stance Tendency Recording Packet

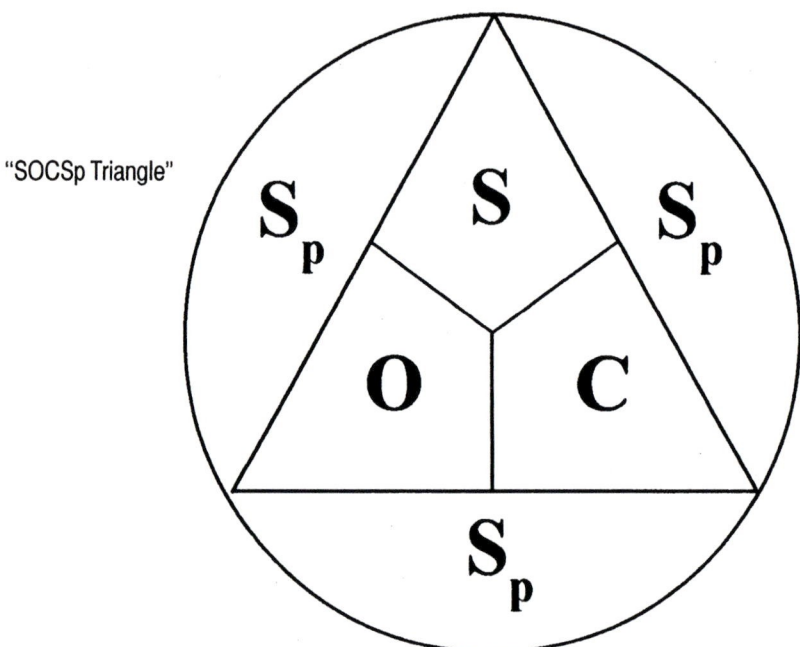

"SOCSp Triangle"

The "SOCSp triangle" serves as a way to assess individual and interpersonal functioning within the family system. The "SOCSp triangle" is based on the proposition that, for human beings, there are four realities (reality = what is). The human being's conscious experiences of reality may be classified as either (1) self, (2) other, (3) context, or (4) spiritual. In a schema similar to one proposed by Sir John C. Eccles, *self* is defined as subjective reality, *other* is defined as the world of physical objects and states, both organic and inorganic. *Context* is defined as the work in the objective sense, and *spiritual* is the supreme force that governs the universe (God). All that has existed, now exists, or will exist fits into one of the realities.

Based in considerations of the four life realities, specific individual patterns of behavior–life stances–may be identified. Intrapersonal patterns between and among family members may be assessed using the life stance schema. The SOCSp model is based on (1) experiences as a clinical social worker in a variety of mental health settings and (2) feedback from professionals who have attended my seminars in family therapy.

LIFE STANCE TENDENCY: RESPONSIBLE
Functional Tendencies

Compliant: A "yes" person, an agreeable person, a strong tendency to defer own needs to the needs of others or the context. Hope is to win by being nice. Self is diminished.

Assertive: A "no" person, comfortable with disagreement, a tendency to meet own needs within "shoulds" and "oughts" of the context. Goal is to win by being first, other is diminished.

Objective: A "know" person, comfortable with rules, logic, and facts. A tendency to avoid emotion. Goal is to win with logical expressions and arguments. Self and other are diminished.

Distractor: An "unknown" person, a totally disorganized appearance, moves from subject to subject and idea to idea, a tendency to be unfocused. Avoids losing by constant shifting and moving. Self, other, and context are diminished.

Self-Concerned: An "I want" person, comfortable seeking own needs at the expense of others. Intent is to win by fulfilling own wishes. Other and context are diminished.

Sensor: An "emotionally oriented" person, a feeling person who is tuned into feelings. Wins through emotions. Context is diminished.

Loyal: A "you oriented" person. Comfortable attending to the needs and wishes of one other person. Goal is to win by serving another. Self and context are diminished.

All of the functional tendencies are appropriate at one time or the other.

Humans tend to be most comfortable in one or two of the responsible stances and able to move from one tendency to another as is appropriate to self, other, and context.

LIFE STANCE TENDENCY PROFILE RECORDING

Following is a paper and pencil procedure for developing some comparisons about how you or your spouse may look on the life stance profile. The procedure has not been tested for its validity or reliability. This is a procedure for recording your impressions of yourself or another person.

In recording page A, the procedure applies to the person completing the list of self-impressions. Depending on the extent to which an item applies to the recorder, a rating of 1 to 5 is selected. After all of the items have been rated, use the "Rating Key" on the last page of the Life Stance Tendency Recording Packet to score the items. For instance, all the compliant items are listed to the right of compliant. In the rating key, items 1, 14, 19, 24, and 27 are compliant items.

Items listed to the right of assertive are scored as assertive (2, 8, 15, 22, and 35). The ratings given each stance item are listed under the appropriate stance in the profile score box. The total score of each stance is listed on the bottom *score* line.

For recording page B, the procedure applies to another person. It is your impression about how he or she deals with each item on the recording sheet. After all the items have been completed, the "Rating Key" on the last page of the Life Stance Tendency Recording Packet is used to score the items.

There are various ways to use the Life Stance Profile Recording Packet. Recording sheet A records my impressions about myself. Recording sheet B records my impressions of another person or my impressions about how the other person would score each item.

The scores and profiles from sheets A and B may be compared to get an impression of how the two people function as a couple. On the other hand, the profile of my impressions of my spouse and her impressions of herself may be compared to get a view of how we see ourself and how another sees us. The life stance tendency profile recording may be used to create dialogue with one's self about one's self. The uses of the Profile Recording are limited only by the creativity one may use to come up with valuable uses. It is to be remembered that the Life Stance Profile tells us the preference we have for each stance. There is no right or wrong score, only the preference or comfort we have for each stance.

(I owe a debt of gratitude to Ms. Marion L. Sharp of Jacksonville, Florida, for her vital contributions to the Life Stance Tendency Profile Recording.)

LIFE STANCE TENDENCY PROFILE RECORDING A

DIRECTIONS: This is not a test. This is a recording of your impressions of yourself. Mark each item in the following manner:

5 = always, 4 = frequently, 3 = some, 2 = seldom, 1 = never

Work as quickly as you can. It is generally accepted that our first response is the most accurate.

Rating

_____	1.	I try very hard to get along with people.
_____	2.	I can say "no" very easily.
_____	3.	I prefer to deal in facts.
_____	4.	I enjoy telling jokes in serious situations.
_____	5.	I am very comfortable with expressing feelings.
_____	6.	I believe in being loyal.
_____	7.	It is very important for me to take care of myself.
_____	8.	I get my point across regardless.
_____	9.	I am concerned about the logic of the situation.
_____	10.	I am uncomfortable with tension in a situation.
_____	11.	I am very aware of the feelings of others.
_____	12.	I have a very important other person in my life.
_____	13.	Getting my needs met is very important.
_____	14.	I tend to think of me last.
_____	15.	I speak my mind.
_____	16.	I see feelings as a hinderance to solving problems.
_____	17.	I have a lot of different ideas about a lot of different areas.
_____	18.	I tend to speak before I think.
_____	19.	I am a peacemaker.
_____	20.	It is important to me that I make the significant person in my life happy.
_____	21.	I have to do what I think is best.
_____	22.	I rather enjoy conflict.
_____	23.	I believe rules are very important.
_____	24.	I try to help people find areas of agreement.
_____	25.	Sometimes I have trouble staying focused for very long.
_____	26.	I say what I feel.
_____	27.	I believe in helping others.

—————— 28. It is hard to be happy if my significant person is not happy.
—————— 29. I tend to think of me first.
—————— 30. I tend to think of the needs of the situation first.
—————— 31. I believe in distractions.
—————— 32. I believe feelings are very important.
—————— 33. It is my responsibility to make life pleasant for a certain important person.
—————— 34. My own feelings, thoughts, and wants are what count most.
—————— 35. It is important that I assert myself.

COMPLIANT	ASSERTIVE	OBJECTIVE	DISTRACTOR	SENSOR	SELF CONCERNED	LOYAL
C	**A**	**O**	**D**	**S**	**Sc**	**L**
TOTAL						

Profile Score Box*

Scoring Procedure—Use the rating key found at the back of the Stance Tendency Exercise Packet to identify which items apply to a specific responsible tendency. List the score given each item under the appropriate tendency column. Each tendency will have five item scores in its column. Add the five scores in each column to get the comparison score for each tendency.

IMPORTANT OTHER LIFE STANCE TENDENCY PROFILE RECORDING B

DIRECTIONS: This is not a test. This is a recording of your impressions of a person important to you. Mark each item in the following manner:

5 = always, 4 = frequently, 3 = some, 2 = seldom, 1 = never

Work as quickly as you can. It is generally accepted that the first response is the most accurate.

Rating

_____	1.	He tries very hard to get along with people.
_____	2.	He can say "no" very easily.
_____	3.	He prefers to deal in facts.
_____	4.	He enjoys telling jokes in serious situations.
_____	5.	He is very comfortable with expressing feelings.
_____	6.	He is a loyal person.
_____	7.	It is very important for him to take care of himself.
_____	8.	He gets a point across regardless.
_____	9.	He is concerned about the logic in a situation.
_____	10.	He is uncomfortable with tension in a situation.
_____	11.	He is very aware of the feelings of others.
_____	12.	He has a very important person in his life.
_____	13.	Getting his needs met is very important to him.
_____	14.	He tends to think of himself last.
_____	15.	He speaks his mind.
_____	16.	He sees feelings as a hinderance to solving problems.
_____	17.	He has a lot of different ideas about a number of subjects.
_____	18.	He tends to speak before he thinks.
_____	19.	He is a peacemaker.
_____	20.	It is important to him that the significant person in his life is happy.
_____	21.	He has to do what he thinks is best.
_____	22.	He enjoys conflict.
_____	23.	He believes rules are very important.
_____	24.	He tries to help people find areas of agreement.
_____	25.	Sometimes he has trouble staying focused for very long.
_____	26.	He expresses feelings openly.

_____ 27. He believes in helping others.
_____ 28. It is hard for him to be happy if his significant person is not happy.
_____ 29. He tends to think of himself first.
_____ 30. He tends to think of the needs of the situation first.
_____ 31. He enjoys distracting others.
_____ 32. He believes feelings are very important.
_____ 33. He makes it his personal responsibility to make life pleasant for a certain important person.
_____ 34. His own feelings, thoughts, and wants are what count most.
_____ 35. It is important to him that he be assertive.

COMPLIANT	ASSERTIVE	OBJECTIVE	DISTRACTOR	SENSOR	SELF CONCERNED	LOYAL
C	**A**	**O**	**D**	**S**	**Sc**	**L**

TOTAL

Profile Score Box*

*For scoring procedure instructions for Life Stance Tendency Profile see Recording A in this packet.

IMPORTANT OTHER LIFE STANCE TENDENCY PROFILE RECORDING B

DIRECTIONS: This is not a test. This is a recording of your impressions of a person important to you. Mark each item in the following manner:

5 = always, 4 = frequently, 3 = some, 2 = seldom, 1 = never

Work as quickly as you can. It is generally accepted that the first response is the most accurate.

Rating

_____ 1. She tries very hard to get along with people.
_____ 2. She can say "no" very easily.
_____ 3. She prefers to deal in facts.
_____ 4. She enjoys telling jokes in serious situations.
_____ 5. She is very comfortable with expressing feelings.
_____ 6. She is a loyal person.
_____ 7. It is very important for her to take care of herself.
_____ 8. She gets a point across regardless.
_____ 9. She is concerned about the logic in a situation.
_____ 10. She is uncomfortable with tension in a situation.
_____ 11. She is very aware of the feelings of others.
_____ 12. She has a very important person in her life.
_____ 13. Getting her needs met is very important to her.
_____ 14. She tends to think of herself last.
_____ 15. She speaks her mind.
_____ 16. She sees feelings as a hinderance to solving problems.
_____ 17. She has a lot of different ideas about a number of subjects.
_____ 18. She tends to speak before she thinks.
_____ 19. She is a peacemaker.
_____ 20. It is important to her that the significant person in her life is happy.
_____ 21. She has to do what she thinks is best.
_____ 22. She enjoys conflict.
_____ 23. She believes rules are very important.
_____ 24. She tries to help people find areas of agreement.
_____ 25. Sometimes she has trouble staying focused for very long.
_____ 26. She expresses feelings openly.

_____ 27. She believes in helping others.

_____ 28. It is hard for her to be happy if her significant person is not happy.

_____ 29. She tends to think of herself first.

_____ 30. She tends to think of the needs of the situation first.

_____ 31. She enjoys distracting others.

_____ 32. She believes feelings are very important.

_____ 33. She makes it her personal responsibility to make life pleasant for a certain important person.

_____ 34. Her own feelings, thoughts, and wants are what count most.

_____ 35. It is important to her that she be assertive.

	COMPLIANT	ASSERTIVE	OBJECTIVE	DISTRACTOR	SENSOR	SELF CONCERNED	LOYAL
	C	**A**	**O**	**D**	**S**	**Sc**	**L**
TOTAL							

Profile Score Box*

*For scoring procedure instructions for Life Stance Tendency Profile see Recording A in this packet.

RATING KEY

Responsible Stance Tendency	Item Number				
Compliant (C)	1	14	19	24	27
Assertive (A)	2	8	15	22	35
Objective (O)	3	9	16	23	30
Distractor (D)	4	10	17	25	31
Sensor (S)	5	11	18	26	32
Self-Concerned (Sc)	7	13	21	29	34
Loyal (L)	6	12	20	28	33

BIBLIOGRAPHY

Bandler, R. and Grinder, J. (1982). *Reframing*. Andreas, S. and Andreas, C., (Eds.). Moab, UT: Rand People Press.

Bardill, D. and Ryan, F. (1964). *Family Group Casework*. Washington, DC: Metropolitan-Washington Chapter of NASW.

Bell, J. (1961). *Family Group Therapy*. Public Health Monograph #64. Washington, DC: Dept. of Health, Education, and Welfare.

Bowen, M. (1966). "The Use of Theory in Clinical Practice," *Comprehensive Psychiatry*, 7.

Bowen, M. (1978). *Family Therapy in Clinical Practice*. New York: Jason Aronson.

Carter, S. (1993). *The Culture of Disbelief*. New York: Basic Books.

Colapinto, J. (1991). "Structural Family Therapy," in A. Gurman and D.K. Kniskern (Eds.). *Handbook of Family Therapy*, Vol. III. New York: Brunner/Mazel.

Eccles, H. (1993). *Evolution of the Brain: Creation of the Self*. London and New York: Routledge.

Eccles, J. (1973). *The Understanding of the Brain*. New York: McGraw-Hill.

Frankl, V.E. (1967). *Psychotherapy and Existentialism: Selected Papers on Logotherapy*. New York: Washington Square Press.

Frankl, V.E. (1975). *The Unconscious God*. New York: Simon and Schuster.

Friedman, E.N. (1985). *Generation to Generation: Family Process in Church and Synagogue*. New York: Guilford.

Friedman, E.N. (1990). *Friedman's Fables*. New York: Guilford.

Friedman, E.N. (1991). "Bowen Theory and Therapy," in A. Gurman and D.K. Kniskern (Eds.). *Handbook of Family Therapy*, Vol. II. New York: Brunner/Mazel.

Glasser, W. (1981). *Stations of the Mind*. New York: Harper and Row.

Goleman, D. (1995). *Emotional Intelligence*. New York: Bantam.

Gottman, J. (1994). *Why Marriages Succeed or Fail.* New York: Simon and Schuster.

Kerr, M.E. (1981). "Family Systems Theory and Therapy," in A. Gurman and D. Kniskern (Eds.). *Handbook of Family Therapy.* New York: Knopf.

Kerr, M.E. and Bowen, M. (1988). *Family Evaluation.* New York: Norton.

MacLean, P. (1985). "Brain Evolution Related to Family, Play and the Isolation Call," *Archives of General Psychology,* 42.

McGoldrick, M. and Gerson, R. (1985). *Genograms in Family Assessment.* New York: Norton.

Minuchin, S. (1974). *Families and Family Therapy.* Cambridge, MA: Harvard Press.

Notarius, C. and Markman, H. (1990). *We Can Work It Out.* New York: Perigee Books.

Olsen, D., Russell, C., and Sprenkle, D. (Eds.) (1989). *Circumplex Model.* Binghamton, NY: The Haworth Press.

Papero, D. (1990). *Bowen Family Systems Theory.* Boston, MA: Allyn and Bacon.

Peck, S. (1978). *The Road Less Traveled.* New York: Simon and Schuster.

Peck, S. (1983). *People of the Lie: The Hope for Healing Human Evil.* New York: Simon and Schuster.

Satir, V. (1972). *People Making.* Palo Alto, CA: Science and Behavior Books.

Satir, V. and Baldwin, M. (1983). *Satir Step by Step.* Palo Alto, CA: Science and Behavior Books, Inc.

Satir, V., Stachowiak, J., Jaschman, H. (1980). *Helping Families to Change.* New York: Jason Aronson.

Satir, V., Banman, J., Gerber, J., Gomori, M. (1991). *The Satir Model.* Palo Alto, CA: Science and Behavior Books, Inc.

Schwartz, R. and Grace, P. (1990). "The Systemic Treatment of Bulimia," in P. Tolan (Ed.). *Multi-Systemic Interventions for Child and Adolescent Behavior Problems.* Binghamton, NY: The Haworth Press.

Smotherman, R. (1980). *Winning Through Enlightenment.* San Francisco, CA: Context Publications.

Smotherman, R. (1982). *Transforming No. 1.* San Francisco, CA: Context Publications.

Schnarch, D. (1991). *Constructing the Sexual Crucible.* New York: Norton.

Steinke, P.L. (1993). *How Your Church Works.* Washington, DC: The Allan Institute.

Steinke, P.L. (1994). *New Creation.* Austin, TX, Vol. 1, No. 1.

Watzlawick, P. (1964). *An Anthology of Human Communication.* New York: Science and Behavior Books.

Watzlawick, P., Beaven, J.H., and Jackson, D.D. (1967). *Pragmatics of Human Communications: A Study of Interactions Patterns. Pathologies and Paradoxes.* New York: Norton.

Index

Page numbers followed by the letter "f" indicate figures.